FORGING LINKS:
EFFECTIVE SCHOOLS AND EFFECTIVE DEPARTMENTS

Dr Pam Sammons is an Associate Director of the International School Effectiveness and Improvement Centre (ISEIC) at the London Institute of Education. She is a co-author of *School Matters* an influential study of primary schools, and has conducted major studies of both secondary and primary schools during the last 15 years.

Dr Sally Thomas is also an Associate Director of ISEIC. She is a leading expert in the study of value added at both GCSE and A level and has worked with a number of LEAs on the development of value added frameworks in different contexts.

Professor Peter Mortimore is Director of the London Institute of Education and is an internationally recognized authority in the field. He co-authored the seminal British school effectiveness research *Fifteen Thousand Hours* and directed the *School Matters* study.

Forging Links:
Effective Schools and
Effective Departments

Pam Sammons, Sally Thomas
and Peter Mortimore

with

Adrian Walker, Audrey Hind, Rebecca Smees, John Bausor
and Rosemary Cairns

P·C·P

Paul Chapman
Publishing Ltd

Paul Chapman Publishing Ltd
144 Liverpool Road
London N1 1LA

British Library Cataloguing in Publication Data
Sammons, Pam
    Forging links : effective schools and effective departments
    1. Effective teaching 2. Teacher effectiveness
    I. Title II. Thomas, Sally III Mortimore, Peter

379.1'5

ISBN 1 85396 349 6

Typeset by Dorwyn Ltd, Rowlands Castle, Hants
Printed and bound in Great Britain

A B C D E F G H 9 8 7

Contents

Acknowledgements

We are very grateful to all the schools involved in this research, especially to the staff of the schools and departments who agreed to co-operate in the case study phase of the project.

Many colleagues at the International School Effectiveness and Improvement Centre have provided support during the two and a half years of the project and we are grateful for their contribution. Other school effectiveness researchers, including Peter Coleman, Bert Creemers, Peter Daly, Harvey Goldstein, John Gray, David Reynolds and Jaap Scheerens, have also provided valuable comments on the study.

From start to finish, Ros Marsh, our project administrator and secretary, has been the linchpin of the entire enterprise, displaying unfailing patience in dealing with the production of many academic papers, project reports and the manuscript of this book, as well as liaising with schools – all this in addition to her normal duties. We are extremely grateful to her for her support and good humour.

Also, we would like to thank Ashley Hay for her helpful contribution in checking the manuscript of this book for consistency and clarity, and assisting in its word processing.

This study would not have been possible without the financial support of the Economic and Social Research Council (R000 234130).

Finally, we wish to pay tribute to the pioneering work of Professor Desmond Nuttall. His thinking stimulated many of the ideas in this book. But for his early death in the autumn of 1993, he would have been a co-director of this project.

Foreword

The conventional wisdom maintains that there are sizeable differences in effectiveness between schools. Researchers have concentrated their efforts, therefore, on trying to understand what 'makes the difference' at the level of the school. Such efforts have proved fruitful. What the present study suggests, however, is that by looking at the differences *between* schools they have run the risk of ignoring equally important differences within schools. The conventional wisdom has simply been a (convenient) fiction.

Anyone who has ever looked at a secondary school's prospectus will have noticed that exam results differ subject-by-subject. Some departments seem to get all the best grades. Unfortunately, relatively little can be grasped from such 'raw' results. Some subjects may, for example, have attracted more able pupils than others; we should not be too surprised, therefore, if their pupils seem to have done somewhat better. This study goes beyond such simplistic comparisons and (through the use of sophisticated, state-of-the art statistical procedures) tries to assess how much value different subject departments have added to their pupils' progress, taking account of the different starting points.

So far, so familiar. Nothing to get worried about here. Until one reaches Chapter 4 where three particular findings are delivered with the precision and technology of a high-velocity rifle. A widely-held assumption falls here, another is questioned there – it is only later that one realizes that these were bombshells!

First, only 'a minority of schools perform consistently across subjects' – a very small minority on some criteria. Few schools, in other words, are uniformly good at teaching Maths, the Sciences, English and Modern Languages; conversely, only a few are uniformly bad at teaching them. In the vast majority of schools, performance in one department is only weakly linked to performance in another. You can have a good Maths department and a poor Science department, a competent English department and a poor French one – plus, of course, all the numerous combinations in between. Virtually every school, in other words, faces considerable challenges in terms of departmental improvement.

Second, only a (very) small minority of schools and departments perform consistently over time, in the majority of cases schools' and departments' 'effectiveness' fluctuates from one year to the next. This year's results are not a particularly good guide to next year's.

Third, there is some evidence that both schools *and* departments are differentially effective with pupils from different social and ethnic backgrounds as well as high and low attainers. For reasons that are not, as yet, well understood, some simply do better with some kinds of pupils than others.

Other researchers will doubtless want to replicate these findings on their own data. Is part of the 'inconsistency', one wonders, down to the fact that, with relatively high levels of teacher turnover, key players are constantly changing? Is there, in other words, a very real sense in which this year's 'school' or 'department' differs from last year's or next year's? And there again, is this just a London phenomenon, confined in the main to communities experiencing relatively high levels of social stress? There is doubtless something in both these arguments but only enough, I suspect, for the conclusions to be slightly modified rather than overturned.

The factors contributing to differences in performance, in terms of departmental practices, form the meat of the case studies which follow on from the statistical analyses. Some of this is familiar but much of it is new. The implications are certainly different – the need to reconceptualize who 'the leaders' in a school are, for example, and the need to consider and facilitate patterns of professional interchange about what it means to teach a particular subject well. One is forced to the conclusion that an overriding interest in school-level factors has led to some important features of teachers' collective practices and interactions being simply ignored or under-valued. In short, one ignores the evidence that much of the crucial action in a secondary school takes place at departmental level at one's peril.

The authors call for future research to be focused simultaneously on school *and* departmental effectiveness. Indeed, they begin to argue that the whole field might usefully be relabelled and reconceptualized along these lines. Their study certainly offers some important stepping stones towards this destination. Their call reminds me, however, of the still bigger prize to be pursued over the next few years. Some three decades ago, around the time that work on school effectiveness was being established, there was a parallel concern with *teacher* effectiveness. Unfortunately, for much of the intervening period, the two fields of research went their separate ways. What might have happened if researchers in both traditions had put more effort into trying to integrate the different levels of the educational process (schools/departments and teachers/departments) is regrettably a matter for speculation. A firm commitment to 'forging the links' undoubtedly offers one of the main ways ahead.

John Gray
Cambridge
July 1997

Preface

The government White Paper, *Excellence in Schools*, published in July 1997, sets out a five-year strategy for raising standards. At the heart of the strategy is the school which takes responsibility for its own improvement. The government expects that each school will set targets for future performance, compare its progress to other similar schools and constantly review its practice in the search for improvement.

If schools are to be able to do all this successfully, then government at local and national level must provide them with good quality performance data, guidance on proven best practice and a coherent approach to professional development for teachers, whatever stage of their career they happen to have reached. It is also the responsibility of government to hold schools to account through inspection and other means and to intervene where there is evidence of underperformance.

It is no exaggeration to say that this policy is founded on the work of researchers in school effectiveness and school improvement over the last twenty years. Moreover, its success will depend to a large extent on how that work is taken forward. Systematic research in this field will surely be the cornerstone of our understanding of best practice in the future. Schools involved in self-review will need to be able to draw on studies which constantly refine our understanding of what creates success.

The work of Pam Sammons, Sally Thomas and Peter Mortimore, which they describe in this book, represented a ground-breaking advance on previous school effectiveness studies. By searching beneath the level of the school as a unit, examining individual subject departments and developing our understanding of 'differential effectiveness', they provide a host of new insights into schools which will be of value to practitioners as well as policymakers.

Pam Sammons, Sally Thomas and Peter Mortimore are acknowledged to be one of the world's leading teams. This book shows why. It will undoubtedly be read across the globe by the growing international community of researchers in this field.

Most important of all, headteachers and teachers will find the lessons of this study – founded as they are on a firm and refined research basis – of direct value in their constant search for improvement.

Michael Barber
Head of the Standards and Effectiveness Unit, DfEE
July 1997

1

Introduction

Twenty years ago studies of school effectiveness were just beginning. Of course, schools must have always had variable qualities and different effects. Quality has probably varied right from the time of the first recorded formal education apparatus established by Plato and the Greek intelligentsia. It undoubtedly did in the middle ages, a time when many schools for choristers and craftsmen were created. During the nineteenth century, as our national system of education was slowly evolving, schools were judged formally by inspectors to be *excellent*, *good*, *fair* or *bad* as part of the Revised Code of '*payment by results*' introduced by the Newcastle Commission. Those with money, of course, have always been able to choose what they consider to be a quality education for their sons and daughters. Increasingly, in the decade following the 1944 Act, other parents seemed to believe that schools could make a difference and went to elaborate lengths to secure places in the maintained school of their choice. No one, however, thought about researching school effects until the appearance in the 1970s of the pioneering studies by Rutter *et al.* (1979) in England, and Edmonds (1979) in the United States.

Despite these individual efforts, the received wisdom – accepted by many researchers, officials and teachers – was that one school was much the same as another. This view sees a student's success as stemming from his or her own talent and motivation or from their family background. In a country as aware of class differences as England, it should not be surprising that teachers' expectations tend to favour children from respectable, well-off families.

The research published on both sides of the Atlantic in 1979 challenged these established views. In the United States, Edmonds – a black academic from Harvard – toured the country proclaiming that 'all children can learn'. If a nation really wants *all* its children to succeed, it will ensure that they do so – was his message. In England, the reactions to *Fifteen Thousand Hours* – the results of the Rutter *et al.* study of secondary schools – were mixed. The Teachers' Associations and a number of educational researchers were critical of the pioneering methodology and of the general approach which sought to identify the school component in a student's success or failure. Some academics felt that the authors were exonerating society of its responsibility for equity because of their focus on the school, a point we discuss further in Chapter 2.

What the studies of school effectiveness did in a systematic way was what Her Majesty's Inspectors of Schools – and indeed the inquiring parent – had been trying to do all along: they made judgements about the quality of learning, teaching and the care of students. The problem was how to do so in a way which took account of the often very different intakes of students entering schools.

Some schools regularly receive new cohorts of students with the highest levels of what we call 'prior achievement' gained during an earlier phase of schooling in a nursery or through the quality of home care invested in them. Schools which receive high proportions of successful students with everything going for them are clearly at an enormous advantage compared with those which receive, predominantly, students with negative early experiences.

Over the last twenty years, a number of other studies of effectiveness have been carried out in the UK, the United States, the Netherlands and, increasingly, in Australia, Hong Kong and other countries in Asia. One of the most comprehensive is the *School Matters* study of fifty inner city primary schools (with which two of us were closely associated: see Mortimore *et al.*, 1988). This study built on the methodology of *Fifteen Thousand Hours* by increasing the scope of the research instruments and the quality of the statistical analyses. The research team drew on the newly written multilevel modelling programmes (Goldstein, 1987) which had been developed to deal with data clustered at different natural levels – classes, year groups and schools.

The research project we have recently undertaken, and on which this book is based, was established to explore a number of important issues that had emerged from the earlier studies of school effectiveness. In particular, we wished to investigate effectiveness in secondary schools and the specific issue of departmental differences in examination results. The study was also designed to measure effects over different time periods and differential effectiveness for different types of students (males and females; different ethnic and social groups; and those with different levels of prior achievement). The project involved the detailed multilevel analysis of examination results for a large sample of over ninety secondary schools and nearly 18,000 students from 1990 until 1992.

During the project, we studied the academic effectiveness of schools through the use of seven measures constructed from the results of the examination commonly taken by all sixteen year old students at the end of compulsory schooling in England and Wales – the General Certificate of Secondary Education (GCSE). The measures of individual student achievement are: a total performance score and six separate subject scores in English, English literature, French, history, mathematics and science. These measures were used to develop models of school and departmental effectiveness which permitted us to undertake a simultaneous examination of the stability, consistency and differential effectiveness of the schools' results.

In addition to the collection of examination data, we carried out in-depth qualitative case studies of six schools and thirty subject departments. The case study schools were chosen from three groups: academically more effective; academically ineffective; and highly mixed effects in different subjects. These outlier schools had significant, stable and consistent effects on students' GCSE outcomes over several years. Our fieldwork involved interviews with head-teachers, deputies and heads of subject departments which provided information about the school during the past five years, as well as about current policies and practices.

In the next chapter of the book we discuss the concept of quality in education. We provide a fuller account of school effectiveness research and, drawing on the increasingly international literature, endeavour to respond to some of the criticisms and challenges associated with it. In this chapter we also report the aims of the study and explain the rationale for its multi-stage methodology.

The main findings of the project are divided into three sections. Part 1 (Chapters 3 and 4) deals with the *measurement* of academic effectiveness. Chapter 3 presents the results of the first phase of our study and focuses on the size of variations in school effectiveness recorded over three years. Chapter 4 deals with the nature of internal variations in schools' GCSE performance for different student groups (categorized by gender, ethnic background and socio-economic status). Part 2 (Chapters 5, 6 and 7) concerns the *explanation* of differences in academic effectiveness. Chapter 5 presents the case study results from the second, qualitative phase of our research, while the results from the third phase appear in Chapters 6 and 7. These cover practitioners' views of effectiveness in some detail and investigate the extent to which it is possible to account for variations in school and departmental academic effectiveness. Part 3 (Chapters 8 and 9) examines the *implications* of our findings for research and practice. Chapter 8 discusses the theoretical implications, and a model of secondary school effectiveness is put forward. Chapter 9 endeavours to deal with the messages for policy and practice for all concerned with school improvement. We tease out how all these apply to *policy makers* in central and local government (judging performance, researching of schools, and inspection): *practitioners*, the headteacher and senior management team (leadership, monitoring strategies for improvement and staff morale): *classroom teachers* (teaching styles/practice, planning, management and feedback) and *students* and *parents* (choosing schools and parental involvement).

In this book we provide as full an account as we can of the differences between schools and departments and of the impact of such differences on the academic success of their students. We also aim to provide an overview of the value added methodology we have employed to measure school and department effects in order to assist educational practitioners in their own evaluations. Needless to say, there are numerous issues which we will not have the space to address in this publication, which is aimed at the general reader interested in the state of our education system as well as the specialist researcher. For those seeking technical information about the study or who are interested in our other work there are a number of references in the index. At intervals throughout this book, we outline the chief elements of certain key concepts such as 'multilevel modelling', 'value added' and 'school effectiveness'. This inevitable overlap occurs because these concepts are central to an understanding of all three phases of the project – measurement, explanation and implications – and we are concerned that our readers should be reminded of the central features of these complex but important ideas.

Current theories of evaluation maintain that it is impossible to measure a situation without somehow changing it. For those of us who work in and with schools, this is a daunting inhibition. We have sought to minimize this *researcher effect* by employing independent practitioners to collect the case study information and, wherever possible, by testing the validity of our data through the use of crosschecks and appropriate statistical techniques. To the best of our knowledge our conclusions accurately reflect the nature of the schools we have studied. Our project was carried out in an inner city of the UK. Nonetheless, we believe that many of the issues involved in conducting this research and some of its findings are relevant to a far wider context.

We are extremely grateful to the headteachers, governing bodies, teachers and students who have at any stage been involved with this study. We hope that they will see the book as a valuable contribution to the collective understanding of how secondary schools work, how they influence student achievement and how they might be improved.

2

The Study of Departmental Differences in Academic Effectiveness

INTRODUCTION

The question of what constitutes quality in education is a vital one for policy makers, as well as for practitioners and consumers of the service. Of course the question is not a new one and, as we have observed elsewhere, is 'intimately bound up with more fundamental questions about the nature of education itself' (Mortimore and Stone, 1991, p. 69). In this country, concern about quality in education and educational standards has grown apace during the last two decades and these topics have become a major focus of public debate.

It is almost impossible to judge whether, as some claim, standards have fallen over the last thirty years, given the lack of reliable evidence following the abolition of national monitoring by the former Assessment of Performance Unit (APU) – and the many changes in curriculum and syllabus – not to mention the much greater numbers of young people entering public examinations and going on to further and higher education. Nonetheless, it is clear, as Hopkins (1994) observed, that 'student achievement still lags behind society's expectations' (p. 89). We think it is this mismatch between *actual* achievement levels and *expectations* which helps to explain the continuing attention given to educational issues by politicians and the media. Government has increased its powers in relation to education considerably during the last ten years (a topic we discuss in more detail in Chapter 9). The main driving forces behind such centralization – of the curriculum, the institution of national assessment and regular national inspection – arose from perceptions of the need to improve educational quality and raise standards to meet the requirements of the economy and society in the twenty-first century. Recent comparative research tends to support those who believe that, in order to maintain and improve economic competitiveness, student achievement levels need to be raised. Although comparative studies are complex and controversial (Goldstein, 1996; Alexander, 1996), they suggest that in some key areas, such as the teaching of mathematics, UK students under-perform (Reynolds and Farrell, 1996). In addition, there is evidence of greater school-level variation in achievement levels in the UK than in many other systems (Reynolds, 1995), and growing acceptance of the view that the UK produces a much larger 'trailing edge' in terms of student achievement levels than many other countries. In other words, it is particularly those who make up the bottom 25 to 30 per cent of the range who are poorly served by our secondary educational system (a theme we return to in Chapter 9).

The UK is not alone in its interest in raising standards and concern about educational quality, as the publication of an international report by the OECD (1989) entitled *Schools and Quality* makes clear. This report articulated a multidimensional view of educational quality which stresses the inter-relationships between five key areas: the curriculum; the role of teachers; school organization; assessment, appraisal and monitoring; and resources.

Lawton's (1994) discussion of the issues involved in defining educational quality stressed the continuing relevance of the OECD's conclusion that 'education is not an assembly-line process of mechanically increasing inputs and raising productivity' (p. 1). He concluded that in the UK reliance on 'two false gods' – parental choice and market mechanisms – to raise quality in education, as evidenced in the 1988 Education Reform Act and later in *Choice and Diversity* (DFE, 1992), is fundamentally mistaken. Rather he drew attention to the potential value of school effectiveness research, such as Rutter *et al.*'s (1979) *Fifteen Thousand Hours* study of secondary schools and Mortimore *et al.*'s (1988) *School Matters* investigation in the primary sector. Lawton went on to stress that a better understanding of what constitutes an effective school culture, and the complex question of how to encourage school-based cultural change, has more to offer those interested in promoting educational quality than beliefs in the efficacy of parental choice and market forces as major agents of change.

In 1989 the OECD report on *Schools and Quality* concluded that:

> The assessment of quality is thus complex and value laden. There is no simple unidimensional measure of quality. In the same way that the definition of what constitutes high quality in education is multidimensional, so there is no simple pre-scription of the ingredients necessary to achieve high quality education; many factors interact – students and their backgrounds; staff and their skills; schools and their structure and ethos; curricular; and societal expectations (p. 27).

We argue that school effectiveness research can help to *disentangle* and *clarify* such interactions, and because of this it has a vital role to play in analysing the constituents of quality in education (Sammons, 1994), and in improving our understanding of the way school and classroom processes can influence student achievement for good or ill.

Values in education

School effectiveness research uses students' educational outcomes as the fundamental criteria for determining school effectiveness. In terms of underlying vision, the concept of equity – raising the achievement of all students regardless of background characteristics such as sex, ethnicity or socio-economic status – has been a driving force in both UK and USA studies in the field. School effectiveness research seeks to disentangle the often powerful impact of students' background characteristics from the influence of the school (Mortimore, 1995a). By focusing on the concept of progress or the *value added* by the school to student achievement over a period of years, for example, in the case of secondary schools from entry at age 11 to public examinations at age 16, it is possible to investigate whether some schools are more effective than others in promoting their students' progress and thus their final level of achievement (Mortimore, Sammons and Thomas, 1994).

The concept of school effectiveness thus depends fundamentally on the choice of measures of students' educational outcomes (Sammons, 1996). Stoll and Fink (1996) have argued that schools should measure what they value. We are in favour of using a broad range of students' educational outcomes to judge school performance, and UK school effectiveness research has, on the whole, paid more attention to social and affective outcomes, i.e. behaviour, attitudes, attendance, than is the case in other countries (Reynolds *et al.*, 1996b). However, whilst academic outcomes are not the only ones which should be valued, we argue that they are of crucial importance: in a society such as the UK where 'high stakes' testing is institutionalized via the public examination system, those examination results remain a major indicator of school performance and have a substantial impact on young people's employment prospects and likelihood of entering further higher education (Mortimore and Sammons, 1997). It is essential, however, that any comparisons of individual schools' results are made on a 'like with like' basis, taking into account the influence of student intake. Otherwise comparisons, such as those presented in the school league table annual publication of raw results, tell us more about the intakes to schools than about their contribution to student achievement. Thus they are more liable to misinform than to increase our knowledge of educational quality, a topic we discuss in more detail in Chapters 3 and 9.

In recent years some authors (for example, Pring, 1995; Elliott, 1996; Hamilton, 1996) have criticized the basis and values underlying school effectiveness research. These criticisms have focused on the methodology employed, particularly the emphasis given to measures of students' educational outcomes, contrasting this adversely with notions of educational quality in which the process – in particular the quality of teacher-student relationships – is all important. Thus, Elliott (1996) has argued that teachers should focus on the quality of the teaching-learning process rather than on its outcomes since, if the former is right, then the students themselves will take care of the latter. Elliott also disparages the concept of effectiveness in comparison with ideas of a 'good' school, suggesting that the learning process rather than outcomes is all important. We find such arguments both circuitous and unconvincing (for a detailed response see Sammons and Reynolds, 1997). Learning, by its very nature, is not observable and can only be gauged indirectly by measuring the outcomes of student learning in some way. Assessment, both informal and formal, for a variety of purposes – formative, diagnostic and summative – is hence an essential part of every teacher's repertoire.

Rather than attempting to define 'good', and thus by implication 'bad', schools, school effectiveness research focuses deliberately on the narrower concept of effectiveness which concerns the achievement of educational goals measured by student progress. We argue that *promoting progress* lies at the heart of the educational process and is accepted by teachers and students as well as parents and policy makers as one purpose, and probably the *fundamental purpose*, of all schools.

By contrast, we doubt whether agreement could, or indeed should, exist concerning the more amorphous concept of a 'good' school. Naturally, individual students' and parents' and teachers' views will often differ, reflecting their own values, cultural backgrounds and preferences. Some may favour single sex education or strict rules about uniform; some prefer church schools or small ones; others may seek the range of provision typical of larger institutions or favour co-education. Music, sports and other facilities will likewise vary in their importance for different parents, students and practitioners. Indeed parents' views of a 'good' school may differ for individual children in the same family, reflecting their perceptions of what would best suit a particular child's needs.

School effectiveness research quite deliberately does not seek to make judgements about what makes a 'good' school – see Silver (1994) and Gray and Wilcox (1995) for detailed discussions of this topic. Rather, it takes as its 'touchstone' the criteria of impact upon students' educational outcomes in evaluating school and classroom practices (Reynolds, 1995). This we think is its one great virtue. Rather than being influenced by passing fashions in policy and practice, school effectiveness research seeks to investigate empirically through longitudinal research the ways in which schools can promote student progress. In our experience it is this very focus on the *links* between practice and student outcomes which makes the field of such interest to practitioners as well as policy makers, and accounts for its rapid growth in recent years.

Thus, although we would not argue that an effective school would invariably be a good one, we conclude that it is a necessary, if not a sufficient, precondition. In addition, we find it hard to believe that any acceptable definition of a 'good' school could be proposed which did not include academic effectiveness – by which we mean the extent to which student progress is fostered – as an essential component.

The contribution of empirical research

In 1996 the former President of the British Educational Research Association argued the case for educational researchers to seek to inform policy and practice on the basis of their findings (Bassey, 1996). At a time when education is high on the political agenda, the need for educational policy to be driven by evidence rather than ideology has never been greater. All too often schools, and therefore both students and teachers, have suffered from ill-founded beliefs that structural changes, for example in the status of schools, are the solution to all their educational ills (real or imagined). No hard evidence has been produced that the institution of grant maintained (GM) or City Technology Colleges (CTCs) or increasing selection will improve standards or quality. Without longitudinal research focusing on student progress and taking into account the undeniable fact that schools vary markedly in their intakes, it will not be possible for a proper evaluation of the impact of such changes to be made. In our view, it is unfortunate that so much educational change has taken place so rapidly on a national level, without the advantage of carefully evaluated pilot schemes to examine the costs and benefits of proposed changes for different groups of students.

We also contrast what can be learnt from school effectiveness research with currently fashionable 'back to the 1950s' prescriptions that streaming, selection, uniforms, caning and traditional 'chalk and talk' whole class teaching are the key to raising standards (Phillips, 1996). Only by monitoring student progress in different schools and examining the relationships between school and classroom practices and students' educational outcomes systematically can we gain a better understanding of whether and why some schools may be more effective than others.

The need for a new study of secondary school effectiveness

Despite their potential to inform policy and practice, relatively few studies have examined the links between school processes, using information about variations in school and classroom organization, policy and practice, and students' educational outcomes (Reynolds, 1994a). The most influential studies in recent years have examined primary school influences. In the UK, for example, Mortimore et al.'s (1988) School Matters research examined junior education and Tizard et al.'s (1988) study focused on the infant years. The ten year Louisiana School Effectiveness project in the USA was likewise conducted on elementary schools (Teddlie and Stringfield, 1993).

In the UK, only the early seminal studies by Rutter et al. (1979) and Reynolds (1976, 1982) address both the question of the extent of differences between secondary schools in their impact upon students' educational outcomes **and** the underlying reasons behind such variations in effectiveness. In other words, what factors bearing on school and classroom organization, policy and practice help to make some secondary schools more effective than others? These two important studies took place during the 1970s and involved small numbers of schools. They were also conducted before more recent methodological advances in school effectiveness research, particularly the application of multilevel models (Paterson and Goldstein 1991; Goldstein, 1995) which facilitate the study of value added by schools to student progress – a topic we discuss in more detail in the next chapter.

Of more recent studies of the secondary years, that by Smith and Tomlinson (1989) is probably the most notable. This important research on multi-racial comprehensives addressed the issue of differences in schools' examination performance, and studied student progress. It focused, in particular, on the topic of ethnic differences in achievement and the school's role in relation to this. However, little data about school or classroom processes were collected, due to industrial action by teachers at this time, and thus the research lacked explanatory power and is of limited value in terms of implications for policy makers and practitioners interested in the key question of *why* some schools are more academically effective than others.

ISSUES IN SCHOOL EFFECTIVENESS STUDIES

In a discussion of school effectiveness research in 1993, conducted at the start of a seminar series funded by the Economic and Social Research Council (ESRC), it emerged that the issue of consistency in school effectiveness is a vital one. This review of research was subsequently published in a volume of seminar papers (Sammons, Mortimore and Thomas, 1996.) There is now substantial academic agreement as to the most appropriate methods of estimating school effects and the data required for valid comparisons to be made (Gray, Jesson and Sime, 1990; Scheerens, 1992; Goldstein *et al.*, 1993; Sammons *et al.*, 1994; Creemers, 1994a; Goldstein, 1995; Thomas and Mortimore, 1996). However, while such studies have pointed to the existence of differences between schools in their effects at all levels – i.e., primary, secondary and post sixteen – only relatively recently has the issue of consistency been addressed. Our 1993 review pointed to the need to 'unpack' the notion of consistency in school effectiveness and focus in particular on three sub-themes. These are consistency in promoting different educational outcomes, stability over time, and differential effects.

Little research has examined the extent of internal variations in effectiveness – that is to say to what extent schools vary in their impact on different measures of student outcomes, particularly at the secondary level. This we define as consistency across outcomes. In other words, are schools which are effective in promoting a particular outcome – reading, for example – equally effective for other areas such as mathematics? At A-level, work has been conducted by Fitz-Gibbon and colleagues (1991, 1992) examining departments' results in different subjects, while the earlier study by Smith and Tomlinson (1989) studied relationships between English, mathematics and overall examination outcomes at age sixteen years, but most secondary school effectiveness studies have focused on overall measures of academic outcomes.

In addition to variations in terms of different outcome measures, another important aspect of internal variations within school concerns the concept of differential effectiveness. By this we mean are some schools more effective at promoting the progress of particular student groups – for example, girls rather than boys, or students from particular ethnic or socio-economic groups? Work on this sub-theme was conducted by us in an earlier study of primary schools (Mortimore *et al.*, 1988), and some secondary research had also explored this topic (Nuttall *et al.*, 1989). However, limitations in the nature of the data available in this latter study meant that the results needed to be treated with some caution. Research by Jesson and Gray (1991) on the topic of differential effectiveness suggested that such effects might be fairly modest, but, given the important implications for equity, this has remained a question of considerable practical as well as research interest during the last six years.

The third sub-theme we identified relates to consistency in school effectiveness and in terms of stability in effects from one year to another. This acknowledges the need for explicit recognition that schools are not static institutions but are subject to considerable amounts of change both internally and externally. For this reason measures of effectiveness related to only one point in time are of limited value and need to be compared from one year to another so that any trends – stability, improvement or decline – can be identified.

As noted earlier, in addition to questions concerning consistency, differential effectiveness and stability, perhaps the major limitation of the school effectiveness field during the early 1990s was the relatively small number of studies, particularly at secondary level, which had examined the school and classroom processes which influence effectiveness. Those studies which had been conducted in the UK were relatively small in size and, as a result, suffered from methodological limitations. From our review it became clear that no recent secondary school effectiveness research had attempted to link processes and student outcomes directly. None met the six criteria cited as necessary for an adequate study of school effectiveness by Scheerens (1992):

- the tapping of sufficient natural variance in school and instructional characteristics;
- the use of adequate operationalizations and measures of the process and effect variables, preferably including direct observations of process variables and a mixture of quantitative and qualitative measures;
- an adequate adjustment of effect measures for intake differences between schools;
- units of analysis that allow for data analyses of sufficient discriminative power;
- adequate techniques for data analysis (e.g. multilevel models); and
- use of longitudinal data.

Moreover, no research had attempted both to investigate in detail the concept of secondary school effectiveness in relation to the three sub-themes described earlier (consistency, stability and differential effectiveness), *and* account for any variations in effectiveness by examining differences in school and classroom processes and their relation to student outcomes.

In 1993, therefore, we began a research project which was intended to address all four of the key areas in which we considered that further school effectiveness research was urgently needed. We decided to focus on the topic of school and departmental differences in secondary school academic effectiveness because at the time there was no recent research which focused on the explanation of variations in effectiveness, nor on both the school and departmental levels simultaneously. In particular, we wished to use the research to inform the development of public policy in the light of the greater emphasis given to schools' raw examinations results following the first publication of league tables in 1992 (DFE, 1992).

Our research had three major aims:

(1) to extend current knowledge about the size, extent and stability over time between secondary schools in their overall effectiveness in promoting students' GCSE attainments;
(2) to explore the extent of any internal variations in school effectiveness at
    (a) the departmental level, and
    (b) for different groups of students, and
(3) to investigate in detail the reasons underlying any differences in effectiveness in relation to school and departmental processes.

It was intended to make a contribution to the continuing debate about how schools' performance may best be judged by exploring internal variations in effectiveness as well as measuring trends over time. Our study was designed to investigate the applicability of the concept of overall school effectiveness to the secondary sector and whether schools can be divided validly into broadly effective or ineffective groups. In other words, it was an attempt to test the validity of policy developments in the 1990s, which had increasingly labelled schools with adjectives such as 'good' and 'bad', 'successful' and 'failing'.

In addition, it is widely recognized that much more is known about the measurement of school effectiveness than about its underlying causes and the field has been particularly criticized for this weak theoretical basis (Scheerens, 1992; Creemers, 1994b; Reynolds et al., 1994). We hoped that our study would improve understanding of the processes which influence effectiveness and feed into the theoretical development of the field, by the formulation of a new model of secondary school effectiveness. We were keen to establish the extent to which it is possible to account statistically for variations in secondary school effectiveness using more appropriate multilevel modelling techniques. In other words, we wished to go beyond correlational studies of associations between process indicators and measures of school effectiveness, and to test out the continued applicability of the results of earlier secondary school studies, such as *Fifteen Thousand Hours* (Rutter et al., 1979).

Equally important was our concern to increase the value and accessibility of school effectiveness research for practitioners and policy makers. At a time when the quality of education and school improvement is high on the political agenda and a focus of interest for bodies such as the DfEE, SCAA and OFSTED as well as for schools themselves, it is vitally important that research and practice is informed by carefully conducted empirical studies, which investigate the impact of different school and classroom policies and practices on students' educational outcomes.

Our study was designed to address five key questions which are of considerable relevance to practitioners and policy makers, as well as to the educational research community.

Key questions

(1) Are differences between the effects of departments on students' GCSE attainments in selected subjects greater or less than differences between secondary schools in their overall effects upon students' total GCSE scores?

(2) Is there any evidence that some schools are generally more effective (across subjects) in promoting students' attainment at GCSE and that others are less effective in most areas, or is the concept of overall effectiveness too simplistic for the secondary age group?

(3) Is the pattern of differences at the school or departmental level stable from year to year?

(4) Is there any evidence that some schools and departments are *differentially* effective in promoting GCSE attainment for different groups of students (categorized by gender, ethnicity, prior attainment and entitlement to free school meals) or are secondary schools and departments equally effective, or ineffective, in promoting attainment for all groups?

(5) What factors to do with school status and processes relate to differences between secondary schools in effectiveness in promoting GCSE attainment? In particular, is there evidence that different factors and processes are important in promoting good results for different departments?

RESEARCH DESIGN AND METHODOLOGY

In order to try and answer these questions we designed a research project with three phases. The three phases combined detailed quantitative analyses of students' GCSE results for three consecutive Year 11 cohorts with qualitative analyses of specific schools and individual subject departments. Empirical methods attempted to identify patterns in data and examine relationships between variables through studies of large numbers of students and schools, using statistical concepts of probability to assist in generalization. By contrast, our qualitative case studies sought to illuminate our understanding of practice by a focus on individual institutions in their specific context. We believe that a combination of these two approaches is likely to be more fruitful than an exclusive reliance on only one methodological approach.

Phase 1

The first phase of our study concerned the measurement of school effectiveness and involved the analysis of variations in school and departmental GCSE performance. Our focus was on academic effectiveness at GCSE. In order to study school effects it is essential to obtain measures of the value added by individual secondary schools to students' GCSE results. By focusing on relative progress of students with similar characteristics in different schools, we were able to make 'like with like' comparisons.

Our study involved a total of nintety-four secondary schools in eight inner London LEAs. We had information for GCSE candidate cohorts of roughly 7,000 students in any one year and our study analysed examination data for a three-year period (1990–92), the minimum needed to identify any trends. Because our study involved inner London LEAs we were able to access (from former ILEA databases) suitable, common prior attainment measures of student-performance at secondary transfer for each of the three examination cohorts. Further details of the sample and methods are given in Chapters 3 and 4.

It is important to recognize that the most appropriate studies of school effectiveness adopt a longitudinal approach and look at the full period of time students are in secondary school. In our view it is vital to use information about the prior attainments of students at intake to secondary school (Year 7 in our study) so that progress can be established over the five years (Year 7 to Year 11) until students reach the end of this compulsory schooling and enter for public examinations. There are significant theoretical as well as methodological limitations in studies which take measures of student achievement some time after entry to secondary school (e.g. at Key Stage 3) because schools will have already had an influence on students' progress. In addition, it is helpful if curriculum related measures of prior achievement are used since these are usually better predictors of later GCSE results, and thus provide a more appropriate control of intake differences to secondary school than IQ-type tests.

We used multilevel modelling techniques (Paterson and Goldstein, 1991; Goldstein, 1995) for the analyses of school effectiveness and took account of two measures of students' attainment at the end of primary schooling prior to secondary transfer. In addition, we were able to examine the relationships between a wide variety of student background characteristics of relevance to academic performance (age, gender, ethnic background and socio-economic disadvantage) as well as contextual measures of the composition of the student intake to individual schools – the percentage of students eligible for free school meals.

In order to explore internal variations in academic effectiveness, we collected details of individual students' total GCSE performance score (derived from all subjects entered) and GCSE scores in six specific subjects: English, English literature, mathematics, French, history and science. We chose these subjects to cover the three core curriculum areas and to ensure adequate numbers of students at the departmental level for the maximum number of schools. For our sample, history and French were the two non-core subjects taken by the largest numbers of candidates.

Because of the detailed prior attainment measures and student background data we collected, we were able to adopt appropriate multilevel models to explore the first four research questions which relate to:

- stability over time (in this case across the three years 1990–92);
- consistency in performance in terms of overall GCSE results and for five subject departments;
- differential effectiveness for different student groups, including males and females, low and high ability students and for different ethnic and socio-economic groups.

Both the second and third phases of our study concern the fifth question addressed by our research, about the explanation of differences in effectiveness.

Phase 2

At the time we planned our Differential School Effectiveness project, the need for more detailed case studies on effective schools was becoming increasingly recognized as one method of developing our understanding of the ways in which different aspects of the functioning of schools can influence student progress (Levine, 1992; Reynolds, 1992). Reynolds (1992) argued: 'To improve our understanding of the complex interaction of persons, methods and processes that generate an effective school we need to undertake greater use of case study and qualitative methods . . . This is particularly important if the school effectiveness work is to be made more accessible to practitioners and policy maker communities' (p. 16).

As well as studies of more effective schools, there was also a need to examine the less effective end of the spectrum, since it was likely that the characteristics and functioning of such institutions would differ fundamentally and not merely exhibit the obverse of the characteristics and processes of more effective schools. In addition, in our view, case studies of schools with mixed effects (e.g. in terms of specific subjects) are required because they may help to illuminate the ways in which the organization and personnel in some departments in the same institution are able to promote greater student progress while progress in other departments is depressed. Such studies may also contribute to the development of theory in the related field of school improvement where the focus is on the process of educational change (Stoll, 1996).

The second phase of our study involved detailed qualitative case studies of six schools and thirty subject departments. These were conducted to examine the processes and characteristics of schools and departments which varied significantly in effectiveness in promoting their students' examination outcomes. We selected the case study schools on the basis of their consistency and statistical significance of the value added estimates of school effects based on the quantitative analysis of examination results conducted during Phase 1.

Initially we chose schools on the basis of a two-year analysis of the examination data for 69 of the 94 secondary schools (73 per cent). (The selection of the case study schools was confirmed by later analyses conducted over three years.) We found that 12 (17 per cent) of these 69 schools could be identified as *outliers*. By this we mean that they had consistent, stable and significant effects over two years. Two schools were chosen from each of three groups.

Group 1   Academically ineffective – broadly negative effects on student progress.

Group 2   Academically more effective – broadly positive effects on student progress.

Group 3   Highly mixed effects – highly effective and highly ineffective departments co-existing in the same institution.

Schools in groups one and two can be seen to represent more extreme cases which differ markedly in terms of their overall academic effectiveness controlling for intake. This finding highlights the existence of a small number of outliers generally academically more effective and ineffective schools, and point to the need to look at overall school factors, as well as focusing on the departmental level in the process analysis. Nonetheless, our results also demonstrated that in some schools departmental effects on particular subjects may be highly significant and that effective and ineffective departments may co-exist within the same school.

The two schools chosen from each of the three groups described above were selected for detailed case studies. We were fortunate that two experienced consultants (a former headteacher and a former LEA adviser) were able to assist in this phase of the research. These consultants were involved in the construction of the interview schedules and the topics covered were also informed by a review of relevant literature (Sammons *et al.*, 1995) for key personnel – the headteacher, deputy head, and heads of five subject departments. The consultants also conducted the interviews and although aware of the nature of the research design, they were not told which schools or departments had been identified as particularly effective or ineffective on the basis of the Phase 1 examination analyses. By collecting information from three different groups of personnel in each school we were able to explore similarities and differences in respondents' perceptions and views.

The case studies adopted an explicitly retrospective approach, in that a strong emphasis was laid on comparing the current situation in the school or department with that of five years previously. Inevitably, this has a number of limitations, including the continued availability of staff from that period and the potential problems of recall and of *post-hoc* rationalization. Nonetheless, it also had some advantages in allowing an explicit focus on the extent of change over a five-year period to be added to the project. Providing school staff with the opportunity to reflect on past events/policies and changes and the reasons for these also gives a picture of school and departmental histories. All staff were assured of both personal and institutional confidentiality and anonymity in the presentation of the interview results. The results of the case studies are described in Chapter 5.

In designing our study we recognized that, as with all tests and assessments,

GCSE examination results can only provide indicators of past performance. Students' learning experiences over the five preceding years in secondary schooling will be reflected in their GCSE achievement. It should be noted that the problems of linking process information and judgements – about management, policies, teaching practices and student learning – concerning aspects of schools' functioning with information about their educational standards are also experienced in the inspection process. This is because examination and Key Stage results, inevitably, relate to the quality of teaching and learning over several previous years.

Ideally, by following an age group from entry at age eleven until sixteen, information about school and departmental policies and classroom practices could be related directly to a given group of students, as it was in an earlier primary study (Mortimore *et al.*, 1988). Such studies are, however, extremely expensive and time-consuming. In addition, because of our interest in stability in performance across years it would be desirable to follow more than one age cohort. Given these constraints of time and resources, this was not a feasible strategy for the present study. Moreover, it would not be possible to identify which schools would be of particular interest as case studies until after an age group had completed their GCSEs, when progress over five years could be ascertained.

In view of these methodological considerations, we believe that our three phase project design maximized opportunities to address all four areas in which we had identified the need for further school effectiveness research. By identifying patterns of consistency and stability in value added analyses of more than one year of examination results we were able to identify schools of particular interest for the second, qualitative phase of study. We recognized that, because the relevant age groups had already taken their GCSEs and left the schools, it would not be appropriate to conduct classroom observations in the schools. Nonetheless, via our retrospective approach we were able to collect information about past school and departmental policies and practices which may have influenced students' GCSE performance in the three years for which data were available (1990–92). This was also a particularly interesting period in which to study schools due to the many changes they experienced from 1989/90 to 1993/4.

Phase 3

The third phase of our research design was also concerned with investigating the relationships between variations in school and departmental processes factors and their relationships with students' GCSE performance. The aim was to establish the extent to which it is possible to account statistically for differences in value added measures of schools' academic effectiveness – in terms of overall GCSE performance and in specific subjects.

Building on the results of our six detailed case studies schools and departments conducted in Phase 2, we were able to develop a small number of instruments for the Phase 3 collection of a more limited set of data about school and departmental process for a larger number of schools. Postal questionnaires were piloted with four non-project schools before being sent to all schools in our sample. In order to minimize demands on schools, separate questionnaires were sent to the headteacher (HT) and two heads of department (English and mathematics HoDs). A total of 264 questionnaires were sent to 88 of our 94 study schools – 4 schools had closed by 1994 and 2 had opted for GM status and, due to staff changes, declined to be involved. All respondents were assured of confidentiality and provided with individual prepaid reply envelopes. Responses were received from 55 schools (61 per cent). Two or more responses were received from 40 schools and just over a third (31) returned all three questionnaires. Schools for which questionnaires were received and those which did not respond were found to be similar in terms of our value-added measures of academic effectiveness. Thus we did not find that staff in the relatively effective schools were more inclined to respond to our survey than others.

Our questionnaires were designed to examine HTs' and HoDs' perceptions of their schools' and departments' academic performance. As with Phase 2 of the study we asked HTs and HoDs to compare the current situation with that in the school or specific departments five years previously. We also questioned respondents about the factors which they perceived as contributing to or inhibiting effectiveness currently and in the past. Their views about the school's principal educational goals and about judging both school and departmental effectiveness were also sought. Chapter 6 describes the results of our analyses of HTs' and HoDs' views and examines similarities and differences in perceptions for different groups of respondents.

The third phase of the research was used to test out some of the conclusions we drew concerning the factors which distinguished more and less effective schools and departments. In addition to simple descriptive statistics and correlations exploring patterns of relationships, we used more sophisticated statistical analyses. As in Phase 1, multilevel modelling techniques involving value added analyses of students' GCSE outcomes were adopted, but in this phase we were able to include process indicators derived from the questionnaire survey. The relationships between HTs' and HODs' questionnaire responses and value added estimates of school effectiveness were examined to establish which school and departmental process items (if any) differentiated between schools in terms of academic effectiveness. In addition, our multilevel models were used to establish whether such items made a statistically significant contribution to the *explanation* of school and departmental variation in GCSE performance over three years (1990–92) after controlling for differences between schools in their intakes.

SUMMARY

Our project research design thus had the strength of combining quantitative and qualitative approaches in order to improve our understanding of academic effectiveness and enhance the development of school effectiveness theory. Part 1 of this book presents the results of the first phase of the study and focuses on measuring academic effectiveness. We had a particular interest in the question of *internal* variations in effectiveness for different student groups and at the departmental level. Also of relevance is the topic of stability in school and departmental effectiveness over time and trends (improving or declining) in performance. Chapter 3 examines the size and extent of variations in academic effectiveness using GCSE results for three consecutive age groups, and Chapter 4 focuses on internal variations or differential effectiveness.

The explanation of variations in academic effectiveness are the focus of Part 2. Findings from the qualitative second phase of the research are given in Chapter 5. We analyse the extent to which the study of particular institutions chosen from three groups in terms of their impact on student progress – academically more effective, academically ineffective and highly mixed – can illuminate our understanding of the ways schools influence student progress.

The results of the third phase of the research, which used a questionnaire survey of HTs and HoDs to collect process information from a larger sample of schools, are presented in Chapters 6 and 7. Chapter 6 examines HTs' and HoDs' views and perceptions of effectiveness and the factors they regarded as influential in their institutions and specific departments. In Chapter 7 we examine the associations between process items and school and departments' value added results, and test the extent to which it is possible to account for differences in overall GCSE performance and specific subject results, after taking account of intake factors.

Part 3 examines the implications of the research for theory, policy and practice. In Chapter 8 we consider the extent to which the project's results add to the theoretical development of the field and present a model of secondary school academic effectiveness. The practical implications of our research are the subject of Chapter 9. Here we examine the main messages for three key groups – policy makers, practitioners and consumers (students/parents), who are concerned with improving the quality of secondary school education. In Chapter 10 we look to the future and suggest principles which we feel would create a better partnership between practitioners and politicians for the benefit of the education service.

PART 1: MEASURING SCHOOL EFFECTIVENESS

3

How Can We Measure School Effectiveness?

INTRODUCTION

We have noted in Chapter 2 that the demand for information about the functioning of the educational system from politicians, managers and consumers of the service has increased markedly during the last decade. But when does information become misinformation, or even disinformation? The purpose of this chapter is to provide an overview of current approaches to measuring school performance and, in particular, value added measures.

The issue of how to provide appropriate and valid ways of reporting on schools' performance is of vital importance. Elsewhere we have discussed the need to employ a wide range of student outcomes including affective, vocational and academic measures. This chapter compares school performance in terms of students' General Certificate of Secondary Education (GCSE) outcomes at age 16, the end of their compulsory schooling. The GCSE is part of the UK's National Curriculum Assessment framework and provides assessment outcomes at the end of Key Stage 4. Our aim, therefore, is to illustrate key issues in measuring school performance by utilizing the data and findings of our Differential School Effectiveness Project, which deals with the topic of secondary school effectiveness and, in particular, focuses on the departmental level.

It has been argued strongly – by educational practitioners as well as academic researchers – that, taken on its own, information about schools' raw examination results, such as that published by the DfEE, will always be an inadequate measure of performance. Without any knowledge of the context of the school, it can be misleading (see Nuttall *et al.*, 1989; Sammons *et al.*, 1993; Mortimore *et al.*, 1994; Thomas and Goldstein, 1995; Thomas and Mortimore, 1996; Goldstein and Spiegelhalter, 1996; Gray *et al.*, 1996). For example, in connection with proposals to publish school league tables, Nuttall (1990) stated that:

> Natural justice demands that schools are held accountable only for those things that they can influence (for good or ill) and not for the pre-existing differences between their intakes. (p. 25)

Raw results are the appropriate answer to the question 'how has my son or daughter performed?' but not to questions about a school's performance. For these questions other information is needed in order to identify what researchers call the *value added* component (Mortimore, Sammons and Thomas, 1994). Moreover, measuring educational value added serves the important purpose of stimulating school self-evaluation and school improvement. This objective is equally, if not more, likely to have a direct impact on educational standards than the limited and slippery goal of accountability. The concept of value added is of considerable value in focusing the minds of HTs and teachers on the contribution that the school makes towards the effective learning of individual students (a topic we return to in Chapter 9).

What is meant by value added?

There are various ways of defining value added and these encompass both qualitative judgements and quantitative measures. Value added approaches also differ in the balance of emphasis placed on evaluating student outcomes directly, or indirectly, via the quality of the teaching and learning process. However, in a broad sense, all definitions of value added have the common aim of assessing the quality and extent of a school's effectiveness in promoting student achievement. For the purpose of clarity we define the term value added more precisely. It is an indication of the extent to which any given school has fostered the progress of *all* students in a range of subjects during a particular time period – for example, from entry to the school until public examinations in the case of secondary schools, or over particular years in primaries – in comparison with the effects of other schools in the same sample. As noted, we are focusing on academic progress in this chapter, but this is not to ignore the value and importance of other outcomes, such as student attitudes to learning. In this case, however, our definition refers specifically to academic attainment and can be stated as the relative boost a school gives to a student's previous level of attainment in comparison with similar students in other schools. Therefore, in order to calculate the value added component, accurate baseline information about students' prior attainment is vital (Sammons *et al.*, 1993; Thomas, 1995a; Sammons, 1996; Thomas and Mortimore, 1996).

An important issue concerns which value added methodology should be employed when prior attainment data are lacking, whether at the national or local level. In the absence of prior attainment data, socio-economic information and other student characteristics – such as fluency in English, gender, age, education of parents – have sometimes been used as proxy measures of attainment at entry to school given the evidence of relationships between attainment and such factors. An example of this approach is described in an OFSTED report (Sammons *et al.*, 1994) which proposes the institution of an interim procedure for evaluating school performance in the absence of nationally available attainment data on entry to secondary schools. The methodology developed for OFSTED has also influenced current thinking about making benchmarks and setting targets (SCAA, 1995). However, it is important to note that several researchers have addressed the issue of comparing different models for separating and measuring the effects of the school and of student intake characteristics, such as prior attainment and socio-economic factors. The findings by Thomas and Mortimore (1996) and Sammons *et al.* (1994) indicate that a number of schools, (perhaps 20 per cent of the whole) may obtain different results when intake attainment data are available for the analysis, in contrast to results based only on student background data – such as age, gender and entitlement to free school meals. Interestingly, when adequate baseline assessments have been used, the inclusion of socio-economic information in the calculation adds little in accounting for the differences between students. But it is useful as a way of 'fine tuning' the value added scores (Willms, 1992; Sammons, 1996; Thomas and Mortimore, 1996). Therefore, it is essential that, wherever possible, value added systems are based on a longitudinal design to measure student progress, where both the baseline and the outcomes are measured in terms of what is taught in schools: the National Curriculum.

The development of value added measures

The development of value added measures has arisen from a variety of sources, rooted in both academic research and policy related issues. First, many school effectiveness studies, in particular those carried out prior to the mid 1980s, were hampered by the limited statistical techniques available (for a review see Scheerens, 1992) and did not have access to the recently developed, sophisticated and now widely preferred method of analysis, multilevel modelling (Goldstein, 1987, 1995). Secondly, the requirements of the 1980 Education Act and the 1991 Schools Bill (section 16) for schools to publish their 'raw' public examination results placed a much greater emphasis on the search for fairer and more accurate measures of school performance. A danger of using league tables – based on raw results alone – is that this can lead to complacency amongst schools serving educationally advantaged communities. The progress made by students in some of these schools may in reality be poorer than that of other schools which serve less advantaged intakes: their examination results which, on the surface, may seem relatively good, are actually lower than they might be. Conversely, there are schools in disadvantaged inner city communities in which students make much better progress than in schools with more advantaged intakes and yet, in terms of raw results, their performance still appears mediocre. Thus, neither kind of school is assisted by the publication of raw league tables. In the former, the need for improvement may not be appreciated; in the latter, serious demoralization of staff may occur. This point was powerfully illustrated in the *Guardian* newspaper's publication of schools' raw and value added A-level examination results in autumn 1992 and 1993 (Thomas *et al.*, 1992, 1993a).

Concern about the use of raw examination results has led to the increasingly widespread and systematic collection of student data by local education authorities (LEAs), including information about student examination and assessment outcomes and other student and school characteristics (see Hill, 1994 for a review). Individual schools have also addressed the issues of school performance and effectiveness as an aspect of internal evaluations and external inspections, such as those carried out by the LEA and, at the national level, by OFSTED. Consequently, the advances in statistical techniques and data collection have facilitated a move towards more accurate and appropriate measures of school effectiveness in the UK.

In recent years, schools and LEAs have employed a wide variety of different statistical procedures using either student background factors, such as socio-economic status, or student prior attainment data, or both, as well as different levels of sophistication in the analysis e.g. employing individual student level data or cruder aggregated school level data (see for example, Gray, 1993; Thomas et al., 1993b, 1994a, 1995, 1997c; Hill, 1994). As noted previously, OFSTED has proposed interim procedures for assessing school effectiveness at the national level that employ contextual information about students and schools but not student prior attainment data (Sammons et al., 1994). And so far no optimal value added model for measuring school effectiveness has emerged. Importantly, the government has now accepted the need for value added measures to provide complementary measures to the raw results (Dearing, 1993) and SCAA has published interim recommendations for a national value added framework (Fitz-Gibbon, 1995). The major difficulty in introducing a national framework for value added measures is the lack of reliable standardized assessments to measure the prior attainment of students on entering school. There are no national assessments of students entering primary school and the National Curriculum assessments at Key Stages 1–3 may not differentiate sufficiently between students, nor be sufficiently reliable for measuring value added. What is required ideally may be impossible to achieve in practice: a system of National Curriculum assessments that will both maintain the benefits of standard and teacher task assessments in enhancing the quality of teaching/learning and provide baseline assessments that can be used for the purpose of measuring value added. This fundamental issue requires the attention of all those who seek to employ the same method of assessment for different purposes.

A value added example

Before looking at the value added results of our ESRC study in detail, it may be helpful to consider how value added measures are calculated using a simple example of data aggregated at the school level – i.e. school mean scores. Just as individual teachers estimate the outcomes for students and HTs estimate the outcome for particular subjects, it is possible – using numerical measures of students' prior attainment – to create an estimate of the 'expected' school performance, on the basis of the statistical relationship between the students' attainment at intake and the GCSE performance measure.

For example, Figure 3.1 shows a plot of the mean London Reading Test (LRT) prior achievement measure (horizontal axis) set against the mean GCSE scores (vertical axis) for each school in our ESRC project sample in 1991. Each data point represents one of the 94 schools that make up our inner London sample. The line, or regression slope, indicates the degree of association between the two measures and the strength of this association is estimated by calculating the correlation using a simple formula. In this case the correlation is 0.82 which suggests a strong association. As a rough indication, 0 indicates no relationship where the line is more or less horizontal and few of the data points fall on or near the line; 1 or –1 indicates a perfect relationship where the line is sloped and all the data points fall on or near the line. The regression slope is used to estimate an expected score for each school. The further the position of a school from this line, the more likely that its 'raw' results differ from the expected one, and that the school will have better or worse value added results. The difference between a school's expected GCSE score and its actual result provides a measure of the value added: this is technically called the school residual. Schools above the line are performing better than expected and have positive residuals, schools below the line are performing worse than expected and have negative ones. Clearly, schools with high or low prior attainment scores may obtain *either* better or worse value added scores. This simple example illustrates the basic methodology of value added analyses. Our ESRC results follow the same principle but employ a more sophisticated technique, known as multilevel modelling, to calculate each school's expected and value added scores.

Methodology for measuring value added

Goldstein (1987, 1995) has emphasized the importance of using multilevel techniques and detailed student level data about individual students in the calculation of value added measures. It is not necessary to go over the technical details of multilevel modelling here as there are several publications which have provided this information – for example, Paterson and Goldstein (1991). As a brief comment, the advantage of multilevel modelling is that it exploits the hierarchical structure of the data – students clustered within classes, schools and LEAs. Also, like multiple regression, it can be used to look at potentially interesting differences, such as those between the performance of girls and boys, having taken account of their attainment on entry, thus allowing a fair comparison of like with like. Once the impact of a range of different factors has been established, the analysis can provide an estimate of the value added score or residual for each school, as noted in the example above. Crucially, a measure of uncertainty, e.g. the 95 per cent confidence interval, can also be attached to each school's results, so that the residuals can be compared (see Figure 3.2) where residuals are anchored to the overall school mean. These confidence limits enable us to establish the statistical

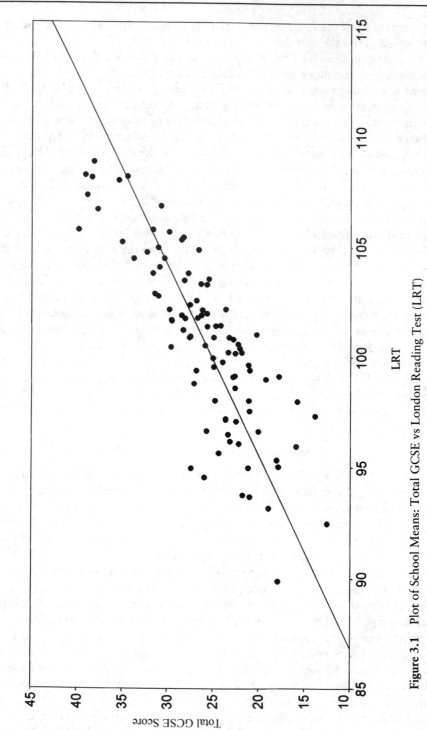

Figure 3.1 Plot of School Means: Total GCSE vs London Reading Test (LRT)

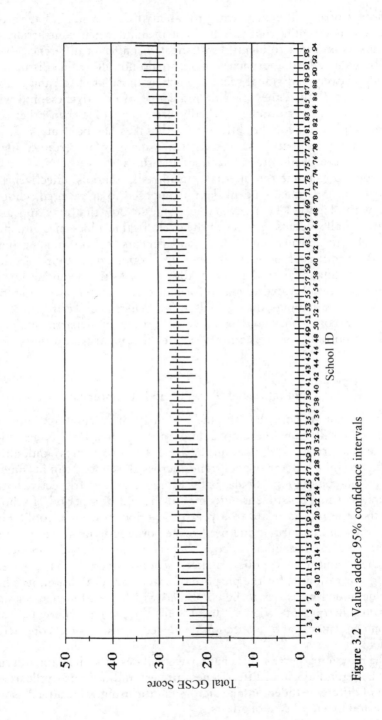

Figure 3.2 Value added 95% confidence intervals

significance of any differences (the probability that they might have arisen by chance). It is essential that this be kept in mind when contrasting school performance in order to identify statistically significant differences between schools. Value added approaches therefore do not allow fine distinctions to be made between individual schools, such as those used to rank schools in league tables. Rather, they provide indicators of effectiveness and whether some schools are performing markedly better or worse than other schools once an adjustment for the differences in intakes has been made. It is also worth pointing out that the same statistical principle of uncertainty applies to raw measures, as well as to value added measures.

In order to examine the internal variations in schools' effectiveness it is essential that individual student data as opposed to aggregated school data (as shown in Figure 3.1) are available. Some schools that may appear to be effective for all students in terms of the overall value added measure may not be so effective, when individual departments or different groups of students or different periods of time are examined in more detail. The analysis of individual student data allows a sensitive examination of all aspects of a school's value added performance. In Chapter 4 we will return to this issue, examining differential effectiveness for different student groups, the consistency and stability over time of departmental effects, and the importance of evaluating educational standards at a more detailed level.

Limitations of the value added approach

It is important to note that the methodology of calculating value added measures is still being developed and thus is imperfect. Issues such as measurement error and data accuracy are difficult to address and, although not likely to influence the overall trends across all schools, can in some cases affect the outcomes for particular ones. Moreover, the retrospective nature of the data, focusing on student outcomes at the end of a period of schooling, mean that the results relate to a previous period of each school's history. These issues are important and need to be borne in mind when interpreting the data for an individual school, whether the reader is an academic researcher, educational policy maker, school governor, HT, parent or student. For example, for the purpose of school self-evaluation, it is helpful for value added measures to be combined with other information such as student/teacher/parent views, local and regional contexts, school development plans and inspection evidence, rather than considered in isolation.

In the remaining part of this chapter we will describe the data and sample of our Differential School Effectiveness project and use this to illustrate the impact of different student intake factors in measuring value added as well as the size and extent of school effects.

MEASURING ACADEMIC EFFECTIVENESS USING A VALUE ADDED APPROACH

Our study sought to contribute to the debate about the effectiveness of schooling and addressed several key issues on the topic of how value added can be measured. The five key research questions are described in detail in Chapter 2 but here we would like to focus on one in particular:

Key question I

Are differences between the effects of departments on students' GCSE attainments in selected subjects greater or less than differences between secondary schools in their overall effects upon students' total GCSE scores?

Two underlying questions have first to be answered and we will address these:

● How important are different intake factors in measuring school performance?

● What is the impact on student outcomes of particular intake factors?

Sample and data

The sample and data employed for our Differential School Effectiveness project study were originally collected for the 1990, 1991 and 1992 studies of GCSE results initiated by the Association of Metropolitan Authorities (AMA) and funded by individual LEAs (Nuttall *et al.*, 1992; Thomas *et al.*, 1993b, 1994a; Mortimore *et al.*, 1994). The database was extended to include an additional finely differentiated measure of prior reading attainment, the LRT taken at the end of primary school.

The data comprised the GCSE examination performance, gender and age of GCSE candidates in 69 (1990), 94 (1991) and 77 (1992) inner London schools, drawn from a total of eight LEAs, and were provided by the National Consortium for Examination Results (NCER). Each student record also included: the London Reading Test standardized score (LRT), the verbal reasoning band (VR) assigned to each student as part of the secondary school transfer procedure i.e. a measure of general attainment on entry to secondary school – the student's ethnicity, and whether or not he/she was entitled to free school meals (FSM, an indicator of low family income). An additional variable designed to describe the context of the student in the school – the percentage of students entitled to free school meals – was calculated for each school. This provides an overall *approximate* measure of disadvantage in a school. Table 3.1 shows a summary of the data in terms of the percentage of students who are girls, entitled to a free school lunch, or from an ethnic minority.

Seven measures of student GCSE performance were employed: the total examination score (tscore) and six subject scores – mathematics, English,

Table 3.1   The characteristics of the student sample (1990–92 GCSE candidates)

	1990	1991	1992
% Ethnic	n=1,423	n=2,593	n=2,254
minorities	36.9%	34.0%	35.4%
% Girls	n=2,035	n=4,006	n=3,249
	52.8%	52.6%	51.0%
% FSM	n=844	n=1,953	n=1,832
	21.9%	25.4%	28.7%

English literature, science (maximum grade obtained), history, French. These particular subjects were chosen because of the relatively high numbers of entrants from the sample schools. The scores were calculated in a standard way by assigning each GCSE examination grade a numerical score (A = 7, B = 6, C = 5 and so on, see Nuttall et al. (1989) for a description of performance scale employed). The mean and standard deviation for each score[1] is shown in Table 3.2, along with the correlation between each measure and the London Reading Test standardized score. For the English and mathematics analyses, the GCSE candidates in the 15+ age cohort who were not entered (or absent) for GCSE examinations in these subjects were given an examination score of zero. The rationale underlying this procedure is that all students are taught English and mathematics and therefore the achievement or non-achievement of all students, where possible, should be included in these measures. However, for the remaining subjects (English literature, science, history and French), only students entered for these individual GCSE examinations could be included in our analyses.

It would have been desirable to include the achievement of *all* students in the 15+ age cohort in each school to take account of differences in examination entry policy. It was only possible, however, to obtain data for GCSE candidates over three years. In other words, information is not included for the relatively small number of students not entered for any GCSE examinations, approximately 10 per cent of the total 1991 cohort, and therefore the mean school performance is slightly higher than would otherwise be the case. Evidence from 6 of the LEAs in our study in 1991 shows that the mean GCSE score of all 15+ students (n=8,049) is 23.2 GCSE points, whereas the mean GCSE scores of all 15+ GCSE candidates (n=7,212) is 25.9 points. However, to address the issue of differences in schools' examination entry policies, an additional analysis of the 1992 data was carried out which included all 15+ students with valid scores, including non-examination students. The results were found to be sufficiently similar to those from the analyses of the 15+ GCSE candidate sample to allow valid interpretation of the findings.

It was also necessary to exclude information on 2,640 candidates in 1992 (29 per cent of the original sample of 9,013 candidates), 2,836 candidates in 1991 (27 per cent of the original sample of 10,458 candidates) and 4,325 candidates in 1990 (53 per cent of the original sample of 8,180 candidates) because of incomplete data records. As an illustration of the impact of

Table 3.2 Mean scores for seven GCSE outcome measures

| | 1990 | | | 1991 | | | 1992 | | |
	n	Mean	SD	Corrn with LRT	n	Mean	SD	Corrn with LRT	n	Mean	SD	Corrn with LRT
Total GCSE score	5867	25.27	15.14	0.59	7851	26.18	15.62	0.58	6475	28.11	16.41	0.59
Mathematics	5867	2.63	2.06	0.50	7851	2.62	2.10	0.51	6475	2.78	2.10	0.56
English	5867	3.95	1.83	0.56	7851	3.92	1.79	0.57	6475	4.00	1.77	0.58
English literature	4056	4.36	1.54	0.55	6143	4.28	1.53	0.56	5288	4.39	1.51	0.58
Science (maximum grade)	4865	3.30	1.84	0.57	6699	3.13	1.88	0.54	5601	3.49	1.91	0.59
History	1647	4.00	1.93	0.57	2438	3.95	1.93	0.54	1992	4.01	1.95	0.58
French	1797	3.53	1.90	0.55	2531	3.56	1.92	0.53	2265	3.78	1.92	0.52

excluding these cases, the mean total GCSE score of the 1991 multilevel sample of candidates (26.1 GCSE points) is systematically higher than that of *all* 15+ candidates (25.5 GCSE points). Consequently, there is a slight overall upward bias in the estimates of school and student performance. This indicates that the least able candidates are somewhat more likely to be excluded due to missing data. Furthermore, it is important to note that some schools have a number of students taking GCSE examinations who are not within the 15+ age group and the achievement of these students is not included. The representativeness of the data should always be borne in mind when interpreting the results for an individual school. However, most schools in our sample had a similar level of missing data and our project sample in total is sufficiently representative to enable us to draw valid conclusions about systematic differences between schools and departments.

The multilevel analysis

In order to examine the size and extent of school and departmental effects we conducted multilevel analyses of students' GCSE examination results over three years (1990–92) for the total sample of ninety-four inner London secondary schools drawn from eight LEAs. An analysis for each outcome measure – tscore, English, English literature, French, history, mathematics and science (highest score in any science subject) – was carried out, which separately estimates the variation in student scores due to the school, year and student levels in order to provide a single measure of school effectiveness that reflects average performance over the three year period. In this way the impact of fluctuations in results over time – in this case three years – is removed.

In total we have employed four types of model to illustrate how the impact of different student intake factors (prior attainment and background) on students' GCSE outcomes can provide evidence of which is the best approach:

Model (I)   Intercept   includes: no explanatory variables
Model (II) Background only   includes: gender, age (in months), ethnicity, entitlement to free school meals (FSM), percentage FSM.
Model (III) Prior attainment only includes: LRT, VR Bands 1–3.
Model (IV) Complete   includes: gender, age (in months), LRT, VR band, ethnicity and entitlement to free school meals (FSM), percentage FSM.

For each model, identical statistical controls for student intake were employed for each of the seven outcome measures. This procedure means that we can make direct and valid comparisons across the school and department residuals from each model (I-IV). By contrasting the results of the four models

Table 3.3 Percentage of total and school level variance explained by three different value added models

	T score	English	Mathematics	English Literature	French	History	Science
Model II total variance explained	11.6	9.5	6.9	7.6	8.3	8.2	6.0
Model II school variance explained	43.8	52.7	37.1	40.8	39.2	29.6	28.7
Model III total variance explained	40.4	36.5	33.7	37.0	34.2	36.2	36.0
Model III school variance explained	57.4	57.3	48.1	42.1	53.1	41.2	49.2
Model IV total variance explained	45.9	40.9	36.6	40.6	38.1	39.2	38.0
Model IV school variance explained	70.0	68.2	53.9	51.1	62.6	49.8	46.6

Note: Model II includes all student background factors but not prior attainment
Model III includes only prior attainment
Model IV includes student background factors *and* prior attainment

(I-IV) in the next section we can address the question:

> • How important are different intake factors in measuring school performance?

Comparing different value added models

We have already noted the importance of accurate baseline assessments for measuring value added performance and our ESRC data provide a unique opportunity to illustrate this with a large sample of inner London schools. The overall 'goodness of fit' of the models II-IV is shown by the percentage of total variance explained for each outcome (Table 3.3). As can be seen, using the prior attainment measures alone as explanatory variables (Model III) produces poorer results than the complete Model IV. This indicates that controlling for additional student background measures, such as gender, is necessary to obtain accurate school effectiveness measures (residuals). Importantly, using only background variables (Model II) explains a substantially lower percentage of total variance than Models III and IV, strongly suggesting that Model II – where the analysis lacks prior attainment data – is inadequate in providing proper controls for student intake.

Table 3.3 also shows that the reduction in school level variation between Models I – which essentially represents the 'raw' scores – and IV – the complete value added model – is 70 per cent for our measure of overall GCSE performance (tscore) and this finding is illustrated for a random sample of 34 schools in Figure 3.3. Interestingly, the reduction of school variance is much greater for the overall performance measure (tscore) and English than for the other GCSE subject scores showing the importance of intake for these outcomes.

In a similar analysis using a different sample in a non-inner city context, Thomas and Mortimore (1996) have compared five multilevel models of varying complexity in order to establish the best value added approach. Thomas and Mortimore's best model involved controlling for a range of individual student intake factors – students' prior attainments in verbal, quantitative, and non-verbal cognitive ability tests, their gender, age, ethnicity, mobility and entitlement to free school meals – in the calculation of the value added measures. In line with our findings, the prior attainment measures were found to be the most important factors to control for in their analysis and similar findings have also been reported by Gray et al. (1995).

Having investigated which factors are important to control for in value added measures we now turn to the related question:

> • What is the impact on student outcomes of particular intake factors?

Total examination score
The results in Table 3.4 show the average effects of the explanatory factors fitted simultaneously in the complete Model IV. They show that, although

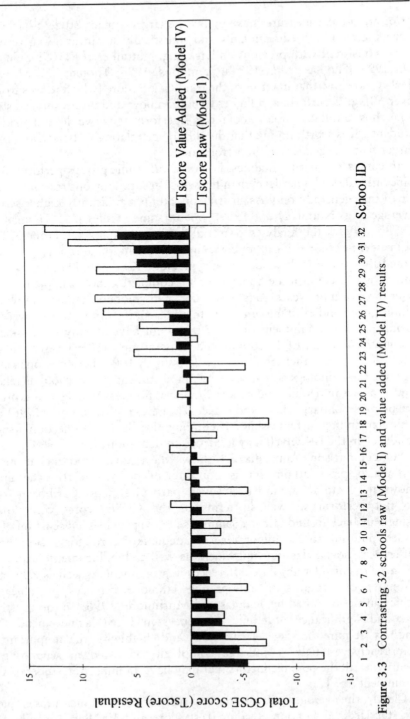

Figure 3.3 Contrasting 32 schools raw (Model I) and value added (Model IV) results

prior attainment measures have by far the larger impact, student background effects remain both educationally and statistically significant. Our results are fairly consistent with previous findings (e.g. Nuttall *et al.*, 1989; Goldstein *et al.*, 1993; Thomas *et al.*, 1994a; Sammons, 1995; Thomas and Mortimore, 1996) and show that in terms of the total GCSE score (which ranges from 0 to over 50), girls perform at a higher level than boys and disadvantaged students – i.e. those entitled to free school meals – perform at a lower level than all other students. It is worth noting that the difference relating to free school meals is larger than the gender gap in performance.

In contrast to earlier findings, however, *all* ethnic groups perform at a significantly (0.05) higher level than the white group. Previous research has indicated that generally only Asian students attain significantly higher scores on average (e.g. Nuttall *et al.*, 1989), but in some studies (e.g. Thomas *et al.*, 1993b, 1994a) the analyses were only able to employ the crude VR band adjustment i.e. for prior attainment. In considering these results, it should be noted that the sample students only include GCSE candidates. It would be interesting to confirm the findings with a complete cohort sample of students over three or more years, to take account of any possible relationship between ethnic group and examination entry. In addition, the differences between these groups in their attainment on entry to school have already been taken into account. The mean LRT score for the white group is 103, whereas the mean LRT score for all other ethnic groups is less than 100. Therefore, one explanation for these findings is that some bilingual students start school as relatively low attainers in reading and make substantial progress in language skills while attending secondary school and indeed Thomas and Mortimore (1996) report a similar finding in Lancashire. There may also be a 'self-selection' aspect to residency in the UK which may influence student motivation.

For comparison, Appendix 3.1 shows the equivalent results in analyses for which prior attainment is not controlled (Model II). The findings show that ethnic minority groups, particularly of Caribbean origin, do not perform so well in terms of the GCSE scores contextualized using only background factors. Sammons (1995) provides a discussion of these issues, pointing to the importance of adequate control for socio-economic differences, social class/unemployment as well as low income indicators, and the need to consider absolute differences in attainment, as well as value added estimates of progress in interpreting ethnic differences in educational achievement. As noted by Thomas and Mortimore (1996) on the question of size and significance of ethnic differences in GCSE achievement: 'These findings require further clarification and highlight the importance of comprehensive analyses and the complexity involved in separating and identifying all the possible factors that may have an impact on students' GCSE attainment' (p. 12).

Clearly, the average impact of the two prior attainment measures employed, the standardized London Reading Test score and VR Band, is substantial. The significance of both measures indicates that, in addition to the finely graded reading measure, the fit of the model is significantly improved by including a crude measure of general ability as assessed by primary school teachers prior to secondary transfer. Large differences appeared between the performances of students in the three different VR bands: Band 1 students scored 13.4 GCSE points more than Band 3 students, and Band 2 students scored 5.5 points more than Band 3 students. For comparison, a difference of 12 points is equivalent to the difference between six GCSE grade Bs and six grade Ds, while five points is equal to an extra grade C GCSE.

Finally, the results show that, on average, student scores were approximately three GCSE points higher in 1991, and approximately four points higher in 1992 than in 1990. This finding illustrates that there was an overall upward trend in student GCSE performance over the three years once all other factors, notably prior attainment, have been taken into account in line with national trends in raw results.

Subject scores
Similar analyses were conducted separately for English, mathematics, English literature, science (maximum grade), history and French. In all cases the score range is much less than for the total examination score, the maximum possible being 7 (Grade A) and the minimum 0 (ungraded). For each subject analysis the explanatory variables included were identical to those described for the total GCSE score Model IV. The results for English and mathematics and the other subjects can be found in Table 3.5.

The findings indicate some differences between subjects in the estimates of the average effects for different groups. For example, girls attain significantly higher scores than boys in English, English literature, history and French but significantly lower scores in mathematics and science once other student intake characteristics have been taken into account ($p<0.05$). Clearly, these findings contribute important evidence to the continuing debate about gender equity and have implications concerning the differential learning experiences, expectations and GCSE subject choices of boys in comparison with girls.

However, the overall pattern of results for subjects is broadly similar to that obtained for the total examination score, allowing for some specific differences between groups for individual subjects. For example, for all subjects a significant negative impact on performance is systematically associated with individual student disadvantage as measured by student entitlement to free school meals. However, the overall level of student disadvantage in each school – the percentage of students in each school entitled to FSM – has a significant negative impact only on the English score, for the other outcome measures the impact is negative but is not statistically significant. In other words, individual student disadvantage and, for English alone, higher overall levels of disadvantage within a school are both significantly associated with lower GCSE performance. Previous evidence of contextual effects related to disadvantage have been identified in some other secondary studies, such as that by Willms (1986) and Sammons *et al.* (1994), and also in a previous analysis of the current data

Table 3.4   Model IV Analysis of total GCSE examination score (1990–92)

Fixed Part	TSCORE	
	Estimate	Standard Error
Intercept	15.61	0.69
LRT	0.45	0.01
LRT^2	0.00	0.00
VR1-VR3	13.44	0.36
VR2-VR3	5.52	0.25
Girls-Boys	2.10	0.22
Age-Mth	0.06	0.02
Year 91-Year 90	2.71	0.33
Year 92-Year 90	4.13	0.36
African-White	5.48	0.46
Caribbean-White	0.55	0.25
Indian-White	8.45	0.46
Pakistani-White	10.48	0.61
Bangladeshi-White	9.88	0.58
Other-White	5.68	0.28
PCTFSM	−0.02 ns	0.02
FSM-NO FSM	−3.29	0.20

Random Part		Estimate	Standard Error
Between Schools	(σ^2)	7.99	1.39
Between Years	(σ^2)	1.26	0.35
Between Students	(σ^2)	98.57	4.09

Notes: Students = 17,850   Cohorts = 213   Schools = 94
Where: LRT   = London Reading Test Score
       LRT^2 = (London Reading Test Score)^2
       VR1   = Verbal Reasoning Band 1 (approximately top 25 per cent)
       VR2   = Verbal Reasoning Band 2 (approximately middle 50 per cent)
       VR3   = Verbal Reasoning Band 3 (approximately bottom 25 per cent)
       FSM   = Entitlement to free school meals
       PCTFSM = Percentage of students in school entitled to FSM
       ns   = Not significant (at 0.05 level)

set for a single year 1991 (Thomas *et al.*, 1994b). However, other recent work (Thomas and Mortimore, 1996) has indicated that school context factors (such as percentage FSM) may only be significant (at 0.05 level) in predicting student outcomes when rich and wide-ranging student level data are lacking. An alternative explanation which may influence the statistical significance of school context variables may be found in the range and extent of advantaged versus disadvantaged intakes in the total sample of schools. In other words, contextual effects may be more likely in LEAs or regions where a policy of selection is employed by a minority of schools. To summarize, it appears that the findings of this study of inner London schools – which historically have had an explicit policy of comprehensive education – indicate that, when examination

Table 3.5 Model IV Analysis of English, mathematics, English literature, science, history and French examination scores (1990–92)

Fixed Part	English Students = 17,850 Cohorts = 213 Schools = 94		Mathematics Students = 17,850 Cohorts = 213 Schools = 94		English Literature Students = 13,694 Cohorts = 212 Schools = 93		Science Students = 15,174 Cohorts = 213 Schools = 94		History Students = 5,338 Cohorts = 204 Schools = 92		French Students = 5,757 Cohorts = 210 Schools = 94	
	Estimate	Standard Error	Estimate	Standard Error	Estimate	Standard Error	Estimate	Standard Error	Estimate	Standard Error	Estimate	Standard Error
Intercept	2.98	0.09	1.61	0.12	3.38	0.10	2.40	0.12	2.53	0.17	1.93	0.18
LRT	0.05	0.00	0.05	0.00	0.05	0.00	0.06	0.00	0.06	0.00	0.06	0.00
LRT²	-0.00	0.00	0.00	0.00	-0.00	0.00	0.00	0.00	-0.00	0.00	0.00	0.00
VR1-VR3	1.32	0.04	2.04	0.05	1.18	0.04	1.45	0.05	1.54	0.09	1.48	0.09
VR2-VR3	0.58	0.03	0.85	0.03	0.49	0.03	0.60	0.04	0.62	0.08	0.54	0.08
Girls-Boys	0.43	0.03	-0.13	0.03	0.31	0.03	-0.11	0.03	0.25	0.05	0.31	0.05
Age-Mth	0.01	0.00	0.00	0.00	0.01	0.00	0.01 ns	0.00	0.00 ns	0.00	0.01 ns	0.00
Year 91-Year 90	0.18	0.05	0.15	0.07	0.08 ns	0.05	0.05 ns	0.07	0.29	0.09	0.38	0.11
Year 92-Year 90	0.25	0.05	0.27	0.07	0.18	0.06	0.34	0.08	0.35	0.10	0.57	0.11
African-White	0.65	0.06	0.38	0.07	0.47	0.05	0.34	0.06	0.34	0.10	0.40	0.10
Caribbean-White	0.20	0.03	-0.16	0.04	0.10	0.03	-0.20	0.04	-0.14	0.07	-0.12	0.06
Indian-White	0.75	0.06	0.87	0.06	0.54	0.05	0.72	0.06	0.67	0.12	0.78	0.10
Pakistani-White	0.87	0.08	1.17	0.09	0.61	0.07	0.90	0.08	0.80	0.16	0.81	0.13
Bangladeshi-White	0.93	0.07	1.05	0.08	0.72	0.07	0.86	0.08	1.01	0.18	0.99	0.16
Other-White	0.46	0.03	0.49	0.04	0.39	0.03	0.44	0.04	0.30	0.07	0.63	0.06
SCHFSM	-0.00 ns	0.00	-0.00 ns	0.00	-0.00 ns	0.00	-0.00 ns	0.00	-0.00 ns	0.00	-0.01 ns	0.00
FSM-NO FSM	-0.33	0.03	-0.31	0.03	-0.21	0.02	-0.24	0.03	-0.29	0.05	-0.26	0.05
Random Part												
Between Schools (σ²)	0.08	0.02	0.16	0.03	0.10	0.02	0.13	0.03	0.37	0.07	0.18	0.05
Between Cohorts (σ²)	0.03	0.01	0.09	0.02	0.05	0.00	0.11	0.02	0.08	0.02	0.18	0.04
Between Students (σ²)	2.20	0.04	1.89	0.07	1.38	0.04	1.64	0.08	2.06	0.09	1.71	0.08

Where: LRT   = London Reading Test Score
LRT²   = (London Reading Test Score)²
VR1   = Verbal Reasoning Band 1 (approximately top 25 per cent)
VR2   = Verbal Reasoning Band 2 (approximately middle 50 per cent)
VR3   = Verbal Reasoning Band 3 (approximately bottom 25 per cent)
FSM   = Entitlement to free school meals
PCTFSM = Percentage of students in school entitled to free school meals
ns   = Not significant (at 0.05 level)

Figures are shown to two decimal places

results for three consecutive cohort years are taken into account, school context is less significant than individual student factors, except for English, where the influence of the socio-economic context seems to be particularly strong.

Size and extent of school and departmental effects

In the last section we addressed the important question of which variables should be controlled for when calculating value added scores. Having established that the complete model IV provides the best fit of the data, we now turn to our first key research question concerning the size and extent of school and departmental effects.

Key question I

Are differences between the effects of departments on students' GCSE attainments in selected subjects greater or less than differences between secondary schools in their overall effects upon students' total GCSE scores?

Even when the average impact of the student intake factors has been taken into account, using the complete model IV described in the previous section, evidence of significant differences between schools in their effects on students' total GCSE performance scores are still to be found. By utilizing data drawn from three years, the statistical power of the analysis is boosted and the possibility of generalizing from our value added results strengthened. In other words, the value added scores provide a single average measure of school effectiveness for each outcome measure over the three year period and the variation in student scores *across* the three GCSE cohorts is estimated separately. In Table 3.6 the results for students' total GCSE performance score are shown[2] and the equivalent figures for individual GCSE subjects are also provided. Shown separately is the percentage of variation in student outcomes due to fluctuations over time, based on the three GCSE cohorts (1990–92).

In considering our key question, these results indicate that while important

Table 3.6 Percentage of variance in students' total GCSE performance and subject performance due to school and cohort: a comparison of one year with results across three years

	% Variance due to school 1991*	% Variance due to school 1990–92**	% Variance due to cohort 1990–92**
Total GCSE performance score	7	6.2	1.1
English	6	4.1	1.8
English Literature	12	6.9	3.4
Mathematics	9	5.9	3.6
Science	11	6.1	4.7
French	14	7.8	7.8
History	20	15.3	3.6

Note: * 2-level variance components model using 1991 cohort data
** 3-level variance components model using 1990–92 cohort data

school differences in terms of total GCSE score exist, subject differences – which give an indication of departmental effects – are also marked. For English literature, French and history, the variation between schools is larger than the overall difference in exam performance. Importantly, these subject differences have been calculated over a three-year period – any variation due to instability over time has been removed and separately estimated. Therefore the evidence strengthens and supports previous similar findings (Thomas *et al.*, 1994b) where only a single year's data (1991) was used – also shown in Table 3.6. In other words, variations between schools in their effects on students' performance in optional GCSE subjects – such as English literature, French and history – are generally greater than those found in overall GCSE performance. Only for English – which we have shown to be particularly susceptible to home influences – is the percentage of variance due to school substantially lower than that for the total GCSE performance. Our findings clearly demonstrate that it is helpful to look at both overall and subject value added scores when evaluating secondary schools' academic performance.

The percentage of variance in student performance attributable to variations over time is small but not insubstantial. The impact of year-to-year variations for successive GCSE cohorts is greatest for French and least for total GCSE performance score. This finding is also reflected in the correlations reported between the school results for the three years 1990–92, which we describe in more detail in Chapter 4 (see Table 4.2). It is noteworthy that when the contribution of both the school and the time effects are analysed in comparison to a single year's results, the percentage of variation due to the school is somewhat reduced (see Table 3.5). Nonetheless, the overall pattern of subject results is similar and generally the findings are in line with previous research by Willms and Raudenbush (1989) as well as conclusions by Smith and Tomlinson (1989), Fitz-Gibbon (1991), Luyten (1995) and Witziers (1994) on the need to examine the departmental level in studies of secondary school effectiveness.

CONCLUSIONS

Our large scale study of secondary school effectiveness provides clear evidence of the importance of taking background factors and prior attainment into account and using appropriate value added models to estimate the influence of the school. We have demonstrated that prior attainment is much the most important factor required to control intake differences in measuring value added using a unique sample of inner London schools. Moreover, our results show that the inclusion of socio-economic factors in the analysis is highly relevant, and that gender and age within each year group also have a significant impact. Therefore, for research investigating overall patterns in school performance, it is appropriate to examine the impact on attainment of the socio-economic context of students and schools. For example, it is important to examine whether local policy regarding selection is likely to affect the size and significance of the relationship between school context factors and attainment. For the purpose of school self-evaluation, however, it is important that HTs and teachers are aware of the assumptions and expectations built into a value added measure that adjusts performance on the basis of student characteristics such as gender, age and entitlement to free school meals, *in addition* to prior attainment.

Our findings show that trying to make judgements about effectiveness from schools' 'raw' examination performance inevitably leads to misleading conclusions. This has important implications for the validity of comparison between schools using 'raw' GCSE examination results, such as those published annually in the UK from 1992 onwards. The large differences observed between schools' raw results are considerably reduced when value added scores are employed, as we have shown in Figure 3.2. Moreover, some schools identified as having below average raw results are actually performing well in terms of value added, while other schools with very good raw results are demonstrably performing below expectation, once allowance has been made for the nature of their student intakes.

This powerfully demonstrates that schools do indeed make a difference. There remains a significant school effect on students' GCSE performance after controlling for intake. In the most extreme case, the difference between the most and least effective inner London school can be interpreted for a hypothetical average student as the difference between gaining six GCSE Grade Bs rather than six Grade Ds. Interestingly, the results of our analysis shows that there is greater variation in schools' value added performance for optional GCSE subject results, such as English literature, French and history) than for the core subjects like English, mathematics and science, and for the overall total examination scores. This finding suggests that the largest differences exist in the effectiveness of departments teaching optional GCSE subjects. One possible explanation is that this may reflect the government policy of encouraging subject specialization in non-core GCSE subjects. It is also useful for practitioners to be aware that in the key areas of mathematics, English, science and overall examination performance there are more similarities in the effects of schools and departments than for other GCSE subjects. Our findings show that it is important to look at more than total GCSE results when evaluating any schools' academic performance, although we think that total GCSE performance remains an important indicator of both overall achievement levels and schools' examination entry policy.

The evaluation of subject results leads to a shift in emphasis from comparisons between the overall performance of students in different schools to the performance of students in different subject departments *within* schools. This approach highlights the existence of internal variations in school effectiveness. As will be discussed further in Chapter 9, this is a crucial aspect of school self-evaluation and improvement because it provides a framework for examining in considerable detail a variety of different value added measures of a school's performance.

In Chapter 4, therefore, we go on to examine in more detail internal variations in three aspects of schools' value added performance: (i) the consistency of subject results; (ii) the stability of school and departmental effects over time; and (iii) the differential effects for different groups of students such as low and high attainers.

NOTES

1. The scores were approximately normally distributed and preliminary analyses indicated that the use of normal scores (with mean zero and standard deviation 1) had little impact on the significance and relative magnitude of estimates. Not using normal scores has the added benefit that the results can be interpreted more easily in terms of GCSE grades.
2. The percentage of variance attributable to years and schools was calculated using the 3-level variance components model including fixed part explanatory variables: LRT, LRT^2, VR Band, gender, age, FSM, ethnicity, per cent FSM, Year 1991, Year 1992 (Model IV).

4

Differences in Academic Effectiveness

INTRODUCTION

In this chapter we examine, in detail, schools' internal variations in effectiveness. This approach involves us in looking at patterns within schools, of differences in effectiveness, and addressing, for example, the question of whether schools that appear to be average in one measure of performance, such as the overall examination outcomes of all students (e.g. total GCSE score or % grades A-C), may, in reality, show considerable differences in performance on a range of more detailed indicators (Thomas *et al.*, 1995b, 1997a, 1997b). We again focus on academic outcomes and three aspects of GCSE performance are examined for our sample in ninety-four inner London schools. These are:

- consistency across subject departments;
- stability of results over three years (1990–1992), and
- differential effects for different groups of students (such as high and low attainers).

In order to illustrate the findings we also examine the results of grouping schools results on the basis of different value added measures. As described in Chapter 3, a value added approach is adopted which controls for selected student background measures of prior attainment (at secondary transfer), gender, age, ethnicity and low income (Model IV). Similarly, we use the same set of seven different GCSE outcome measures as the focus for the investigation: total GCSE score, and scores in English, English literature, mathematics, science, French and history.

The extent of departmental differences

This phase of the research project addressed the key question of consistency across subject departments:

Key question 2

Is there any evidence that some schools are generally more effective (across subjects) in promoting students' attainment at GCSE and that others are less effective in most areas, or is the concept of overall effectiveness too simplistic for the secondary age group?

As we noted briefly while outlining the research design in Chapter 2, a relatively neglected area of school effectiveness research is the extent of consistency in schools' effects on different outcomes at the same point in time. This issue is particularly relevant in the light of the published performance tables which report only overall measures of the raw results, such as the percentage of students gaining five or more GCSE grades A-C. Clearly, the difficulty of interpreting the raw examination results is compounded if large differences exist between the performance of subject departments. Moreover, Sammons, Mortimore and Thomas (1996) in their review of this topic note that very few studies have considered schools' effects on a range of outcomes, both cognitive and non-cognitive (social/affective outcomes). Of the studies which have examined schools' effects on different academic outcomes, most have focused on the performance in the basic skill areas of reading and mathematics and have only examined primary schools. Only a few have looked at effects on different subjects at the secondary level (see, for example, Cuttance, 1987; Willms and Raudenbush, 1989; Smith and Tomlinson, 1989; Fitz-Gibbon, 1991; Goldstein *et al.*, 1993; Thomas *et al.*, 1993a, 1994a; Luyten, 1994; Thomas and Mortimore, 1996).

Our study builds on and extends earlier research on this topic. Analyses of secondary schools' overall performance and subject results were used to estimate the strength of the relationships between schools' effects on total GCSE performance and on six specific subjects over a three-year period (Thomas *et al.*, 1997a). By conducting the analysis across three years we were able to allow for annual fluctuations and obtain more robust estimates of effectiveness. Table 4.1 shows the correlations between the value added scores (i.e. school residuals) of each performance measure.[1] In all cases the correlations are positive but the associations range from *fairly strong* in some cases to *fairly weak* in others. This means that in some schools, particular departments appear to be somewhat more or less effective than others. Schools' effects on science were most closely correlated with those on total GCSE performance score (r=0.58), closely followed by those on English (r=0.57). As would be expected, effects on English and English literature were fairly strongly related (r=0.72), but the correlation for mathematics and science effects was surprisingly low (r=0.35).

Our evidence strongly suggests that substantial differences exist within some schools in terms of departmental effectiveness over a three-year period, because 7 out of the 15 (47 per cent) subject correlations reported are less than 0.3. Such differences may be masked by a reliance on a single measure of total GCSE score. The underlying reason for the differences or similarities in subject results within schools may be due to a variety of factors such as whole school policies, exam entry policy, school development planning or other process factors related to what teachers do in different departments. These issues concerning process are examined in Part 3 of the book which focuses on the *explanation* of variations in effectiveness (Chapters 5, 6 and 7). The findings are in line with previous research (e.g. Willms and Raudenbush, 1989; Smith

Table 4.1   Consistency in effectiveness: correlations between the value added subject scores

	Tscore	Maths	English	English Literature	French	History	Science
Tscore		0.48	0.57	0.38	0.52	0.42	0.58
Maths			0.24	0.24	0.45	0.25	0.35
English				0.72	0.38	0.31	0.26
English Literature					0.25	0.25	0.20
French						0.33	0.34
History							0.37

Note: Students = 17,850 Schools = 94 Years = 3

and Tomlinson,1989; Thomas and Mortimore, 1996) and suggest strongly the need to look at school performance in detail – not just at total GCSE performance but also at subject results. Investigating internal variations in academic effectiveness and possible explanations for these is also relevant to practitioners interested in school and departmental improvement, a topic we return to in Chapter 9.

How stable are school and departmental effects?

Key question 3
Is the pattern of differences at the school or departmental level stable from year to year?

The question of stability over time in schools' effects – involving comparisons based on more than one age cohort – has received relatively little attention in school effectiveness research in comparison with that given to the question of the size of differences between schools in their effects for any given age cohort. However, this is a question of considerable practical as well as theoretical significance as reviews by Bosker and Scheerens (1989), Scheerens (1992) and, more recently, Sammons, Mortimore and Thomas (1996), Gray *et al.* (1993), Mortimore *et al.* (1994) and Thomas *et al.* (1997a and b) note.

Our analyses for the Differential School Effectiveness project extend previous findings and show that despite broad consistency – indicated by the fact that only positive correlations were identified – the correlations between schools' effects for 1990, 1991 and 1992 are far from perfect (Thomas *et al.*, 1997a). The evidence concerning the stability of results over the three years (1990–92) shows that schools' effects on total GCSE performance score were notably more stable than the subject measures (see Table 4.2). For the total GCSE measure the correlations, estimated by the multilevel analysis, ranged from 0.82 to 0.88. At the subject level, results for French were the least stable (with correlations ranging from 0.38 to 0.57) and those for history the most

Table 4.2 Stability in effectiveness: correlations between value added scores across years 1990, 1991, 1992

	1990 vs 1991 Model IV	1990 vs 1992 Model IV	1991 vs 1992 Model IV
Tscore	0.88	0.82	0.85
English	0.86	0.40	0.77
Mathematics	0.59	0.56	0.83
Science	0.52	0.41	0.59
History	0.92	0.71	0.83
English Literature	0.84	0.38	0.71
French	0.48	0.38	0.57

Note: Students = 17,850 Schools = 94 Years = 3

stable (with correlations ranging from 0.71 to 0.92) over the three years. These correlations are slightly lower than similar research that relies solely on total GCSE score (Gray *et al.*, 1993). However, this may be due to the special influence of teacher and student mobility in inner city schools. Thus, despite evidence of broad stability in some areas, our study indicates that, at the subject level, there can be a substantial degree of change over time and points to the value and necessity of looking at results in more than one year. Gray *et al.* (1993, 1996) have argued that three years is the minimum required for the identification of any trends over time and the present research supports this view.

Finally, it is important to draw attention to the comments of Willms and Raudenbush (1989) and Gray *et al.* (1993, 1996) who have argued that fluctuations or changes in schools' results over time may reflect 'real' improvement or deterioration in school performance as well as random variations. The latter relates to the random sampling error associated with schools' successive GCSE examination cohorts, whereas the former points to 'real' changes in school policy and practice that have a lasting impact on GCSE performance. Ideally, data are required over a longer period of time (e.g. five to ten years) than the three years available for our ESRC study in order to investigate significant changes in school performance. This important issue requires further investigation which could be carried out by comparing the pattern of school residuals over time with information about changes in school processes, and thus identify the factors which help to ensure lasting improvements in school performance.

Differential Effectiveness

The topic of differential effectiveness focuses on the question of whether schools are equally effective for all student groups.

Differential school effects is a topic of increasing interest in school effectiveness research especially in the UK. Differential school effects concern the existence of systematic differences in attainment within schools for different student groups – for example, those with different levels of prior attainment or different background characteristics – once the *average* differences between these groups has been accounted for. Again, as we noted in Chapter 2, this topic had received relatively little attention from researchers when we commenced this study.

Key question 4

Is there any evidence that some schools and departments are *differentially* effective in promoting GCSE attainment for different groups of students (categorised by gender, ethnicity, prior attainment and entitlement to free school meals) or are secondary schools and departments equally effective (or ineffective) in promoting attainment for all groups?

In order to investigate in more detail the nature of differential effectiveness, our ESRC study involved an examination of schools' differential effects in terms of an overall GCSE measure as well as subject outcomes, using our sample of inner London schools.

Because of the size of the data set (over 17,000 students covering three years of results) we were able to investigate evidence for differential effects in connection with ethnicity, gender, socio-economic disadvantage simultaneously. The aim of our analysis was to test the differential school and departmental effects for the following student characteristics:

- prior attainment (LRT);
- gender;
- ethnicity; and
- socio-economic status (eligible for FSM).

Once the average impact of the student intake factors had been taken into account (using the complete Model IV described in Chapter 3) evidence of significant differences between schools in their effects for particular student groups for total GCSE performance and subject scores was tested using multilevel analysis. In other words, to examine differential school effects it is necessary to investigate whether the overall variation due to the school, or department, for *all* students reflects the significant within-school (or -department) differences in GCSE attainment between *particular* groups of students in some schools.

Previous research using the same data for two years (1990, 1991) (Thomas *et al.*, 1994b) has reported that, in general, the more effective schools tended to promote the performance of higher ability students to a greater extent than other schools. Therefore, LRT was the first student intake characteristic we

Table 4.3 Summary of differential results

	Prior Attainment	Free School Meals(FSM)	Gender	Ethnicity*
Tscore	SS	SS	SS	SS
English	SS	SS	SS	SS
Mathematics	SS	SS	SS	SS
Science	SS	S	N	SS
History	SS	N	N	N
English Literature	SS	S	SS	SS
French	SS	S	N	SS

Note:
SS = significant when tested individually and jointly
S = significant when tested individually
N = Not significant
*The ethnic categories were collapsed into three groups: white, Caribbean, other

tested in the differential analysis for each outcome measure. The previous findings were confirmed and it was found that school slopes and intercepts varied significantly (at $p<0.05$ level) for total GCSE score as well as for each subject score. In other words, schools varied in both the average progress made by students and the gap in attainment between the most and least able students. In addition to the LRT student intake measure, differential school and departmental effects were tested for the following groups:

• boys vs girls,
• white vs other[2] (not Caribbean) and white vs Caribbean,
• students not entitled to FSM vs students entitled to FSM.

The findings show that in addition to the prior ability measure, schools and departments were found to be differentially effective for most of the student characteristics tested (Thomas *et al.*, 1997b). School means varied significantly ($p<=0.05$) for students entitled to FSM (versus students not entitled) for total GCSE score, English and mathematics. For students of the Caribbean group (and the other ethnic group) differential schools effects were found for total GCSE score, mathematics, English, English literature, French and science. Gender was also found to be significant with differential effects being identified for total GCSE score, English, English literature and mathematics. The results are summarized in Table 4.3.

Importantly, it also emerged that individual schools and departments were not necessarily consistent in their effects for different groups of students. Thus, using total GCSE as an example, the correlations between the value added scores for different student groups ranged from +0.88 to +0.97 (further details are provided in Thomas *et al.*, 1997b). However, the results suggest that, overall, all students in effective schools and departments (with high LRT intercepts for average LRT students) are likely to perform relatively well at GCSE but that particular groups of students (such as non-FSM students) are likely to perform especially well.[3] In contrast, it appears that all students in ineffective schools and departments (with low LRT intercepts for average LRT students) are likely to perform relatively poorly at GCSE. Nonetheless, particular groups of students – such as 'other (not Caribbean)' ethnic minority – are likely to perform somewhat better. It should be noted that the results for individual schools can, in some cases, be complex and may have important implications for whole school equal opportunities policy. Therefore, further detailed research is required to examine the overall school effects for specific groups of students as well as the gap in attainment between specific groups.

It should be noted that the results reported earlier in Chapter 3 (see Table 3.6) show that some of the variation in student scores can be attributed to average changes in results over time (three years) across all schools. Therefore, it was also important to test whether some school results varied much more (or less) than average over time than other schools. For this purpose an indicator of each cohort year was tested to examine whether the time trend co-efficient for each performance measure varied significantly across schools, over and above the average improvement in GCSE results for all schools.

Significant differences between schools were found in trends over the three-year period for English, English literature and mathematics but not for total GCSE score, French, history and science. This finding is important because it shows that for three outcome measures (English, English literature and mathematics) significant increasing or decreasing trends in GCSE attainment can be identified for some schools. In other words we can conclude that some English and mathematics departments were improving over time – in comparison with the average department – in terms of promoting student GCSE attainment, whereas others were declining. These findings suggest that further research into the processes associated with improving schools and departments would be particularly relevant for the core curriculum areas of English and mathematics as some schools appear to have been very successful in improving GCSE performance in these subjects over a relatively short time period. In Chapters 6 and 7 we explore information about departmental processes obtained from HTs and HoDs of mathematics and English in detail.

Thus, in terms of Key Question 4, it appears that schools and departments are indeed differentially effective for different groups of students. This is particularly notable in terms of total GCSE score, English and mathematics. Our finding strongly suggests the need for schools to examine in detail the value added performance of different groups of students in their schools, especially by level of prior attainment, gender, low income and ethnicity. They also demonstrate the existence of differences between schools in performance over time (the year effect) and the importance of monitoring trends in GCSE performance using overall measures, and specific subject measures over several years.

GROUPING SCHOOLS CONSISTENCY AND STABILITY OF SCHOOLS' VALUE ADDED RESULTS

In order to provide an example of how the profile of an individual school's results can vary dramatically in terms of two different aspects of performance, we have used a procedure for grouping similar schools. In particular we have grouped schools according to whether GCSE performance is *both* consistent, over a range of subjects and for total GCSE examination score, *and* stable over time, that is for successive student cohorts. Our criteria for selecting schools involve establishing the extent to which schools' actual GCSE performance differs significantly (at the 0.05 level) from that expected, taking into account their student intake, in terms of prior attainment and background factors. In other words, schools are categorized according to whether the size of the residual is approximately two or more times the standard error for each outcome measure. An alternative approach could have been to define a set cut-off point for each school residual using, for example, the results of the tenth highest and lowest ranked schools. Both approaches use arbitrary but predefined criteria to identify groups of schools as being 'effective' or 'ineffective'. However, for our purpose it was decided that the first – and more stringent approach – was preferable because of changes in the number of schools included for different analyses. This means that the rankings cannot be compared. A second rationale for our chosen approach is that statistical significance (at the 0.05 level) is the standard criteria used to infer that a result is unlikely to have occurred by chance.

Using the criteria shown in Table 4.4 schools are grouped into seven categories. As can be seen, in any single year's analysis, only a minority of schools were significantly more effective in promoting students' total GCSE performance and had significant positive effects on several specific subjects (and *no* significant negative effects). For example, in the analysis of the 1991

Table 4.4 Grouping schools by stability and consistency of value added measures

		1990 Number of Schools (n=69)	1991 Number of Schools (n=94)	1992 Number of Schools (n=77)	1990–1992 Number of Schools (n=69)
Positive Scores	Criteria [1]	10	13	12	3
Positive Scores	Criteria [2]	11	14	12	1
Negative Scores	Criteria [3]	10	15	7	3
Negative Scores	Criteria [4]	8	12	13	1
Mixed Scores	Criteria [5]	14	18	22	4
Mixed Scores	Criteria [6]	8	12	6	0
Other Scores	Criteria [7]	1	3	2	0
No Significant Scores		7	7	3	0

Note:
Criteria [1] significant +ve total score *and* 2 or more significant +ve subject scores (no significant -ve scores)
Criteria [2] significant +ve total score *or* significant +ve subject scores (no significant -ve scores)
Criteria [3] significant -ve total score *and* 2 or more significant -ve subject scores (no significant +ve scores)
Criteria [4] significant -ve total score *or* significant -ve subject scores (no significant +ve scores)
Criteria [5] 3 or more significant +ve *and* -ve subject scores
Criteria [6] 2 or more significant +ve *and* -ve subject scores
Criteria [7] any other combination of significant scores

GCSE cohort, 13 (14 per cent) out of the 94 schools were identified in this group (see Table 4.4). However, far fewer schools were categorised as significantly effective for all of the three GCSE cohorts (1990–92), only 3 (4 per cent) out of 69 schools with data for all three years.

A further 15 schools (16 per cent) could be classified as broadly ineffective for 1991 (significant negative effects on total GCSE performance scores and on two or more subjects and *no* significant positive effects) but only 3 schools (4 per cent) across three years. Thus for 1991 just under a third of schools (30 per cent) could be adequately classified as broadly more or less effective. However, for three years the equivalent figure is much lower, at only 9 per cent.

For the majority of schools in 1991 (70 per cent), no clear cut picture emerged. There were 30 schools (32 per cent) which recorded significant negative effects in some subjects and significant positive effects in others taking account of prior attainment and background (reflecting the non-perfect subject correlation results shown in Table 4.1). These schools thus had very mixed effects at GCSE. This finding further demonstrates the extent of marked within-school variation in GCSE performance in some schools. In certain cases these schools' total GCSE performance was not significantly different from expected, substantial subject differences being masked by the average overall results. Only in a small number of cases did schools record no significant effects – positive or negative – in terms of total GCSE and/or subject results.

In summary, the results of grouping schools (on the basis of three single year analyses) in terms of overall and subject effectiveness show that just under a fifth, 12 out of 69 schools (17 per cent), were categorized in the same groups, with very few schools being placed in the most effective group (3) or in the least effective group (3). We would argue that this stringent procedure for categorizing schools in terms of effectiveness is helpful for identifying and separating schools with the most stable pattern of results over a three-year period – to form outlier groups of effective, ineffective or mixed. The results from the first quantitative phase of our research were used to select schools for more detailed qualitative case studies, as we discuss in Chapter 5.

SUMMARY OF RESULTS FROM PHASE 1 OF THE STUDY

The first part of this book has focused on the measurement of schools' academic effectiveness. Our study highlights the importance of taking account of background factors and prior attainment using appropriate value added models, in order to estimate the influence of the school, while pointing to the complexity of making judgements about performance (Thomas *et al.*, 1997a, 1997b; Sammons, 1996). There is some evidence of a broad consistency in schools' effects on GCSE subject results averaged across three successive GCSE cohorts, thus all correlations were positive ranging from 0.20 to 0.72 between the separate subjects and total GCSE performance scores. For a substantial proportion of schools (about a third in 1991), however, there are significant departmental differences in terms of effectiveness and these may be masked by a reliance on a single measure of total GCSE score.

In general, schools' effects on total GCSE performance score were much more stable over the three years 1990–92 (correlations ranged from 0.82 to 0.88) than those for specific subjects. This is also an important finding. At the subject level, results for French were the least stable and those for history the most stable (correlations ranged from 0.92 to 0.71) over the three years. However, despite evidence of broad stability in some areas, the correlations indicate that there can be a substantial degree of change over time in some schools and point to the value and necessity of looking at performance across several years to obtain a picture of trends. Our results are in line with previous studies reporting estimates of stability and change of results over time (such as Gray *et al.*, 1993, 1996) and show that some schools appear to be improving (or declining) in performance. However, as Gray and Wilcox (1995) have pointed out, how an 'ineffective' school improves may well differ from the ways in which more effective schools maintain their effectiveness. Reynolds (1992) has drawn attention to the fact that ineffective schools may differ in fundamental ways from those which are more effective – a topic we explore in connection with the case studies in Chapter 5. Moreover, school improvement is a relatively less well researched area than school effectiveness. Further studies are required to examine the pattern of changes in schools' effectiveness from year to year in relation to school policy and process factors.

The evidence concerning differential school effects we have obtained in our study shows that some schools do indeed achieve differing value added results for different groups of students. The findings were particularly strong for students categorized by prior attainment measures and by ethnicity, although differential effects were also found for girls versus boys and for those students from low income families versus other students. These results indicate that value added measures which reflect the progress of all students may conceal the under-achievement of particular groups of students within each school. Nevertheless, overall, the results also suggested that all students in effective schools and departments were likely to do relatively well at GCSE but particular groups (such as those not entitled to free school meals) were likely to perform especially well. In contrast, all students in less effective schools and departments were likely to obtain relatively poor GCSE results, but particular groups' (such as Asian students) performance was least adversely affected. We can conclude that effective schools tend to boost the achievement of all students, but that advantaged groups may benefit most. Likewise, in the less effective schools certain ethnic minority groups (such as the Caribbean group) may be most adversely affected.

Overall, the evidence from Phase 1 strongly suggests that within-school performance varies across different outcome measures and over time. Therefore, there is a need to look at trends in school performance in detail – not just at total GCSE performance and subject level – in order to tease out effective departments. It is also important to investigate the relative performance of different groups of students within schools and departments to establish the extent of any differential effectiveness. It is worth noting here that our study was carried out at a time when little or no detailed quantitative information was available to schools about their value added performance, particularly for specific groups of students. If value added data are adopted more widely as a tool for school and departmental self-evaluation then current patterns of consistency and stability in performance may change.

CONCLUSIONS

In this chapter and Chapter 3, we presented the results of Phase 1 of our study, focusing on the performance of schools in terms of examination results. On their own, such results are not sufficient for complete judgements about schools' performance. Other outcomes such as student attendance, attitudes to school and to learning, behaviour, and self-concept are also important. School effectiveness research aims to investigate a broad range of educational outcomes and examples of this approach are provided by previous work reported in *Fifteen Thousand Hours* (Rutter *et al.*, 1979) and *School Matters* (Mortimore *et al.*, 1988). On-going work in the Lancashire value added project (Thomas and Mortimore, 1996) and our current Improving School Effectiveness project conducted in Scotland (MacBeath and Mortimore, 1994; Robertson and Sammons, 1997) also involves the collection of student, teacher and parent attitude data in addition to academic outcomes. Nonetheless, we acknowledge the primacy of academic outcomes and it is for this reason that we believe it is essential that a range of useful information about students' progress is employed in any comparisons of schools.

The results from our research where schools are grouped into strictly defined effectiveness categories show that only a minority of schools perform both consistently (across subjects) and with stability (over time) and that these schools are at the extremes of the effectiveness range (i.e. strongly positive or strongly negative) (Thomas *et al.*, 1997a). Therefore, there is only limited value in trying to make judgements about schools' examination results performance in any one year or by any one outcome measure. Instead our results show clearly that monitoring internal variations in performance in any year and across years should be encouraged to review standards at the departmental (or subject) level and for different groups of students, as well as overall, and how these standards may change over time. Where possible, this should also be done for different year groups within the school.

The findings we have reported are, we think, of both practical and theoretical importance. School performance that varies greatly between departments and/or over time has implications for whole school policies and may provide important evidence about the impact of departmental planning and improvement initiatives. School performance that varies greatly for different groups of students, such as boys and girls, also has implications for equal opportunities policies. These findings also have important lessons for parents who can only make *one* choice of secondary school and hope to select a school which is both broadly effective in all areas and likely to continue to be effective in future years (a topic we return to in Chapter 9 where we discuss the implications of the research).

Effectiveness is best seen as a feature which is outcome- and time-specific. Therefore, one useful approach for the purpose of evaluating school improvement is to establish where results are significantly different from those expected (taking account of intake) over *more* than one year, in terms of overall performance and in specific subjects. In terms of extending Scheerens' (1992) criteria for adequate studies of school effectiveness we conclude that judgements about schools need to address three key questions:

- Effective in promoting which outcomes?
- Effective over what time period?
- Effective for whom?

Or in terms of improvement:

- Improvement in promoting which outcomes?
- Improvement over what time period?
- Improvement for whom?

The task of linking school effectiveness measures to school improvement begins with the premise that analysis is the start, not the end, of the process – that monitoring does not by itself improve performance. Future developments in value added research are likely to build on current findings, such as those of our study, that investigate the relationship between measures of school performance and the *conditions* that appear to enhance, or alternatively form barriers, to school effectiveness in different types of school context. We believe that the Differential School Effectiveness project is especially useful in demonstrating the use of both qualitative and quantitative data by employing a combination of value added methodology to evaluate school performance with interview and questionnaire data to investigate the factors and processes related to greater departmental and school effectiveness. In the next chapter we move on from the quantitative results of Phase 1 to examine the case studies of differentially effective schools (highly academically effective or ineffective or mixed at the departmental level) in order to explore these issues further.

NOTES

1. It is important to point out that any correlations between school value added scores (i.e. residuals) may be viewed as technically 'inflated' estimates due to the fact that there is an element of 'shrinkage' (towards the overall means score) in the calculation of these scores, particularly for schools with very small numbers of pupils. In other words the estimates shown can be interpreted as upper limits and the 'true' correlations would be somewhat lower. Given the large sample size using three years' data such shrinkage will be limited.

2. Earlier analyses indicated that it was necessary to collapse the original ethnicity categories as follows: Caribbean = Caribbean; other = African, Indian, Pakistani, Bangladeshi, other.

3. Importantly, the inclusion in the analyses of a more detailed measure of students' social class and level of parental education, may have an impact on these findings. In other words, the most advantaged students, with parents in professional occupations and a university level of education may be more likely to perform well at GCSE and also to attend the more effective schools. Therefore, further clarification of the results is required in future work to include more detailed measures of student intake characteristics (especially of social class and level of parental education).

PART 2: EXPLAINING DIFFERENCES IN EFFECTIVENESS

5

Case Studies of More and Less Effective Schools and Departments

INTRODUCTION

In the second phase of the research we turn to the fifth key question addressed by our study. This concerns the relationship between school and departmental processes and students' academic performance as measured by GCSE results.

Key question 5
What factors to do with school status and processes relate to differences between secondary schools in effectiveness in promoting GCSE attainment? In particular, is there evidence that different factors and processes are important in promoting good results for different departments?

In order to improve our understanding of the factors which influence academic effectiveness, we undertook detailed case studies of particular institutions and departments. These were selected on the basis of the Phase 1 multilevel analyses of the GCSE results of three consecutive age groups drawn from a sample of ninety-four schools. In this chapter we present the main findings from Phase 2 which involved the study of thirty different subject departments in six of these schools chosen as outliers with significantly positive or negative effects at GCSE. These schools were categorized as follows (with two schools chosen from each group):

Broadly positive effects – academically more effective in terms of overall GCSE results and different departments' subject results – consistently significant positive effects.
Highly mixed effects – schools with consistently highly effective *and* highly ineffective departments located within the same institution.
Broadly negative effects – academically less effective – consistently negative effects, in terms of overall GCSE results and the subject results of different departments.

In recent years, the need for detailed case study research on effective schools has become apparent as an important means of increasing understanding of the ways in which internal functioning of different schools can enhance students' academic progress (Reynolds, 1992; Levine, 1992). School effectiveness research still has a fairly weak theoretical basis (Scheerens, 1992; Sammons, Mortimore and Thomas, 1996; Scheerens, 1995; Scheerens and Bosker, 1997; Creemers, 1995). Case study research, however, can illuminate the complex interactions of context, organization, policy and practice which help to generate more or less effective schools and departments. It can also establish the extent to which similar or different approaches and strategies are adopted in different schools identified as equally effective or unequally ineffective in academic terms (Hargreaves, 1995a).

In addition, case study approaches allow the testing of existing school effectiveness theory and can also contribute to its development and further refinement. Thus the use of case studies enables us to establish whether unusually effective schools do, in fact, exhibit the features, characteristics and processes associated with greater effectiveness identified in past research synthesis and reviews of the school effectiveness field (e.g. Borger et al., 1984; Mortimore, 1991a and b; Mortimore et al., 1991; Levine, 1992; McGaw et al., 1992; Reynolds, 1992; Scheerens, 1992; Creemers, 1994a).

The Phase 2 case studies involved in-depth semi-structured interviews with headteachers (HT), deputy heads (DHT) and heads of five subject departments (HoD). Questionnaires were used to obtain additional background information about schools and departments. School and departmental policy documents were also collected.

All schools and staff involved in the case studies were assured of confidentiality in the presentation of results. Two experienced consultants with different subject expertise were employed to conduct the fieldwork. An important feature of the research design was that consultants were not informed about which schools had been allocated to the three case study groups (broadly negative, broadly positive or highly mixed) until after the completion of fieldwork and analysis of data. Also, to avoid influencing perceptions, schools were not given details of their value added results for the period 1990–92.

A review of relevant school effectiveness research and of practitioner guidance documents related to secondary school effectiveness was used to identify areas/topics to be covered by the research (Sammons et al., forthcoming). The review's results were discussed by the project consultants and research team as part of the process of developing interviews for use with key personnel in each case study school. In this way it was possible to incorporate the understanding developed by experienced practitioners into the data collection process.

Our interviews with the HTs and DHTs lasted between two and four hours. The semi-structured schedule laid a strong emphasis on comparing the situation five years ago with that currently (1993–94). One DHT (where more than one was in post, a DHT was chosen because of particular responsibility for curriculum and examination matters) was interviewed in five schools. In the sixth, which consisted of separate upper and lower schools, both DHTs were interviewed. The HT and DHT interviews included many common questions

Table 5.1   Numbers of departments by effectiveness category

	More effective	Less effective	Not classified or non-significant effect
English	3	3	
French	2	2	2
History	3	2	1
Mathematics	2	4	
Science	3	3	
Total	13	14	3

in order to explore the extent of similarity and disagreement in views and perceptions about a variety of topics.

A total of thirty subject HoDs were also interviewed, five in each school. These covered the three core curriculum subjects (English, mathematics and science), plus history and French. Thirteen of the thirty departments were categorized as academically more effective in terms of value added to their students' GCSE results and fourteen were, by contrast, categorized as academically less effective.[1] Three departments effects were not consistently positive or negative over three years, or could not be classified in one or more years due to small numbers of entrants. Table 5.1 gives the numbers of case study departments by subject and value added effectiveness category – more effective, less effective and not classified/non-significant.

Topics covered by the HT/DHT and the HoD interviews included:

Philosophy and aims
   principal educational goals for students; major successes/achievements of the school and department; major problems/challenges facing the school and departments; levels of satisfaction with different aspects of the school; and current role and leadership approach/style.
School and department policies
   student grouping; assessment; option arrangements; examination entry; homework; marking; classroom organization and pedagogy; and teacher involvement in decision-making.
Senior Management Team (SMT)
   assessment of the SMT including members' roles, effectiveness, commitment, ability to use initiative, leadership quality, creativity and general satisfaction with their performance; and ways in which the performance of the SMT could be improved and how change (if necessary) could be achieved.
Staff generally
   including aspects of their performance; estimates of average additional time spent on job by different members of staff; and teacher shortage and absence.
Parent involvement
   relationship with and feedback from parents; assessment of parental interest in their children's education; parental attendance at meetings; methods of

informing and communicating with parents; and parents' role in homework monitoring.

Student involvement and outcomes

code of conduct; system and use of rewards and sanctions/punishments; judgement of behaviour in school; motivation and attendance; exclusions; judgement of percentage of intake with SEN; E2L; and academic balance.

In addition, HTs were interviewed about each of the five departments/faculties included in the project. They were asked to rate them in terms of ethos and academic emphasis, the leadership qualities displayed by HoD and staff performance. They were also questioned about these departments' particular strengths or major achievements, weaknesses or problems, staff shortages and attendance and about decline/improvement over time.

School and departmental histories

Schools are not static institutions and in the UK, as elsewhere, they have been subject to particularly marked externally-imposed changes during the last decade. In addition, all schools are subject to a variable amount of internal changes, often unforeseen. These can include staff death/sickness, mobility, as well as building problems and changes in enrolment patterns and intakes. The need to focus on change and to take account of school and department histories to gain a better understanding of the functioning of institutions is a strong message from our research. Although case study schools were chosen because they exhibited significant and consistent patterns of effectiveness, in overall GCSE results and/or specific subject results, over three years (1990–92), there was evidence that in at least one of the case study schools, some improvements in student outcomes (on a very low base) were beginning to occur by 1993, as well as organizational and other improvements.

The HoD interviews provided information about school and individual departmental histories. In most schools a significant change in personnel, both at the SMT level and within individual departments, had occurred in the last five years. In some cases this was seen to have been highly beneficial and a catalyst for improvement, particularly in one of the ineffective schools. Moreover, high staff turnover and absence or shortages were noted as a source of particular difficulties in some, but not all, of the ineffective departments. However, in other cases the presence of long-serving staff who were not open to new ideas and disliked change were also identified as barriers to departmental improvement.

As noted above, in one of the less effective case study schools, some improvements in student outcomes had occurred by the end of 1993. The leadership qualities of a new HT and one DHT – both in post for about four years – and the recruitment of a number of new HoDs were seen to be the driving forces behind a change in direction here. Nevertheless, there was evidence that not all HoDs or DHTs in this particular school were in favour of the reforms introduced during this time. A number of long serving HoDs and one SMT member resented, and felt threatened by, the process of change and it was clear that, as yet, a whole school consensus regarding goals had not been achieved. Nonetheless, some improvement was perceived by all five middle managers in terms of different student outcomes, including behaviour, attendance and motivation. These perceptions were supported by the conclusions of its first OFSTED inspection, as well as by an upward trend in examination results for some departments in 1993. In this school the contrast between past policies and practice and that currently reported was especially striking.

A notable and perhaps unsurprising feature of our case studies was that HoDs from both effectiveness categories commented on problems in implementing the NC and NA, and an increased workload for the past five years leading to unusual pressure on staff. Some also commented adversely on revision of GCSE requirements, for example, in relation to the reduction in course work components.

The HT interviews, like those of the HoDs, drew attention to the extent of change over time in subject departments, staffing and performance, and point to the need to take account of the unique history of individual departments. For example, one HT from a school in the mixed effects category commented on 'considerable difficulties' in the history of the mathematics department, assigned to the ineffective group of departments. These included 'poor discipline', 'several weak teachers', and 'some uninspiring senior staff', 'lack of team work', 'poor student-teacher relationships', and a shortage of qualified mathematics teachers in the department. However, this HT reported that a new HoD, a new second-in-command and another qualified teacher had been appointed over the last year. Although not yet satisfied with the department's performance, the HT felt there were now signs of real improvement, the new HoD was very good at managing the department and staff, had good leadership skills, team work had increased, student-teacher relationships were more cordial and the 'whole-school relationship' of the department had become better.

Another example was given by the HT of one of the academically less effective schools concerning their French department (from the less effective departmental group). There had been a good deal of staff movement since 1988. Two changes of HoD had occurred and a DHT had taken over for a while as acting HoD 'so many staff . . . they're always moving'. An 'incompetent' second-in-command in the department had been seen as a long-standing problem. In the HT's view, the new HoD of French and a new second-in-command had improved the department's organization, especially in relation to monitoring student performance. The use of mixed ability grouping, however, was still seen to cause 'problems', examination results continued to be poor, and lack of cohesion and teamwork remained evident. Nonetheless, the HT felt that some positive achievements had been evident recently in the form of productive journeys abroad and exchanges.

A HT from the more academically effective group of schools also commented on the impact of staff changes, in this case in the science department (drawn from the more effective departmental group). This HT noted that, until recently, the science department had benefited from a very strong, well-respected and highly qualified HoD. However, the very new HoD 'lacked confidence with staff'. Recently numerous changes of staff were said to have taken place in the department and this was also perceived to be causing problems. Nonetheless, the HT felt that the science department's examination results were continuing to improve and that the team remained 'well motivated, innovative, hard-working, creative and forward looking', the legacy of an effective and stable past.

The importance of staff stability in effective departments was noted by the HT of the other case study school classified as academically more effective, in describing the English department. This department had a long record of good results and stable staffing. However, during the last five years a new HoD had taken over and had then had a considerable amount of absence before leaving. The department had been mainly run by an efficient second-in-command during this period. The HT reported that he/she had provided 'a lot of input personally' and, despite the upheavals, good English results had been maintained, the NC linked in and consolidated, and IT and good programmes of work had been developed. The appointment of a new HoD, who was seen to be 'very good' had recently taken place and the HT was optimistic about the future.

Our case studies also drew attention to a strong tendency for the staff of less effective schools and departments to blame long-standing demographic or geographical factors for their shortcomings. For example, one HoD said staff at their school 'hid behind the locality' and treated working class children as 'thick'. Others complained about physical aspects such as the poor quality of buildings or the layout of their school(s) e.g. 'split site'. Heads of science in particular drew attention to a lack of physical resources – space, laboratory equipment etc. This was true in the case of both the more and the less effective departments.

Although each school and department has a unique history, a number of common themes also emerged from the case studies, the most important of which are summarized in the next section.

ACADEMIC EMPHASIS AND HIGH EXPECTATIONS

Both HoDs and HTs were asked to rate the academic emphasis of the case study departments. We found marked differences in HTs' ratings of the stress different departments placed on academic achievement according to their value added effectiveness grouping. It should be remembered that neither HoDs nor the HTs had been informed of either their school's or specific departments' effectiveness category. Wide variations in academic emphasis were reported to have existed five years previously, as can be seen in Table 5.2.

Table 5.2 Comparison of HTs' and HoDs' ratings of departments' academic emphasis by effectiveness category

HTs' views
a] *More effective departments (n=13)*
Academic Emphasis

| | Very strong emphasis <·······················> Weak emphasis | | | | |
	1	2	3	4	5
Now	5	5	3	–	–
5 yrs ago	3	6	2	1	1

[b] *Less effective departments (n=13)* *
Academic Emphasis

| | Very strong emphasis < ·······················> Weak emphasis | | | | |
	1	2	3	4	5
Now	4	5	1	3	–
5 yrs ago	2	2	1	8	

*One HT was currently Acting HoD and therefore was interviewed about this department from the HoD perspective

HoDs' views
a] *More effective departments (n=13)*
Academic Emphasis

| | Very strong emphasis < ·······················> Weak emphasis | | | | |
	1	2	3	4	5
Now	10	3	–	–	–
5 yrs ago	10	2	1	–	–

b] *Less effective departments (n=14)* *
Academic Emphasis

| | Very strong emphasis < ·······················> Weak emphasis | | | | |
	1	2	3	4	5
Now	9	5	–	–	
5 yrs ago	3	8	–	2	1

Overall, HoDs' views were more favourable than those of HTs. Respondents from the two effectiveness groups were equally likely to report that their departments had a very strong academic emphasis currently, although for HoDs of ineffective departments the situation five years previously was perceived a little less favourably, three out of fourteen indicating a weak emphasis and fewer reporting a stronger one than before.

These tables indicate that over the past five years HoDs had more positive views of departments' academic emphasis than HTs. In particular, HTs' views of the past academic emphasis in departments classified in our analyses as less effective were notably less favourable than HoDs.

As well as being asked about academic emphasis in general, interviewees were questioned on specific elements of this and we analyse their responses in the following section.

Homework/marking

Headteachers and their DHTs were generally dissatisfied with the current operation of their school's homework policy, although several had revised this in recent years. In the two more effective schools, much discussion with heads of years and of departments had occurred. Both HTs and their DHTs were also of the view that their schools' homework policy was much more organized, rigorous and monitored now (1993–94) than in the past, although homework had always been strongly emphasized. For example, as part of the HTs' regular departmental reviews in one school, all HoDs were asked to provide evidence on the extent to which teachers set and marked, and students completed, homework.

In both the mixed schools, homework policy was being reviewed and discussed. In one no policy had existed five years before, while in the other it was noted that homework had been given low priority and that teachers were very 'inconsistent' in their practice. The current situation in this school was reported to be better than five years previously – but not much.

Both the less effective schools' HTs and DHTs reported *severe* difficulties concerning homework, especially in the past. In the less effective school which nevertheless appeared to be progressing, considerable monitoring had been instituted very recently, on a weekly basis by tutors, fortnightly by heads of years and an annual survey. This had demonstrated significant anomalies between departments which were now receiving attention. In the past notional homework timetables had 'existed' but work was rarely set in practice and marking was of 'a very poor standard'.

In the other school in the less effective group, both HT and DHT commented that the setting of homework was very patchy and some tutors were 'slack'. Marking of homework – if it occurred – was 'perfunctory' with inadequate formative comment. Whereas in the past there had been no policy, one had now been agreed but was not fully implemented,.

Overall, the evidence obtained from HTs, DHTs and HoDs indicated that both homework and marking policy and practice had usually been regarded as much more important and been more consistently applied in the more academically effective departments than in the less effective ones. In addition, marking and homework continued to remain highly 'contentious' topics for HoDs of a number of the less effective departments. The regular setting of homework and provision of prompt and regular feedback by marking was seen to be very important by many HoDs and an influence on ethos and expectations, although some, particularly new ones in less effective departments, were very dissatisfied with their department's current and/or past performance in these areas.

No school was fully satisfied with the operation of its homework policy, and there was a clear message from HT/DHTs and HoDs that this was a major problem area in both the less effective and in at least one of the mixed schools. Inconsistent approaches by individual staff and different departments, as well as low expectations and priority, were much in evidence in these schools.

Examination entry

Headteachers and DHTs were asked about their school's policy for examination entry. Student choice was important, though usually with constraints, e.g. to adhere to National Curriculum (NC) requirements and avoid problems of low take-up by girls of subjects such as science and technology. One of the more effective schools specifically mentioned consultation with parents as well as students. In all schools, HoDs or faculties made decisions about syllabus and examination boards but some differences were evident in response to questions about how students were actually selected for entry. Both the more effective schools stressed a high entry policy: 'We hope to enter everyone for everything' and in these schools this policy was reported to be unchanged over the last five years. By contrast, in the mixed and less effective case study schools, decisions about whether a student could enter were made by the relevant teachers or departments based on records of attendance, judgements about motivation and whether sufficient course work had been completed. In both of the less effective schools, it was felt that insufficient students had been entered hitherto and that examination entry had been given a low priority in some departments.

There were few differences between more and less effective departments in terms of choice of examination boards. We identified several examples of departments which used the same boards for the same subject, but with different levels of success in terms of our value added analyses. There were some indications from HoDs, however, that entering all students for GCSE who had any chance of success was a more common strategy in the more effective departments – in line with reports from HTs and DHTs. While most took note of coursework, in some of the less effective departments high levels of attendance and all course work completed were required. In some of the more effective departments, however, comments such as '60 per cent of coursework completed' were made, indicating a less than stringent approach to entry. The more effective departments also paid much greater attention to assessment, feedback to students and homework – factors which were seen to have a strong influence on the probability of examination entry as well as success. Likewise, in the more effective schools, respondents indicated that examination entry had been accorded a higher priority in the past than it had in the less effective schools.

Student assessment

We found much evidence that many departments, particularly those from the less effective group, laid greater stress on assessment now (1993/94) than five years before. This appeared to be, at least in part, a reflection of changes related to the NC and assessment system and GCSE examinations, worries about OFSTED inspections, and the general publicity attached to league tables. In the past, in the less effective departments, there were indications that assessment policies – if they existed – were not well-developed and very inconsistently applied. In more effective departments, by contrast, assessment had always been fairly frequent and accorded a much higher priority, record-keeping practices were more consistent and assessment results were commonly monitored by the HoD and, in some cases, also at the school level. In effective departments, staff had usually been involved in the development of the assessment policy, engendering a sense of ownership. The regular monitoring and discussion of results by the whole departmental staff was also common in the academically effective departments.

Student grouping

We found no straightforward relationship between overall school effectiveness and policies on student grouping at the school level from the case studies. In all schools, irrespective of effectiveness category, there had been a move away from mixed ability strategies towards some form of setting by ability for selected subjects, especially in Years 10 and 11, during the last five years.

At the departmental level we found no clear evidence that grouping policies distinguished between the more and less effective departments although there were some indications that setting was more typical in effective French and history departments in the past. One HoD of a less effective department appeared to be moving towards setting in response to poor mathematics results, whereas some HoDs of more effective departments that had used setting in the past said they had adopted mixed ability grouping fairly recently. Amongst the thirty case study departments, mixed ability was the most common method of grouping for all subjects except science. Where setting was used it was usually adopted for Years 10 and 11.

In assessing the concept of academic emphasis, we explored overall perceptions, as well as policy and practice, in relation to homework, marking, assessment, examination entry (including Boards and syllabus) and student grouping. With regard to choice of examination boards and syllabi and grouping strategies, there was no clear cut distinction between the setting practices of more and less effective departments or schools. Low expectations and a lack of academic emphasis were clearly recognized by HTs/DHTs as past weaknesses in the two less effective schools, whereas in the more effective ones these had always been central concerns. One of the latter had a long established reputation for academic achievement and for an emphasis on departmental autonomy. In the other, improvements were identified on the existing fairly positive base. Change in staff attitudes were seen as important for bringing about improvements in students' academic achievement in several schools.

The HoDs' interviews showed clear differences in perceptions and indicated that, especially in the past, a lack of academic emphasis was seen as a major failing of the less effective departments. Homework, marking, assessment and emphasis on examination entry were key areas of difference in policy and practice. Inconsistent practice was also a notable feature. Student grouping, although currently a focus of concern, showed no obvious relationship with the academic effectiveness of different departments in our case studies.

SHARED VISION/GOALS

As we have already described, both schools in the more effective group laid considerable emphasis on academic success and there was a strong correspondence between the HTs' and DHTs' accounts of their school's principal educational goals. In one school, this was demonstrated by an underlining of the traditional academic curriculum: departments had considerable autonomy; there was a strong sixth form, and the subject teachers were, in general, highly qualified. Promoting students' self-confidence and encouraging them to express their opinions were thought as important as academic results. No changes in goals or emphasis over the past five years were reported. The view expressed by the DHT in this school was very close to the HT's: 'vigorous teaching and a good learning experience' plus pastoral systems to allow all students to achieve their full potential.

The other more effective case study school served a very socio-economically disadvantaged area. Its HT stressed raising achievement in all senses: valuing everyone, attendance, commitment, homework, standards. Here the emphasis was on providing an 'entitlement' curriculum for all, curriculum differentiation, encouraging students to become independent learners, and developing both self-respect and respect for others. It was suggested that, in comparison with the past, a greater stress was now placed on high expectations for students and demands for rigorous work. The DHT's views in this school corresponded very closely to those of the HTs, with high examination achievement for *all* being the prime goal. Like the HT, the DHT also felt that in the past there had been more emphasis on caring and rather less on learning, although academic matters had always been seen as important.

In the two less effective case study schools, there was a clear recognition by HTs that too little emphasis had been placed hitherto on improving academic standards. In one of these schools (which now seemed to be moving forward) the HT had taken up post in the last four years. Equal opportunities, providing a high quality curriculum and raising achievement for all were now said to be top priorities. Five years previously no written policy on educational goals existed, attendance was very poor and expectations were felt to have been far too low. The need to create 'a well-structured, caring, *working and learning* environment' was stressed. However, there was evidence of differences in opinions between the two DHTs interviewed in this school, as well as divergence between the HT and DHTs. Unlike the HT, neither DHT stressed either academic or pedagogic matters, suggesting that as yet the school had not achieved a shared vision even within the SMT.

In the other less effective school, the HT also reported that, in the past, much more attention had been placed on 'caring' than achievement. The emphasis was now seen to be on 'individual achievement for all' (academic, social, creative), although it was recognized that much more needed to be done to ensure this occurred. Areas thought to require attention included curriculum and staff development and the strengthening of particular departments. Unlike the HT, the DHT in this school did not mention academic results or pedagogy specifically, stressing that students should leave school 'personally and intellectually enriched'. The DHT acknowledged that five years ago the emphasis had been on caring, with work being treated as largely 'incidental' both by staff and students! Major problems in getting all staff to accept the importance of learning and teaching had been experienced in the past and these were still not resolved.

Interestingly, in the schools in the mixed group there was also evidence that HTs felt that, five years previously, the emphasis was on creating order and a caring atmosphere. One commented that their school had been 'bumbling along' and students – especially 'white working class boys' – had been under-achieving. Now raising achievement, equal access to the curriculum, gaining the highest qualifications possible and acquiring independence were stressed. One DHT felt that in the past the emphasis had been too much on discipline and control 'for its own sake', rather than as an aid to learning. The DHTs in these schools from the mixed group emphasized the general aim of equal opportunities but neither noted any specific academic or learning goals.

These results represent the HTs' and DHTs' perceptions of the goals their school tried to achieve. Several felt that now much more emphasis was – or should be – placed on academic achievement, and awareness that in the past academic achievement had been insufficiently emphasized. By the same token, some expressed the view that caring and pastoral matters previously had received too much prominence. It is notable that in the more effective schools, there was much greater similarity in the views expressed by both HT and DHT about educational goals, suggesting the existence of a more fully developed shared vision.

HoDs were asked to describe the ethos of their department, and, if applicable, how this had changed over the last five years. Amongst the HoDs of the more effective group, ten of the twelve who responded laid stress on being 'very co-operative' and 'very supportive' with a 'definite team spirit'; four specifically noted that staff covered for each other when absent; and four emphasized that their departments had 'friendly relations', were 'happy places' or that staff and students 'enjoyed' working in them.

By contrast, HoDs of the less effective group were more likely to stress a change in ethos in the last five years. Nine (out of thirteen who responded) commented on co-operation, teamwork or more supportive relations, although for eight this was seen to represent a *very marked* improvement from the situation five years before. Only one HoD from this group commented that staff 'regularly' covered for each other and another observed that there was no internal cover within the department. 'Dreadful' staff tensions, 'unhappy staff' and poor HoD leadership in the past were seen to have prevented the development of team spirit and co-operation by six HoDs in this group.

Lack of consensus within departments and personality conflicts were perceived to inhibit effectiveness by nine HoDs – all but one from the less effective group of departments – the other was HoD of a department with non-significant effects in a school from the mixed effects category. One commented specifically on an 'obstructive' second-in-command in the department and 'failure to implement agreed policy' concerning the curriculum and organization. Another two noted 'tensions' or 'strong disagreements' between individual members of staff. In all cases teamwork was seen to have suffered badly as a result. In addition, in three instances the heavy workloads and outside commitments of senior teachers within certain departments were seen to inhibit common approaches and teamwork. By contrast, only one HoD from the more effective group mentioned that 'a few' staff were less open to new ideas and less willing than others to work together as a team.

The HT and DHT interviews drew attention to the impact of staff consensus and a shared view about the purposes of the school primarily as a place for working. The emphasis on both teaching and learning was recognized by students as well as staff (Sammons *et al.*, forthcoming). The HoD interviews reinforced this conclusion but also drew attention to the importance of such shared vision for the effective functioning of individual departments. Divisions over matters such as student grouping policies, the choice of courses or examination boards, assessment and homework, and marking policy and practice were commented on to a much greater extent by HoDs in the less effective departmental group, particularly when referring to the past. Personality conflicts and high staff turnover were also factors which HoDs felt inhibited the development of shared vision and agreed goals in some of the less effective departments. Of course, these also have important implications for effective teamwork.

The positive impact of effective and consistent school-wide policies on matters such as student behaviour, marking, homework and assessment were noted by HoDs of more effective departments in the two more academically effective schools. By contrast, other HoDs – respondents from schools in the mixed and academically less effective groups – noted the adverse impact of the absence of consistency.

THE SENIOR MANAGEMENT TEAM

The SMTs ranged in size from four to seven members (including the HT) in the six case study schools, and the functions and responsibilities of the different members varied markedly. In both schools in the more effective group the HT had been a DHT in the school. These schools appeared to have benefited from greater stability or continuity of approach. In one more effective school the performance of all members was rated as uniformly very effective, while in the other and in one mixed case study, most members were seen as very effective or of average effectiveness. In contrast, in schools in the less effective group and one mixed school, several members of the SMT were identified as fairly or very ineffective, not committed and a source of conflict. These members were thought to prevent greater delegation with an effectively-functioning SMT possible only through a change of post-holder. The DHTs' evaluations of the effectiveness of the SMT members corresponded fairly closely to those of the HTs in their schools. Overall, we found that ratings of SMT members were more positive – especially in terms of effectiveness, commitment, ability and creativity – in the more effective schools.

Only one difficulty in running the SMT was noted in one of the effective schools. Here the DHT felt the HT was perhaps not assertive enough, although the HT was otherwise generally rated very positively by this respondent. The need for more teamwork was felt to be a minor problem also. In this school, the HT had laid great stress on the school's long-standing tradition of departmental autonomy. A more pro-active approach to leadership was advocated by the DHT. In contrast, in the other more effective school, more time for SMT meetings was viewed as the only requirement for increased effectiveness.

In one of the mixed schools problems with particular members of the SMT were reported and a lack of team spirit was noted. It was thought that this could only be resolved by acceptance of a 'common goal of student good'. The arrival of a new HT was anticipated as a means of fostering team spirit and developing whole school goals.

The need for better teamwork was also emphasized in the progressing less effective school. Communication and removing 'secrecy' was stressed by one DHT in this institution. The other DHT pointed to great tensions within the SMT – a problem also noted by the HT – and the need for more meetings to overcome this. By contrast, in the other less effective school, inefficient meetings, decision-making and consultation processes were all areas of concern, with renegotiated job descriptions and more closely structured meetings being perceived as potential solutions.

In all schools, HTs and DHTs reported spending 'too many' extra hours on top of the normal school day on their job; somewhere between thirty and forty hours a week extra being cited. However, in schools in the mixed and less effective groups, specific members of the SMT, identified as sources of difficulty, were felt to donate much less extra time than others. This was clearly a source of some resentment for respondents who felt that, as a result, they shouldered a greater burden than 'less committed' colleagues.

Our findings on strained relationships in less effective schools are in line with conclusions by Reynolds and Packer (1992) concerning the abnormal staff culture of failing schools. Clearly difficulties may arise when a new HT takes over a school and an incumbent DHT is passed over for headship. The conclusions of school effectiveness research on the importance of a shared vision and ability to work constructively as a team drawing on, or complementing members' strengths, are supported by HTs' assessments of their SMT. In general, the SMT of the more effective schools appeared to function as coherent and complementary teams in a way which was not evident in the other schools. Indeed, in the two less effective schools conflict in the SMT was a strong feature.

Heads of departments were also asked to rate the current effectiveness, commitment and leadership qualities of members of their school's SMT and compare this with the situation five years before. They were also asked in what ways, if any, could the performance of the SMT be improved and how worthwhile change could be achieved.

A school-by-school analysis of HoDs' ratings and comments revealed that in five out of the six case studies, HoDs views about the effectiveness of, and satisfaction with, their HT varied. However, in one school from the more effective group, in which all departments were in the more effective category, all HoDs gave their current HT – who had taken over within the last five years – the highest effectiveness rating – 'the school is very efficiently run'. Although the SMT clearly received considerable credit for the continued improvement in this school's effectiveness over the last five years, HoDs had some criticisms of style. In common with HoDs in all other schools, the middle managers wanted more day-to-day contact and consultation between the SMT and staff.

Within the other school from the more effective group, in which all departments were categorized as effective, ratings of the SMT were also favourable. Nonetheless, HoDs' comments indicated that they still saw a need for better communication and more consultation in the school, and 'fewer unilateral decisions'. One felt the SMT were too 'cut off' from other staff.

In the two schools in the mixed effectiveness category there was greater variation in ratings, especially of DHTs. In one school, individual HoDs' views also differed considerably. One rated the HT as quite ineffective currently and five years before, two gave average ratings and two quite positive scores. Individual DHTs' ratings also varied strikingly between very effective to quite ineffective. One HoD commented that the school had 'no sense of direction or ethos . . . no feeling of community' – and held the whole SMT responsible.

We turn now to the two schools from the less effective group. In the school that had experienced a series of very difficult inspections and a number of changes of HT, HoDs' views of the SMT also diverged sharply. Two HoDs here rated the relatively new HT as very effective and were more than satisfied with his/her performance. By contrast, out of three HoDs – who had all been in post for a longer period – one rated their HT as average or variable in effectiveness and two as unsatisfactory. All HoDs' ratings of this school's DHTs varied from the extremes of very effective to very ineffective, indicating great divergence of views and satisfaction with individual postholders. One of these HoDs felt the SMT should accept responsibility for the school's failure instead of 'blaming' teachers and criticized the HT for not being decisive enough in 'turning things round', but at the same time wanted the SMT to be 'more democratic'.

HoDs of the other school in the less effective category showed less variation in ratings of effectiveness and satisfaction. Three out of four respondents rated the HT as quite effective now and five years before and one as average or variable. Nonetheless, some SMT members were much less favourably rated. Also two HoDs felt the SMT was 'too detached and formal', and that a greater recognition of staff talents and efforts should occur.

Whilst HoDs in all schools commented on some problems or ways in which their SMT could function more effectively, responses overall indicated greater satisfaction with the functioning of the SMT as a team in the more effective schools. In mixed and less effective schools several SMT members were rated as ineffective. In all schools, middle managers felt that their roles should be better defined and wanted more involvement in decision-making. The remoteness of SMT members and perceived lack of awareness for staff feelings was also a common theme.

Our interviews with HTs and DHTs underline the importance of the SMT – including the HTs' role and leadership – in fostering school effectiveness. Important features include shared goals, commitment, loyalty and hard work, which enable staff to work together as a team and to each other's strengths. The results of the HoD interviews also support the conclusion that an effective and fairly stable SMT is closely connected with greater school effectiveness.

It is notable that, as a whole, HoDs felt the need for greater contact between middle managers and the SMT and desired greater involvement in school policy making. Thus, even in the more academically effective schools, room for improvement was reported in this area.

ROLES AND LEADERSHIP APPROACHES

The headteacher's role

Headteachers varied in identifying the most important features of their role and how this had changed in the last five years. In one of the more effective schools the HT saw marketing as crucial and always said 'yes' to media coverage, while in the other, the HT saw his/her role as an 'enabler/facilitator'.

In the mixed schools one HT laid greatest stress on planning meetings with the SMT and providing an example to staff through teaching two classes. The other HT said they focused more on the classroom to promote 'differentiation and effective learning'. Pastoral and social welfare and relationships with parents were also regarded as important here.

In the two less effective case studies, the fairly new HT of the school which now appeared to be moving highlighted the need to create a 'high personal profile' with parents, students, staff and governors. For example, she/he played an active part in playground and lunchtime duties to increase contact with students. In the other case study of this group, the long-serving HT also emphasized the need for high visibility, vision and delegation, but was vague about how this was achieved.

In terms of 'main activities which take up your time', four HTs complained of excessive paperwork, especially on budget matters connected to LMS. All HTs felt they had too little contact with students or time to observe teaching. However, one HT from the effective group had delegated LMS to a DHT and thus spent more time on personnel, especially giving a high priority to recruitment and teaching-related matters. In the more effective schools and also in the progressing less effective school, short, frequent meetings with SMT, and separately with deputies, and regular conversation with teachers were seen to be important management tools.

Leadership style
Both HTs of effective schools said they were 'firm' in their approach. Although each would frequently consult and collaborate with senior colleagues, they had to make the final decisions. One stressed the importance of the HT as the key 'role model'.

In the mixed case studies, one HT stressed that they came up with ideas to be discussed by staff and was approachable and consultative. In the other mixed school, the HT took pride in being accessible and approachable to staff and students but during the interview mused 'Have I stayed too long?'

Amongst the less effective case studies the relatively new HT of the apparently progressing school emphasized their role as 'very much as leader of a team', consulting staff about 'nearly all matters' but prepared to make final decisions. In the other less effective school, the HT reported a 'friendly, approachable' style, but also noted 'I'm quick to say no', and made no mention of how decisions were actually reached.

Differences in leadership style between HTs appeared to be more a matter of emphasis than of fundamental approach. The importance of the HT's role has been noted in a number of studies and Gray (1990) states that it is one of the clearest of the findings of school effectiveness research. These case studies support this view.

The deputy head's role

Deputy heads with most responsibility for curriculum matters were selected for interview. They varied in their accounts of the most important features of their role, reflecting the different management structures in individual schools.

In one of the more effective schools, the DHT saw their role in terms of direction of the sixth form, overseeing a whole school curriculum, assessment and timetabling. In the other more effective school the DHT also felt their curriculum experience was significant. This DHT had particular responsibilities for monitoring student progress and conducting reviews of different departments' work. It was felt this helped ensure greater focus on learning rather than on caring, which had been the case five years previously.

In the mixed group, one DHT saw the role as being a line manager in charge of several departments but with a bias towards financial matters. In the other mixed school, the DHT saw the role primarily as one of personnel management. This role had not changed in either school over five years.

From the less effective group, one of the two DHTs was responsible for Year 7, specific departments and site management. Five years before, this respondent was in charge of the upper school, responsible for the curriculum and LMS. The other saw his/her role as 'getting staff to move with me'. In the other less effective school, being an effective time manager and maintaining the curriculum were reported as key aspects of the DHT's position, whereas in the past they had been more involved in assessment and work with support staff.

Overall, there was some indication that, in the more effective schools, deputies were involved more in the monitoring of student progress, assessment and reviewing departments, and matters directly related to student learning. Staff management was a more important part of DHTs' roles in both the mixed and less effective schools.

As with the HTs, there were no striking differences between the deputies in their descriptions of their leadership approach or style – variations appeared to be a matter of emphasis. In both the more effective schools in particular there was a close correspondence between the HT and DHT's descriptions, stressing encouraging autonomy while being supportive and working with teachers. Phrases like 'leading by example' were used.

In the ineffective but now progressing case study, one DHT mentioned adherence to procedures and 'lots of talking, planned and informal'. The other underlined the importance of consultation. By contrast, the DHT in the other less effective school stressed being clever at saying 'no' to staff, a point also made by the HT – though both also claimed to be good at listening to people.

The Head of Department's role

Half the thirty departments involved in the case studies had undergone a change of HoD during the last five years, and in some several changes had occurred. In many cases, HTs viewed this positively, especially for the departments in the less effective group.

The HoDs of the three more effective **English** departments claimed they avoided authoritarian approaches. One referred to 'leading by example (but) pretending not to!'. Another commented on this department's different but 'very strong' team and the importance of working with each member, as well as with the whole team. They tried to deal with all routine administration by paper to give meeting time for more important matters. The third (HoD of an effective department in a mixed school) emphasized 'discussion/negotiation' although he/she noted 'if I feel very strongly I will do it'.

Of the HoDs of the three less effective English departments, one – a recent appointee in a school from the mixed effectiveness category – also emphasized the need for consensus and consultation but said they would still make final decisions. In contrast, two HoDs of less effective English departments in schools from the academically less effective group had doubts about their approach. One thought he/she was 'not hard enough' and would be unhappy about being viewed as 'authoritarian and managerial'. The other commented: 'I hope it's (style) not dictatorial' – seeing themselves rather as the source of new ideas and developments which eventually all would share.

Heads of **French** departments interpreted their leadership approach/style in a rather similar manner. One HoD of a more effective department in a school from the academically effective group claimed to have changed from being a 'benevolent dictator' to 'getting people to give their opinions'. The HoD of the other more effective French department tried to be 'not confrontational' but was 'prepared to take people to task if necessary'.

One French HoD (from a school in the mixed group with non-significant effects) commented on being 'informal' and 'approachable'. Another new HoD from a department with non-significant effects claimed to be 'consultative' but 'not good at delegation'. The apparently 'disastrous' leadership of the previous HoD was emphasized by this respondent who stressed the most important feature of his/her role as 'to keep the [understaffed] department together'. Another (fairly new) HoD from the less effective departmental group and also from a school in the academically ineffective category commented on the major task of 'trying to get a group of teachers into a team' and underlined the importance of communicating and introducing new ideas. The other HoD of French did not express a clear view of their role as a HoD.

For **science**, the three HoDs of more effective departments drew attention to the importance of curriculum development as part of their role and the need for appropriate schemes of work, differentiated material and good resources, including teaching and technical staff. One of these HoDs of science stressed that the move to double science (from single subjects) had brought their team closer together. In this school, from the academically more effective group, a broader cross-departmental group was involved in consultation on teaching styles, and was seen to have a positive impact. Although two of these science HoDs had been in post for some years, another had only recently taken up post, but previously had been second in command in the same department.

Amongst the less effective group of science departments, difficulties in motivating staff to 'get to grips' with the NC, and frequent NC changes were seen to have caused problems. One of these HoDs argued that energy should be spent on curriculum delivery rather than bidding for resources which was seen to have diverted staff from their real work.

There was some indication that HoDs in the more effective science departments spent more time on teaching, marking and preparation and none mentioned student discipline as one of the main activities over the year, whereas this problem was referred to by all three HoDs from the less effective group. In one effective science department, located in a school with mixed effects, the HoD noted that the adoption of a whole school approach to student control and discipline had led to improvements in student behaviour and this gave staff more time for teaching and learning matters.

The HoDs of the three more effective **history** departments stressed the importance of adapting to the skills and strengths of team members and staff development which focused on remedying weaknesses. Supporting staff and making them 'feel valued' was also noted as was the need for really good organization of the 'nuts and bolts'. Two stressed that they gave a strong lead and the third felt they were 'less democratic' than they would like but believed that staff were happy with this leadership approach.

One HoD of history from the less effective department group (in an academically less effective school) also commented on their 'low key' leadership approach and felt that encounters with colleagues were best when 'unscheduled'. He/she also said it was 'hard to approach staff over difficult matters'.

For **mathematics**, one HoD from the more effective departmental group stressed managing the department and supporting colleagues in their classroom practice, especially assisting with 'classroom problems'. This respondent felt it important to be a source of new ideas, commenting on the stability of the mathematics teaching staff, and tried to 'ease' the heavy workload on staff. In another effective mathematics department – also located in a school in the more effective group – the HoD stressed supporting staffs' professional development, resource management and running the department effectively, as well as monitoring student performance closely.

Amongst the HoDs of the four mathematics departments in the less effective group, a pressing need to motivate and support staff and 'to make maths more interesting' was recognized by two respondents who had taken over their role fairly recently. One also stressed the difficulty of raising student aspirations. Two mentioned that they had 'responsibility for student achievement/behaviour in maths' but another saw the role purely in terms of managing staff and resources.

As with science, in three of the less effective mathematics departments, HoDs reported spending fairly significant amounts of time on student discipline. One of these HoDs also commented that in their department, much teaching was done by staff with other senior management responsibilities whose attention was diverted 'outside mathematics', which made team building difficult.

Leadership

The importance of the leadership exercised by HoDs was mentioned by HTs in connection with the improvement of departmental performance. In a number of instances the good leadership of a relatively new HoD was perceived to have improved the teamwork and commitment of staff in less effective departments, or led to further gains in more effective ones. In some instances HTs drew particular attention to the benefits of active HoDs monitoring examination results and overseeing the implementation of marking/homework policies. In schools in the mixed effectiveness category, HoDs of more effective departments were seen to provide examples of good practice and a lead for other less effective departments, and there were instances where a specific departmental policy had been adopted as a whole school policy. Poor leadership by HoDs, present and past, and a lack of teamwork were seen as major problem areas in less effective departments by HTs, irrespective of the subject taught.

There was no clear pattern of differences in the amount of extra time HoDs estimated they spent on work-related matters. For example three HoDs from the more and three HoDs from the less effective group said they spent over thirty extra hours a week. Overall, HoDs of the 'core' curriculum subjects tended to give higher estimates of their extra hours than those of French or history. Thus, it is not possible to conclude that more effective departments and the two effective schools were effective simply because their staff worked longer hours.

To summarize, in interviews on leadership approach, all HoDs stressed consultation, consensus and supporting colleagues although four said they would take decisions, even if consensus could not be achieved, and one stressed taking a lead and being prepared to defend decisions. There were indications that HoDs of the more effective departments placed a greater stress on their responsibility for levels of student achievement, monitoring and teachers' classroom practice. Nonetheless, some relatively new HoDs whose departments were in the academically ineffective group also demonstrated similar concerns. Poor HoD leadership was viewed as an important barrier to academic effectiveness by a number of HTs, especially in the past. Effective departments in schools from the mixed effectiveness category were usually recognized as providing a lead and stimulus to less successful departments.

Teamwork

Interviews with the HoDs highlighted the importance they attached to teamwork within departments and HTs also drew much attention to this (or its absence!) in their comments about individual departments. There were clear indications that good teamwork was a stronger feature of nearly all departments from the more effective category, particularly in the past. Moreover, HoDs of less effective departments frequently stressed the need for greater teamwork and commented on ways in which they were attempting to foster this. As might be expected, teamwork was seen to be closely related to the existence of shared vision/goals. A number of HoDs drew attention to the involvement of staff in decision-making, particularly in the development of agreed policies on assessment, marking, homework, or choice of examination boards. Whole department discussion of, and agreement on, policy changes were regarded as important to their successful implementation.

As well as the lack of shared vision/goals, factors seen to inhibit teamwork included personality conflicts, weakness/lack of commitment of specific members of staff, low morale and high staff turnover. High levels of staff absence, staff shortages and inability to recruit subject specialists were also noted as barriers restricting the development of teamwork, especially by HoDs and HTs in school in the academically ineffective and mixed groups.

CLASSROOM ORGANIZATION AND PEDAGOGY

Headteachers and DHTs were asked to describe the overall classroom organization and pedagogy in their school. In the two more effective case study schools, neither were felt to have changed much in the last five years. In one, approaches were perceived to be varied. The HT felt that uniformity was not really desirable, and the DHT also said approaches were mixed. Although they felt some might think lessons were too 'teacher-led', a lot of group work also took place. In line with the emphasis on departmental autonomy, teachers were also given autonomy in these areas. In the other more effective school *all* teachers were expected to ensure differentiation of work. Teaching approaches were felt to be broadly the same in the past, but student participation was widespread. All students were said to be involved in individual action planning which had increased their involvement and motivation. A mixture of teaching styles was reported in this institution.

In the two mixed schools, methods of teaching and pedagogy were reported to vary 'tremendously' and overall quality was believed to be much improved. In one there was now a general move to whole-class 'core' presentation and group work in comparison with the past and the DHT reported a dramatic change from a pattern of 'chalk and talk and death by a thousand work sheets' common five years previously. In the other mixed school the HT felt most staff were now moving towards differentiation and encouraging more student participation. In the past, formal, didactic approaches were said to have been common with little oral work. The DHT in this school commented on much variation in teaching quality, although some teachers were thought to be very purposeful with well-structured lessons using a variety of techniques and conveying clear expectations to students, others were very poorly organized, with unclear expectations for learning. In the past, keeping order was felt to have been far more important than learning.

There was also a great variation in teaching quality in the two less effective schools. In one, it was reported that the best classes relied on varied styles and activities; and students were well-controlled and motivated. In the worst, control was poor, teaching formal to maintain order, there was a lot of copying and work sheets were used extensively. Organisation was poor and goals unclear. In this institution, both the HT and DHTs felt teaching quality had improved substantially over the last five years, although in 'too many' classes poor practice was still found. One DHT observed that, in the past, teachers 'had to be more formal' to keep order because the students 'weren't so co-operative then'. In the other less effective case study, teaching approaches were also reported to have improved a great deal in the last five years. Where they had been more didactic and undifferentiated, there was now more oral work, lots of 'productive, active group work' and 'good whole class teaching'. Students were said to be more involved and classroom display was 'better'. However, a substantial minority of teachers were still perceived to be poorly organized and to have very low expectations of students.

Overall, HTs and DHTs in all schools now reported a wide variety in teaching approaches and most felt this was appropriate and beneficial. There was a general indication of greater differentiation and more student involvement in work in many cases. However, in the mixed and less effective case studies, problems were still perceived in poor quality teaching in a substantial minority of classes. Didactic formal approaches, reliance on worksheets, low expectations, an emphasis on keeping order rather than learning, poor organization and unclear goals were all highlighted.

HoDs were also asked to describe the overall classroom organization and pedagogy in their department currently and how this compared with practice five years before. Thus we were able to compare HoDs' views with those of HTs and DHTs. Greater variety of teacher approaches were reported in humanities departments, with reliance on individualized strategies in mathematics departments and a tendency towards a more formal didactic approach in science, although with a strong practical element. In history, teacher-centred approaches with students playing a more passive role had been prevalent in the past. In contrast to findings from the HT and DHT interviews, there was little evidence of differences between the more and less effective departments in HoDs' descriptions of classroom organization and pedagogy, and most HoDs suggested that teachers used a variety of approaches in most lessons. There were also signs that some departments were attempting to provide more structure to lessons and that the use of whole-class approaches to introduce and end lessons, with individual and group work in the middle, was much more popular now than in the past, especially in science. In interpreting this result it seems that the HTs and DHTs identified broader patterns than HoDs which related to differences in effectiveness between the less and more effective schools as a whole. They also were generally more critical in their view of past practice, as we describe in the next section.

Satisfaction with different aspects of school functioning

Headteachers and DHTs varied in their levels of satisfaction with their schools. The level of satisfaction reported by HTs and DHTs in specific schools mirrored each other fairly closely. In almost all aspects, respondents were more positive about the situation currently than they were five years previously. The main exception was for staff morale which was generally seen to have declined in response to outside pressures relating to the implementation of the ERA (1988), OFSTED inspections and dissatisfaction over teachers' terms and conditions. Only in one school (from the less effective group), which appeared to be improving from an exceptionally low base, was morale said to have risen noticeably, having been reportedly to be at 'rock bottom' five years previously.

Student attendance and behaviour were seen to have improved in four schools, the exceptions being one mixed and one less effective school. In the case of the other less effective but progressing school, changes in these areas were seen to be particularly marked. Academic achievement continued to be rated as 'quite satisfactory' in one of the effective schools and 'not very satisfactory' in one less effective and one mixed school. The most marked improvements in achievement were reported in the progressing less effective school and the second effective case study.

In terms of student motivation, great improvements were also reported in the progressing less effective school and in one of the more effective case studies. Some improvements in three other schools were also noted. In the other more effective school this area continued to be viewed as quite satisfactory.

Both HTs and DHTs tended to be more satisfied with the quality of those with support and pastoral functions than of teaching staff. Nonetheless, greater current than past satisfaction with teaching staff was reported in all schools except one mixed case study where the HT did not respond to this question. Only in the second of the effective case studies was the HT broadly satisfied with all teaching staff. Elsewhere HTs and DHTs were satisfied with the performance of some but not others.

Satisfaction levels with school organization and management had risen most markedly in the progressing less effective case study in the view of the HT and one DHT, although the other DHT in this school expressed a very different view of the impact of the HT, who had taken over in the last four years after the school had received a particularly poor inspection report. The HTs of one more effective and the other less effective school were partially satisfied and, in the case of the latter, this represented a marked improvement on the past. In all schools, satisfaction with the curriculum had risen over the last five years, probably a reflection of the greater structure and coherence provided by the NC, in spite of the strong perception of increased workload, stress and negative impact on morale.

HoDs' satisfaction with work of their department

Heads of Department were asked about their overall satisfaction with the work of their department/faculty. As might be expected, respondents from the more effective group of departments tended to be more satisfied than those from the less effective group. Of the thirteen HoDs of more effective departments, six were 'highly' , 'very' or 'well' satisfied, and five were fairly satisfied but felt there was room for improvement in some areas. Only one – a new history HoD in a 'traditional' department – thought there was a 'long way to go' to encourage students of all ability levels to take the subject at GCSE. Of the fourteen HoDs from the less effective departmental group, by

Table 5.3 HoDs' satisfaction with different aspects of departments' functioning

a] *HoDs of more effective departments (n=13)*

| | Now | | | | | 5 years ago* | | | | |
| | Very satisfied < ······ > Very dissatisfied | | | | | Very satisfied < ······ > Very dissatisfied | | | | |
HoDs' satisfaction with department in terms of:	1	2	3	4	5	1	2	3	4	5
Organisation	2	8	3				3	4	5	
Management	5	6	2			1	3	6		2
Teaching staff	9	2	2			3	5	2	1	1
Support staff**	2	7	3	1		1	4	5		1
Curriculum	2	8	3				5	2	3	2
Staff morale	4	5	2	1	1	1	3	5	2	1
Student academic achievement	4	6	3			1	6	5		
Student attendance	4	6	2	1		4	5	3		
Student behaviour	7	5		1		3	6	3		
Student motivation	5	6	2			2	5	5		

*1 HoD did not respond to these items   ** 1 department had not had support staff 5 years before

b] *HoDs of less effective departments (n=14)*

| | Now | | | | | 5 years ago* | | | | |
| | Very satisfied < ······ > Very dissatisfied | | | | | Very satisfied < ······ > Very dissatisfied | | | | |
HoDs' satisfaction with department in terms of:	1	2	3	4	5	1	2	3	4	5
Organisation	4	6	4			1	2	4	3	3
Management	3	9	0	1	1		4	3	4	2
Teaching staff	1	7	5	1			3	4	3	3
Support staff**	5	3	1	2	1	3	4	1	2	2
Curriculum	2	9	3				7	3	3	
Staff morale	1	6	4	1	2		4	3	3	3
Student academic achievement		4	9	1			2	5	4	2
Student attendance		6	8				6	3	3	1
Student behaviour	2	6	6				6	3	3	1
Student motivation	1	7	5	1			4	5	4	

* 1 HoD did not respond to these items   ** 2 departments had no support staff currently and 1 had had none 5 years previously

contrast only one was 'very satisfied'. Six were reasonably or quite satisfied, four said their satisfaction levels were very varied for different members of staff; one felt there was a lot of room for improvement; one was not at all satisfied, and one felt unable to respond.

The HoDs were also asked to rate satisfaction with different aspects of their department's functioning. Table 5.3 shows their responses, comparing current satisfaction levels (1993/94) with those five years previously (1988/89).

For both groups, overall satisfaction levels had increased for nearly all areas, although the improvement was rather more noticeable for the HoDs from the less effective group. Departmental organization and management showed the greatest increase in HoDs' satisfaction levels over the last five years for both groups. For the HoDs of less effective group of departments, satisfaction levels for student behaviour and motivation were higher than those for student achievement. Interestingly, HoDs from the more effective group showed most change in their satisfaction ratings for the curriculum over the past five years. This may reflect their greater success in the introduction of the NC during this period.

Staff performance

Two of the fourteen HoDs from the less effective group felt unwilling/unable to comment on staff performance either currently or five years before. Both commented that high staff turnover, high absence levels and use of supply teachers made the task 'too complicated'. All these factors can be seen as handicaps in ensuring quality and consistency in teaching. Two new HoDs (taking up post in the last year) felt unable to comment on the situation five years previously, but commented on present practice.

As with their ratings of satisfaction with different aspects of departmental functioning, the responses indicated that HoDs generally had much more positive views of staff performance currently. There were few clear differences between HoDs from the more and the less effective departmental groups in their evaluations of staff performance. For both groups of HoDs ratings were most positive (currently) for staff knowledge of the content of the GCSE syllabus, experience of teaching the subject and qualifications for teaching the subject. These aspects therefore did not account for differences in academic effectiveness. However, ratings of their department now were (e.g. in terms of teacher enthusiasm) somewhat more positive for HoDs of more effective departments, although the differences were small.

The aspects of staff performance rated least positively for the less effective group five years previously included: staff expectations for student performance; ability to exercise effective control; clarity of goals, and the work focus of lessons. The aspects of staff performance rated least positively by HoDs of the more effective group of departments five years before were: promptness in starting and finishing lessons on time; making the subject interesting to students; teacher enthusiasm, and ability to exercise effective control. These results suggest that for both groups views about staff performance in the past varied more than views of present performance.

Overall, HTs' views of the *past* performance of staff in the less effective departments tended to be far more critical than those of HoDs, but as with the HoDs, HTs' ratings were rather more favourable concerning current than past performance. Nonetheless, HTs gave lower ratings for staff in terms of teacher-student relationships, the exercising of effective control, expectations for student performance and behaviour, teacher enthusiasm and promptness starting/finishing lessons in the less than in the more effective departments (see

Table 5.4 HTs' current and past descriptions of the performance of staff in departments by effectiveness category

a] *Staff in more effective departments (n=13)*

	Now					5 years ago*				
	Good < ·····> Average/ < ·····> Poor					Good < ·····> Average/ < ·····> Poor				
			Variable					Variable		
HTs' rating in terms of:	1	2	3	4	5	1	2	3	4	5
Expectations for student performance	5	4	3	1		2	3	5	2	1
Expectations for student behaviour	10	1	1	1		5	5	3		
Exercise effective control (firm but friendly relations)	8	4	1			5	4	2	2	
Teacher enthusiasm	4	6	3			2	3	4	3	1
Teacher/student relationships	5	6	1	1		3	3	4	3	
Promptness starting/ finishing lessons	3	7	2	1		2	5	3	2	1

b] *Staff in less effective departments (n=13)**

	Now					5 years ago*				
	Good < ·····> Average/ < ·····> Poor					Good < ·····> Average/ < ·····> Poor				
			Variable					Variable		
HTs' rating in terms of:	1	2	3	4	5	1	2	3	4	5
Expectations for student performance		5	6	2				7	6	
Expectations for student behaviour		10	3				4	5	4	
Exercise effective control (firm but friendly relations)		6	7					9	4	
Teacher enthusiasm	1	5	7			2	7	4		
Teacher/student relationships	1	7	5			2	8	3		
Promptness starting/ finishing lessons	1	4	8			2	5	6		

* One HT was currently Acting HoD and therefore was not interviewed about this department

Table 5.4). In conjunction with other evidence from HT, DHT and HoD interviews these results suggest that differences in staff performance in these areas played a part in accounting for past differences in effectiveness.

Staff absence and workload

Deputy heads were asked about levels of absence by teaching staff. Absence rates were typically reported to be 'very low' in the two effective case study schools and in both attendance had remained good over the preceding five years. By contrast, in mixed schools they reported slight increases in staff absence during the same time period. Long-term absence by the few was seen to be more of a problem than casual absence. In both the less effective case study schools, staff absence levels were said to have been very high five years previously but had improved slightly. Nonetheless, in the progressing less effective school there was still much variation with some individuals continuing to exhibit very high absence levels.

In line with DHTs' responses, staff absence was also found to be highly significant at the departmental level. Differences between the more and less effective departmental groups in HoDs' accounts of current teacher absence levels were apparent. For the effective group, eleven out of thirteen gave comments such as 'excellent attendance', 'very low', 'hardly any', 'virtually none' or 'minimal' regarding the last year, compared with seven out of fourteen HoDs from the ineffective group. In the other two departments from the more effective group in one instance the (new) HoD had personally had higher absence due to exceptional circumstances but indicated that attendance by other staff in the department had been excellent in past years. Another thought absence rates were now very moderate but, being new, did not comment on the past. Five HoDs from the less effective departmental group indicated that over the last year teacher attendance was individually 'very variable'. Eleven of the fourteen HoDs from the less effective departmental group commented on past attendance patterns, and of these eight indicated that teacher absence had been significantly worse five years before and a major problem area.

Instability in staffing leading to difficulties in ensuring consistency in approaches and teamwork was identified as an important barrier to greater departmental effectiveness by four specific HoDs, all from the less effective departmental group. Taken together, the responses of DHTs and HoDs indicate that more effective schools and departments tended to have a fairly stable history of good staff attendance over the last five years, whereas variable or poor attendance was a feature of many, though not all, of the less effective departments – particularly in the past. Of course, high levels of absence may be as much a symptom as a cause of ineffectiveness and are likely to be closely related to fluctuations in staff morale and teamworking. Clearly high levels of absence over a number of years have implications for curriculum coverage and continuity, the development of shared goals, common practices and teamwork as well as an impact on student motivation. It also made the implementation of major educational changes such as the NC and associated assessment that much more difficult.

STUDENT BEHAVIOUR AND INVOLVEMENT

Headteachers and DHTs were asked about how their school's code of conduct (or rule system) was developed including who was involved in setting it up, and whether it had led to improvements in student behaviour.

In both the more effective case studies, students had been closely involved in developing the school's behaviour policy, especially regarding bullying. In both schools the institution of a code of conduct and a policy on bullying were felt to have led to improvements in behaviour. By contrast, in both the mixed schools significant behaviour problems were reported. Neither school had originally involved students in their policies which were said to be 'old'.

Behaviour, previously a great cause for concern, was reported to have improved substantially over the last four years in one of the less effective (but apparently progressing) case study schools, due to greater awareness of what was regarded as acceptable, especially with respect to bullying and a whole-school commitment to focus on improving behaviour. In the other less effective school, the HT felt that the long-standing policy was fairly well understood but admitted behaviour was still an important cause for concern. The DHT in this school also felt that behaviour had been a significant problem, but reported some improvements in recent years.

Systems of reward were highlighted in several schools. In one of the more effective schools the DHT commented on the creation of 'a praise culture'. Attendance and punctuality certificates and achievement awards were mentioned as very common both here and at the other effective school.

Amongst the less effective schools 'rule by punishment' was reported by one DHT in the past although this was now thought to be dying out. In the other school in this group, detentions, 'every day for individuals', and 'on report' were said to be common practice, while exclusions had increased in the last five years. One DHT sadly acknowledged 'we don't praise enough'. Nonetheless, in both the less effective schools a number of 'good reforms' were said to have been instituted in recent years, including merit marks, letters home, attendance certificates, prize-giving, showing good work to the HT. These were thought to be leading to improvements in both student behaviour and attitudes/motivation.

Our findings indicate that significant student behaviour problems were much more apparent in the mixed and less effective schools, being a particular problem in the past. Exclusion rates had increased in the mixed and less effective schools during the last five years in line with national trends. The use of punishments was said to be far less common in the more effective institutions. There can be no doubt that the high incidence of behaviour difficulties made management and teaching more difficult in these schools.

Parental involvement and interest

Headteachers varied markedly in their estimates of the percentage of parents who were 'very interested' in their child's schooling. In both the more effective schools, over 70 per cent fitted this description, in one levels of interest were thought to be unchanged over the last five years, whereas in the other, whilst the situation had been good in the past, interest was felt to have decreased. In marked contrast, in the four other case study schools only between 5 and 20 per cent of parents were felt to be 'very interested' . In the two less effective case studies five years ago over 60 per cent of parents were classified as 'not very interested' in their child's schooling. In general, the DHTs' perception of parental interest was fairly close to that of the HTs'. The percentage rated as not very interested was again highest in the less effective case study which was not progressing.

Heads and DHTs were also asked to estimate parental attendance at meetings. In all schools attendance at the governors' annual meeting for parents was very low, often in single figures and sometimes described as 'pathetic'. Attendance at educational meetings and parents' evenings was higher (60–70 per cent) in the more effective and mixed schools. While in less effective schools the equivalent figure was around 40 per cent.

Heads of departments also varied in their estimates of the percentage of parents who they felt were 'very interested' in their child's schooling. There was some evidence that HoDs of more effective departments took a more positive view than those of less effective departments, but not invariably. Three out of the thirty HoDs did not give estimates of current levels of parental interest, and nine felt unable to comment on the situation five years before.

Methods of communicating with parents about educational matters involved the production of a newsletter (weekly) or paper (half-termly). Regular letters home and meetings were also used. In both the effective schools and the progressing less effective school more frequent meetings for parents were reported now than before. In terms of the formal provision of information for parents, all schools produced an annual report as statutorily required for all years, plus an option or curriculum booklet in Year 9. In all schools, especially those in the less effective group, it appeared that efforts were being made to improve the flow of information to parents.

Some parental involvement in monitoring students' homework was reported in all schools except one from the effective group where parents were already said to be generally very active. Given the evidence, reported earlier, about variations in the practice of staff setting, checking and marking homework, it is not clear to what extent parents were actually involved in this in the less effective and mixed schools, especially in the past.

The HT and DHT interviews indicate considerable variation in perceptions of levels of parental interest amongst the case study schools. It should of course be acknowledged that negative perceptions of parental interest/motivation may have an adverse impact upon a school's effectiveness. Such perceptions may reflect a tendency by staff to 'blame' the school's intake and a failure to accept responsibility for student performance, reflecting a culture of under-expectation of certain types of students and their families. The HoDs' interviews certainly supported the findings of more negative perceptions of parental interest and support in schools from the mixed and ineffective groups. Respondents in schools from the more effective category generally had a more positive view of parental interest in their child's education than others, although in one school 'pushy' middle-class parents were seen as a threat by some. Within schools in both the ineffective and mixed categories HoDs varied markedly in their perceptions of levels of parental interest/support – some thinking their schools under-estimated parents, and others having a very negative view of parental interest in education. Indeed, our interviews indicated that HoDs were generally less concerned with fostering parental involvement than SMT members.

There were many indications that all schools were more concerned to involve parents than was the case five years ago and this may, in part, reflect the higher profile given to parents in recent legislation. It may also reflect greater awareness of the positive contribution parents can make in supporting the work of the school. Some schools reported very successful developments in relation to providing more feedback in the form of regular newsletters, information about curriculum developments and enlisting parents to monitor homework diaries.

Perceptions of school achievements and weaknesses

Both HTs and DHTs were asked to describe any major successes and achievements of their school over the last five years. They were also asked to describe any major weaknesses or problems experienced during the same time period.

Similarly 'surviving' the introduction of LMS was seen as an achievement in both schools in the effective group. The DHT in one of the effective schools argued that a new found stability and enhanced reputation under the new (within the last five years) HT's leadership was their major success. Continued high levels of academic success and post 16 staying-on rates were noted in the other.

Successes were also reported for the two schools in the mixed group. In one, the HT reported a new focus on achievement which was publicly celebrated as a source of great satisfaction. It was further noted that 'visitors can now be shown round by children', something not previously possible due to poor behaviour. The DHT in this school commented on making schemes of work 'live and relevant', and much better discipline. Again it was thought that the appointment of a new HT (five years before) was largely responsible. The HT of the other school in the mixed group also reported the beginnings of improvement with higher levels of achievement by all ability bands from 1993. Equal opportunities and special education needs (SEN) provision were felt to have benefited from the influence of a new DHT. A more pleasant working environment, better use of resources, an improved management structure and a 'sharper' curriculum were also reported with pride.

Amongst the least effective case studies some successes were also noted, though of a different order. For the HT of one school – which had had a succession of HTs and high staff turnover – it was seen as a *major* success to be currently fully staffed with qualified teachers in contrast to past years. Student attendance had risen and behaviour problems were reduced. The two DHTs in this school, however, again differed sharply in their views. One stressed greater stability under the new (in the last four years) HT and firm middle management, while the other commented on a recent much improved inspection assessment but did not credit the new HT for achieving this.

At the other school in the less effective group some improvements in staff attitudes were highlighted by the HT, as was a greater uptake of vocational courses by sixth formers. The DHT's view differed, focusing on success in establishing a broad and balanced curriculum ahead of the introduction of the NC.

Overall, HTs from the more effective group made specific reference to continuing academic success or improvements in staying-on rates post–16, while in the less effective schools, matters such as improved attendance and behaviour were stressed. Again, it is relevant to note that the views of HTs and DHTs were particularly close in the more effective schools.

Due to the speed of recent educational change, all interviewees felt they had been beset with problems during the preceding five years. Both HTs and DHTs in the more effective group reported difficulties linked with the implementation of the 1988 ERA Act. In one, the introduction of LMS had created 'excessive' work and the HT was a strong critic of the 'imposed' NC. The DHT here also commented on 'constant government-imposed change' and its pressures.

For both the HT and DHT of the other more effective school, working with an 'incompetent' and changing LEA structure after the abolition of ILEA and disagreements over its budget were also reported as problems, as was the pace of NC change. Staff stress was more prevalent, partly as a result of NC pressures – although also perhaps due to the level of expectations from the SMT.

In the mixed schools external sources of difficulty were not highlighted as major sources of problems by the HTs, possibly because of more immediate internal pressures, such as discipline, threat of closure etc. 'Creaming of middle class' children by other local schools leading to a highly skewed intake was noted by one school. Deputies also commented on 'dead wood' in specific departments, lack of coherent policies, and an absence of parental involvement.

Amongst schools in the least effective group, poor attendance compounded by high staff vacancies and *severe* problems related to student discipline had been encountered in past years. The DHTs in one school cited staff 'burn out' and unsuitable buildings. In another, internal factors – low expectations by staff, high absence levels of staff and students – were seen as major sources of difficulty by the HT, but the DHT blamed only external ones – parental indifference, grave social problems, and falling numbers.

It is perhaps necessary to remember that some areas of weakness – HTs who 'couldn't cope' or high staff vacancies/turnover/burnout and discipline problems – are as much results as causes of ineffectiveness. All but one of the case study schools served very disadvantaged intakes by national standards, but only one mixed and one of the less effective schools blamed their weaknesses *directly* on their intake.

SUMMARY

Our case studies of effective schools and departments indicate that they share the following characteristics: academic emphasis and high expectations, a shared vision, strong but flexible leadership, an effective SMT, good quality teaching, a high rate of examination entry and a significant level of parental involvement/interest. Another important finding is that some schools and departments were better prepared to adjust to change, even when imposed from outside. All but one of the case study schools served disadvantaged student intakes, but as our definition of effectiveness – being based on value added analyses – controlled for the impact of intake, this factor cannot account for differences in success.

In the light of these findings important questions about the less effective case study schools can be raised:

- Did the less effective schools follow different *routes*?
- Did the less effective schools/departments exhibit different *definitions* of the constituents and barriers to effectiveness in their schools?
- Did the respondents (or their predecessors) give less emphasis to the *academic matters* in their schools?
- Were the less effective schools/departments unable (for a variety of reasons) to provide *delivery* of the necessary planning, teaching or support for student learning?

Routes
The results suggest that the more and less effective schools did not differ fundamentally in their approaches, although it appeared that the less effective case studies lacked the consensus and shared vision in management and organization evident in the more effective group. Clear leadership from both HT and DHT, and a cohesive SMT, were also seen as important.

Definitions
Overall HTs, DHTs and HoDs generally shared a fair degree of consensus about factors which influence school and departmental effectiveness. Our results suggest that the more and less effective schools and departments did not differ fundamentally in their definitions of the constraints and barriers to effectiveness. Differences in approach seemed to be more related to subject rather than effectiveness category. However, there was evidence that the leadership role of the HoD was seen by respondents as an important contributory factor for greater effectiveness, or, alternatively as a barrier inhibiting past performance in some less effective departments. Staff motivation, hard work and commitment were also more likely to be stressed as constituents of effectiveness by more effective HoDs.

Teamwork was viewed as a major determinant of effectiveness and the cultivation of this was perceived as an important feature of the HoD's and

HT's role. There were marked differences in the extent to which HoDs and HTs reported their departmental staff functioning as a team – the extent of teamwork being more positively viewed in effective departments, especially in the past.

Shared goals, an academic emphasis and high expectations of students (or the absence of these) were also important factors perceived to impinge on departmental effectiveness, particularly past performance.

Academic emphasis
The level of academic emphasis and high expectations emerged as important differentiating factors. A greater emphasis on examination entry, assessment, marking, homework and curriculum matters was evident in the more effective schools. Departmental and whole-school monitoring of students' results were also seen as important. Our findings suggest that the answer to the third question raised by the case studies – is less emphasis given to academic matters in less effective schools? – was broadly 'yes'. Schools in the less effective group acknowledged that too little recognition had been given to student achievement in the past than was now considered necessary, and it was acknowledged that greater efforts were needed to raise teachers' and students' expectations, to change attitudes and to prioritize the schools' teaching and learning functions. Improvements in the overall quality of teaching (organization, the communication of clear goals to students, appropriate feedback and assessment) and the setting and marking of homework were seen to be essential from a significant minority of staff in these institutions. In particular, specific departments in some schools were viewed as a cause for considerable concern and the leadership of some HoDs was reported to be (or have been in the past) inadequate.

There were strong indications that, particularly five years ago, a lack of academic emphasis was perceived as a major problem in many of the less effective departments. Low expectations of students, little emphasis on examination entry, unclear or inconsistent approaches to matters such as assessment, marking and homework were reported as features of many of the less effective departments. In addition, departmental monitoring and use of assessment or examination results was infrequent. Many new HoDs of less effective departments drew attention to the much higher profile given to improving examination results now. In this connection, the impact of the four-year cycle of OFSTED inspections (in 1993) and publication of examination 'league' tables (in 1992) may well have had an impact. There was also evidence of much greater awareness of equity issues, specifically the need to promote the progress and achievement of students for all groups. In some schools HoDs acknowledged that 'working class kids', particularly boys, had suffered from low expectations and that there had been too much emphasis on creating a caring, pastoral environment and too little on teaching and learning.

Delivery

The respondents revealed that the less effective schools were less able to deliver or support effective teaching and learning than the effective ones. Factors such as acute staffing shortages and turnover – especially of suitably qualified staff – allied with management and organizational weakness, a reflection of internal difficulties in the SMT and possibly the quality of past leadership by the HT, were highly relevant. Also low staff morale and high absence rates, and lack of consistency in approach in the implementation of policies, also appeared to be responsible, at least in part, for some schools' poor academic records. Overall, the results of the case studies indicate that the less effective schools failed to develop and emphasize whole school policies as determinants of effectiveness. They were also less likely to foster a (high) overall quality of teaching and shared goals, including high staff expectations of students. Less effective schools were more likely to blame lack of effectiveness on 'external' factors, such as quality of their student intake and lack of parental interest and support. However, the need for greater consistency in approach amongst teachers and between departments was also recognized as a major influence in these institutions.

There were some indications that the more effective schools had put more energy into creating and had a more positive view of home/school partnership, although all schools now saw this as an important concern. Certainly parental involvement and interest appeared to be significantly higher than in the two more effective case study schools. By contrast, in the other schools highly negative perceptions of parents and of student intakes were common.

There were also strong indications that a variety of factors inhibited particular departments from delivering the necessary planning, teaching or support for student learning. It appeared easier for departments in the more effective schools to achieve and maintain effectiveness. This may result from a variety of factors: a stronger academic ethos and higher expectations across a variety of departments may have become mutually reinforcing; while clear whole-school policies were consistently implemented. A climate in which the school and its staff were seen as a learning organization with a strong emphasis on departmental review, and the monitoring of student outcomes (academic, but also behaviour and attendance) was evident in the more effective schools. In some schools, the SMT seemed to function as a cohesive and complementary team, with shared goals. In other institutions, especially the less effective and mixed schools, the SMT were radically divided. A number of HoDs specifically commented on their school's SMT either as promoting or, in the less effective schools, actively hindering their department's performance. In the mixed schools, the need for stronger SMT leadership, and the development of whole school policies on topics such as marking, homework and behaviour (including asking staff about 'what works') was noted by some HoDs of more effective departments.

School-wide problems in student behaviour were seen to hinder teaching in some less effective department in schools from the less effective and the mixed groups, and HoDs emphasized the need for a whole school approach to behaviour management. It was clear that, whilst some HoDs valued departmental autonomy, there was also an appreciation of the inter-dependence amongst departments.

High levels of staff absence (especially in the past), instability and shortages of qualified personnel clearly had a very detrimental effect on some departments' ability to deliver the curriculum effectively, and to cope with the implementation of the NC and NA. Certain schools in the less effective and mixed effectiveness categories found it had been hard to attract and keep good qualified staff, particularly in the late 1980s.

In addition, personality conflicts, an 'obstructive' or weak second-in-command, lack of shared goals and values, and some 'uncommitted' teachers were seen to inhibit team working and the implementation of agreed policies. In some of the less effective schools this was reported by the HT to have been a school-wide phenomenon in the past, suggesting the existence of an unhelpful school culture.

Lack of stability in staffing was not the cause of difficulties in all of the less effective departments, however. In some instances, a core of long-serving, uncommitted staff who were not open to new ideas and unwilling to change were perceived to hinder attempts at improvement by HoDs.

It is notable that for both HoDs and HTs one of the main perceived routes to improvement identified was a change of post holder, or removal of certain 'problem' staff for their departments. Moving 'difficult' staff around (e.g. to teach non-examination groups) was also reported in some instances, as was intensive work by a SMT member with a HoD perceived as needing extra 'support'. In one instance this 'support' was also seen as a lever for exerting pressure for improvement!

Links with other research

The second, qualitative phase of our study provides the opportunity to test the extent to which the results of the earlier influential *Fifteen Thousand Hours* research by Rutter *et al.* (1979), also conducted in inner London, remained applicable – given the considerable changes in the education system in the intervening years. The overall conclusion of Rutter's (1979) research was that, even in a disadvantaged area, schools can be a force for good and can do much to foster good behaviour and attainment. The analysis of schools' value added results reported in Chapters 3 and 4 provides strong evidence of the existence of significant variations in school effectiveness over time (stability) and across different outcomes (consistency). For a small proportion of schools, differences can be striking: some – such as the outliers analysed here – were more or less effective across the board over several years, and others were very mixed. Our case studies indicate that, in terms of value added, some schools serving disadvantaged intakes were much more academically effective than others and the study of these helps to increase understanding of the underlying factors which influence academic effectiveness.

In terms of school processes, the *Fifteen Thousand Hours* study highlighted academic emphasis (including high expectations), the leadership of the HT, teacher actions in lessons, the use of rewards and punishments, student conditions, student responsibility and participation, staff organization and the skills of the teachers. Despite their different historical context, the results of the case studies presented here do not diverge greatly from these found in the Rutter study in many ways, although they provide much more detail about practitioners' views and the importance of school and department histories. Leadership continues to remain important, but the coherent functioning of the SMT seems to be equally significant. Shared vision and goals and a consistency in approach receive more emphasis in this study, as does the important role of middle management (HoDs), while differences in the ways schools encouraged student responsibility and participation are smaller.

The analysis of interviews with thirty HoDs in the six case study schools supported and extended the conclusions of the analyses of HT and DHT interviews (Sammons *et al.*, forthcoming). They demonstrate the need to focus explicitly on the views of both middle managers and SMT members. The retrospective focus of the interviews, comparing the current situation with that of five years previously, also proved helpful in identifying factors related to change and improvement. The value of considering individual departmental and school histories in school effectiveness studies was confirmed by this research. Schools from the mixed group (in which both more effective and ineffective departments co-exist) are of particular interest as case studies and provide rich subjects for those concerned with school improvement.

The need for detailed case studies of individual schools has been noted by Reynolds (1992) and more recently by Brown, Riddell and Duffield (1996). Harris, Jamieson and Russ (1995), have reported research on a study of effective departments in six secondary schools in a West Country city. These were schools chosen on the basis of six performance indicators using a value added approach. Their study focused exclusively on more effective departments. They concluded that departments were good at 'either working with or neutralizing external influences'. Harris, Jamieson and Russ (1995) concluded that while the schools they worked in were broadly supportive, it was 'not a major factor' in the success of specific departments. Factors highlighted by their research include:

- a collegiate management style;
- a strong vision of the subject effectively translated down to the level of the classroom;
- well organised assessments, record keeping, homework, etc.;
- good resource management;
- an effective system for monitoring and evaluating;
- structured lessons and regular feedback;

- clear routines and practices with lessons;
- a syllabus matching the needs and abilities of students;
- a strong student-centred ethos that systematically rewards students;
- opportunities for autonomous student learning; and
- a central focus on teaching and learning.

The present study focused on both more and less effective departments. Moreover, departments were drawn from academically effective and academically ineffective schools, and those with highly mixed effects at the departmental level. A major feature of our study concerned the comparison of past and current practice and events, because examination results are inevitably indicators of past teaching and learning practices and the performances of student groups no longer at the school, and value added indicators, like raw GCSE results, provide retrospective measures of performance.

Nonetheless, there are a number of common features between the outcomes of our case studies and the findings of Harris, Jamieson and Russ (1995). The central focus on teaching and learning, and the need for clear routines and practices with lessons, links with our findings concerning the importance of the quality of teaching and academic emphasis. The importance of effective systems for monitoring and evaluating performance was also noted. Internal monitoring and use of assessment and other results by the department itself were also found to be important in our study, although school systems for reviewing departmental performance, or, conversely, the lack of such systems, were also significant.

The HoDs' leadership was found to be important, collegial approaches and the need for teamwork were highlighted in our study. Consensus and shared goals were important for the department staff as a whole. The value of feedback of results to students, via the prompt marking of work and regular setting and marking of homework, was highlighted. So also was the use of a variety of teaching approaches by teachers, avoiding sole reliance on teacher-led didactic 'chalk and talk' or mainly individualized work. A blend of whole-class, individual and group work in each lesson, clear goals, and introducing and summarizing main points were noted by HoDs of some of the more effective departments. Many HoDs expressed concern about making lessons interesting and relevant to students and encouraging student participation. Good classroom control (firm but fair), positive staff-student relationships, a strong work focus to lessons, teacher enthusiasm and a focus on providing challenges for students of all abilities, were important influences on the quality of teaching.

Our research, however, draws much more attention to the facilitating nature of the whole-school context, particularly the leadership of the HT and role of the SMT, than Harris, Jamieson and Russ's (1995) research. This is perhaps a reflection of the selection of case study schools, which embraced both more and less effective departments and schools. While the departmental level is undoubtably very important, in some schools it was apparently 'much easier' than in others for *all* departments to function effectively. This was due to the influence of a more supportive context, shared whole school emphasis on the central importance of student learning and achievement, and perhaps the mutually beneficial impact of successful departments supporting each others' efforts and spurring each other on.

Gray and Wilcox (1995) have drawn attention to the high stakes involved in making judgements about ineffective schools and the importance of rapid improvement of 'ineffective' schools. However, they also stress that there is little UK research explicitly concerned with 'turning round' ineffective schools. Our present study provides some support for Gray and Wilcox's contention that the correlates of ineffectiveness are not necessarily the reverse of those concerned with effectiveness. The histories of individual schools and departments can exert an important positive or negative influence on academic effectiveness.

The case studies of thirty departments and six schools, chosen on the basis of the quantitative analysis of consistency and stability in their effects on GCSE performance over several years, draw attention to the interconnections between the school and departmental levels. The examples drawn from mixed schools, where effective and less effective departments co-exist, confirm that some departments can be much more successful with the same student intakes than others in the same (or in other) schools, when the impact of prior attainment and background is controlled. However, the existence of consistently academically more and academically less effective schools also points to the impact of whole-school processes.

Our analyses of these case studies provide additional evidence concerning both the factors and processes related to school and departmental academic effectiveness and ineffectiveness and highlight the need to look in depth at the interactions between the two. In this chapter we have used case studies – a qualitative medium – to try and analyse the constituents of school and departmental effectiveness. In the next two chapters we look at the results arising from the quantitative approach embodied in a questionnaire conducted in Phase 3 of the research to assist us in the development of explanations for variations in schools' and departments' academic effectiveness. Chapter 6 focuses on a survey of HTs' and HoDs' views of school and departmental goals and factors influencing effectiveness. In Chapter 7 we examine the statistical relationships between our value added results and details about school and departmental policy and practice obtained from the questionnaire survey. In this way we seek to test the findings from our qualitative case studies using a wider sample of schools and thus examine the generalisability of our conclusions.

NOTE

1. Consistently scoring significantly positive or significantly negative residuals (±2SE) in two or more of the three years or in one-year and in the three-year analysis.

6

Practitioners' Views of Effectiveness

INTRODUCTION

The 'touchstone' of school effectiveness, as we noted in Chapter 2, is the impact of schools on their students' learning, measured by their progress in specified educational outcomes (Reynolds, 1995). Nonetheless, little is actually known about the relationships between practitioners' beliefs and views about the factors which influence effectiveness, and which ought to be taken into account in judging school performance and value added measures of schools' effects on their students' educational outcomes. Yet staff can differ markedly in their views about what constitute appropriate goals for students and for schools (Elliott, 1996; White, 1997). It is a matter of considerable practical as well as academic interest to establish how much senior and middle managers' views on such matters vary, and the extent to which the practitioners' beliefs and perceptions are related to research findings about the key characteristics of effective schools.

In this chapter we investigate the concepts of school and departmental effectiveness and their determinants from the practitioners' perspective. As in the previous chapter, we asked respondents to compare the current situation in schools (early 1995) with that five years before. This enables us to examine perceptions of groups of key personnel about the processes of change and/or improvement during this period.

The third phase of our research was used to test out, empirically, the results of the qualitative case studies (discussed in Chapter 5), using a larger sample of schools. A questionnaire survey was undertaken to obtain information about important areas of school and departmental policy, organization and practice which could be analysed in relation to GCSE outcomes. These questionnaires were informed by the results of the case studies and were piloted in four schools not involved in the Differential School Effectiveness project.

A total of 264 questionnaires (for the HT and two subject HoDs) were sent to 88 schools included in the analysis of GCSE results. The survey was conducted in the spring term of 1995. One or more responses were received from 55 of the 88 schools (62.5 per cent), a fairly good response rate for a postal survey. Forty-seven HTs (53.4 per cent), 40 HoDs of mathematics (45.5 per cent) and 39 HoDs of English (44.3 per cent) submitted returns. Two or more responses were received from 40 schools and just over a third (31) returned all three questionnaires. All respondents were assured of confidentiality and provided with individual pre-paid reply envelopes. Schools for which questionnaires were received and those which did not respond were found to be similar in terms of their academic effectiveness – as measured by the residual estimates from the multilevel value added analysis of examination data, which we described in Chapter 3.

Our questionnaires examined HTs' and HoDs' perceptions of their schools' and departments' academic performance and the factors they perceived as contributing to, or inhibiting, effectiveness. Views about their school's principal educational goals and about aspects they thought important in judging school and departmental effectiveness were also sought. It should be stressed that no feedback had been given to staff concerning their own institution's academic effectiveness as measured by our value added analysis of students' progress. Of course, all schools knew their raw GCSE results and had experienced the publication of national league tables for three years by 1995.

The relationships between HTs' and HoDs' responses and estimates of schools' effectiveness over three years were examined to establish which school and departmental process items, if any, differentiated between schools in terms of academic effectiveness. In addition, multilevel models were used to establish whether such items made a statistically significant contribution to the *explanation* of school/departmental level variance in GCSE performance over three years (total GCSE performance score, English and mathematics), and to establish which combination of variables provided the 'best fit' models for the data. We present these results in Chapter 7.

A higher proportion of HTs (64 per cent) in the survey were female. More HoDs of English than of mathematics were also female. As would be expected, HTs tended to be somewhat older than HoDs – 36 per cent were aged 51 years or over, compared with only 10 per cent of HoDs of English and mathematics alike.

A substantial minority of respondents (43 per cent) had been a HT for under five years and 17 per cent for one year or less. Just over one in ten had been HTs for eleven years or more. Only two HTs had never been a DHT, 43 per cent had been a DHT for four years or less and 17 per cent for eight years or more. Just over a third (36 per cent) had been a DHT in their current school before taking up the headship. For the middle managers, one in five of mathematics HoDs had been in post for one year or less, whereas the equivalent figure for English HoDs was lower at 10 per cent. Proportionally more of the mathematics HoDs had been in this position for eleven or more years – 25 per cent compared with 10 per cent for English HoDs.

Around two-thirds of HoDs possessed a degree in the subject they taught (69 per cent for English and 65 per cent for mathematics HoDs). Despite these differences in the personal and professional backgrounds, we found that they bore little relationship to measures of their school's academic effectiveness, as we describe in Chapter 7. We can conclude, therefore, that such factors are unlikely to be important in explaining the differences between schools' or departments' value-added results.

The questionnaire focused on the following key aspects identified as important by the case studies. For schools in general – principal goals, judging effectiveness, factors contributing to effectiveness, barriers to effectiveness, major successes achieved and major problems encountered were explored. Similarly in considering departments, the focus was on judging departmental effectiveness, major successes and problems faced, factors contributing to effectiveness and barriers to effectiveness.

Headteachers' and HoDs' views and perceptions of these topics were examined in the light of the changing demands and expectations of schools during a five-year period between 1990 and 1995. These include the impact of the implementation of the Education Reform Act, involving a National Curriculum, a greater emphasis on accountability, and changes in the inspection process following the institution of four-yearly inspections after the creation of OFSTED in 1993. The extent to which middle managers and HTs differ in their views and perceptions and the implications of this were also examined.

Schools

Principal educational goals

Headteachers and HoDs were asked to identify up to ten principal educational goals which their school tried to achieve for its students now (1995) and five years ago. The results are shown in Table 6.1a. It was found that HTs cited rather fewer principal goals for students in the past than currently. This suggests that HTs felt that schools now had greater demands placed upon them, possibly reflecting the higher profile attached to education and increased emphasis on accountability.

For HTs, the five most commonly cited principal goals currently were: raising achievement in all senses (first); creating a secure, stimulating and enjoyable school environment and maintaining good standards of behaviour and attendance (joint second); providing a rigorous and differentiated curriculum accessible to all (fourth); and improving examination results (fifth). There was evidence of some movement in HTs' views about the principal goals their schools tried to achieve for students over time. The five most commonly cited goals five years previously were: developing respect for others (first); creating a secure, stimulating and enjoyable school environment and maintaining good standards of behaviour and attendance (joint second); emphasizing equal opportunities (fourth); and preparing students for the world of work (fifth). Goals which showed evidence of a marked change over time included: raising achievement in all senses – noted by 94 per cent compared with 40 per cent as a current principal goal; improving examination results (70 per cent compared with 43 per cent); providing a rigorous differentiated curriculum accessible to all (77 per cent compared with 17 per cent); ensuring each student obtains the

Table 6.1 Principal goals which the school tries to achieve for its students

a]

What would you say are the principal education goals that this school tries to achieve for its students?	Headteachers' Views* [n=47]			
	Now		5 years ago	
	Rank	per cent	Rank	per cent
Developing respect for others	7	66.0	1	70.2
Creating a secure, stimulating and enjoyable school environment	2.5	80.9	2.5	68.1
Developing self-respect	13	42.6	7.5	44.7
Providing an entitlement curriculum for all students	10.5	51.1	9.5	42.6
Increasing students' self-confidence	13	42.6	12	40.4
Education for life	17	34.0	6	46.8
Preparing students for the world of work	16	36.2	5	51.1
Promoting students' ability to learn independently	8.5	53.2	16	21.3
Promoting student responsibility	13	42.6	15	27.7
Promoting a sense of achievement	6	68.1	7.5	44.7
Improving examination results	5	70.2	9.5	42.6
Promoting student progress	15	38.3	12	40.4
Providing a rigorous, differentiated curriculum accessible to all	4	76.6	17	17.0
Ensuring each student obtains the highest qualifications possible	8.5	53.2	14	31.9
Raising achievement in all senses	1	93.6	12	40.4
Emphasizing equal opportunities	10.5	51.1	4	66.0
Maintaining good standards of behaviour and attendance	2.5	80.9	2.5	68.1

b]

What would you say are the principal education goals that this school tries to achieve for its students?	Heads of Departments' Views* [n=79]			
	Now		5 years ago	
	Rank	per cent	Rank	per cent
Developing respect for others	4.5	64.6	2	67.1
Creating a secure, stimulating and enjoyable school environment	4.5	64.6	1	68.4
Developing self-respect	11	49.4	5	54.4
Providing an entitlement curriculum for all students	8.5	54.4	13	35.4
Increasing students' self-confidence	13	46.8	6	53.3
Education for life	16	24.0	9.5	43.0
Preparing students for the world of work	17	17.7	16	26.6
Promoting students' ability to learn independently	10	53.3	11	38.0
Promoting student responsibility	14	45.6	9.5	43.0
Promoting a sense of achievement	3	67.1	8	45.6
Improving examination results	1	74.7	7	51.9
Promoting student progress	15	27.8	14.5	34.2
Providing a rigorous, differentiated curriculum accessible to all	8.5	54.4	17	8.9
Ensuring each student obtains the highest qualifications possible	12	48.1	14.5	34.2
Raising achievement in all senses	2	70.9	12	36.7
Emphasizing equal opportunities	7	59.5	4	55.7
Maintaining good standards of behaviour and attendance	6	62.0	3	59.5

*Respondents were asked to indicate up to 10 goals

highest qualifications possible (53 per cent compared with 32 per cent); and preparing students for the world of work (down to 36 per cent compared with 51 per cent in the past). It is likely that these changes reflect the impact of a variety of factors including the implementation of the NC, publication of league tables of examination results and in many cases a change of school leadership. In 20 of the 47 schools, a new HT had taken over within the last five years. In terms of most important goal, nearly a quarter of HTs identified raising achievement in all senses. The next most popular choices of currently important goals (each named by 15 per cent of HTs) were: ensuring each student obtains the highest qualifications possible; creating a secure, stimulating and enjoyable school environment; and providing a rigorous, differentiated curriculum accessible to all.[1] Five years before, HTs listed: creating a secure, stimulating and enjoyable school environment (15 per cent); followed by raising achievement in all senses (11 per cent); and providing an entitlement curriculum for all students (9 per cent). In all, nearly a quarter of HTs (11) were unable/unwilling to comment on which was their school's most important goal for students five years before.

The analysis of HTs' responses concerning their school's principal educational goals indicated that they gave a greater emphasis to academic goals now in comparison with the situation five years before. In other words, ensuring each student obtains the highest qualifications possible, improving examination results, raising achievement in all senses and promoting a sense of achievement. Relatively less emphasis was said to be given to more general goals such as education for life, preparing students for the world of work, developing respect for others and equal opportunities.

The middle managers' responses provided a rather different picture of schools' principal goals (see Table 6.1b). The five most commonly cited current goals were: improving examination results (first); raising achievement in all senses (second); promoting a sense of achievement (third); and developing respect for others and creating a secure, stimulating and enjoyable school environment (joint fourth). Five years before the most frequently noted were: creating a secure, stimulating and enjoyable school environment (first); developing respect for others (second); maintaining good standards of behaviour and attendance (third); emphasizing equal opportunities (fourth); and developing self-respect (fifth).

Goals which showed the greatest change over time in HoDs' responses were: providing a rigorous differentiated curriculum accessible to all – cited as a principal goal by 54 per cent now compared with only 9 per cent five years before; raising achievement in all senses (71 per cent compared with 37 per cent); improving examination results (75 per cent compared with 52 per cent); and promoting a sense of achievement (67 per cent compared with 46 per cent). It is evident that academic goals were less highly rated in the past than currently.

As with the HTs' responses, the implementation of the NC and publication of league tables, as well as changes in staffing, may have influenced the greater emphasis given to academic goals by HoDs. Furthermore, it is notable that promoting student progress was less highly rated than improving examination results by both groups, presumably because raw results are easy to measure and receive considerable media and parental attention, while student progress may be harder to demonstrate.

The HoDs were also asked to identify which of their school's goals was most important now and five years before. Four HoDs, two from English and two from mathematics departments, were unable/unwilling to identify one goal as most important now, and twelve did not respond to the question about most important goals five years before. Of those who did respond, fifteen (29 per cent) cited raising achievement in all senses as most important currently, followed by providing a rigorous differentiated curriculum accessible to all (15 per cent) and ensuring each student obtained the highest qualification as the most important current goals (13 per cent).

Five years before HoDs were most likely to cite creating a secure, stimulating and enjoyable school environment as most important (27 per cent); ensuring each student obtains the highest possible qualification (18 per cent); emphasizing equal opportunities (9 per cent); raising achievement in all senses (9 per cent); and improving examination results (9 per cent).

In comparison with those of HTs, HoDs' responses laid somewhat less emphasis upon maintaining good standards of behaviour and attendance and providing a rigorous differentiated curriculum accessible to all.

Table 6.2

Factors which ought to be taken into account in judging the effectiveness of any secondary school	HTs		HoDs	
	Rank	per cent	Rank	per cent
An improved staying on rate post–16	18	25.5	18	24.1
A caring pastoral environment	16	29.8	11	44.3
Good progress (value added) for students of all ability levels	1	89.4	2	77.2
The creation of confident, articulate people	11	51.1	8	54.4
A high level of academic achievement in examinations	17	27.7	16	30.4
Positive inter-personal relationships for staff and students	5.5	66.0	3	70.9
High quality teaching	2.5	74.5	1	79.8
A good record of student attendance	9	57.4	17	27.8
Good discipline and student behaviour	4	70.2	6.5	58.2
Preparation for work	21	2.1	21	2.5
The encouragement of students to take responsibility for their own learning	7.5	61.7	4	63.3
The encouragement of a positive attitude to school (pride in school)	15	31.9	15	32.9
The provision of a good range of extra curricular activities	14	36.2	19.5	17.7
The creation of a positive climate for learning	5.5	66.0	5	60.8
Shared goals and values by staff and students	7.5	61.7	12.5	43.0
High expectations of students	2.5	74.5	6.5	58.2
High expectations of staff	10	53.2	9	51.9
Teacher motivation and commitment	12	48.9	10	50.6
High level of student motivation	13	38.3	12.5	43.0
Parent/community satisfaction	20	17.0	14	34.2
Student satisfaction	19	21.3	19.5	17.7

Judging school effectiveness

The HTs and HoDs were asked to indicate up to ten most important factors which ought to be taken into account in judging the effectiveness of any secondary school. Table 6.2 gives details of their responses.

The results indicate that, for HTs, good progress, or value added, for students of all ability levels was the most commonly noted factor which ought to be taken into account in judging the effectiveness of any secondary school. By contrast, less than a third felt a high level of achievement in examinations ought to be taken into account. High quality teaching and high expectations of students were the next most frequently cited factors (joint second), followed by positive inter-personal relationships for staff and students and the creation of a positive climate for learning (joint fourth). In joint sixth place were shared goals by staff and students and the encouragement of students to take responsibility for their own learning.

The list of factors which HoDs thought ought to be taken into account in judging the effectiveness of any school was similar to that of HTs in terms of most commonly cited factors. High quality teaching was in first place, followed by good progress, or value added, for students of all ability levels in second, positive inter-personal relationships for staff and students (third), the encouragement of students to take responsibility for their own learning (fourth) and the creation of a positive climate for learning (fifth). These results showed a fair degree of agreement in views between HTs and HoDs, the rank correlation being 0.84.

Nonetheless, there were some differences in emphasis. HoDs placed rather less stress than HTs on shared goals and values for staff and students. In addition, they were less likely to cite a good record of student attendance, good discipline and student behaviour, and high expectations of students as important criteria for judging school effectiveness.

Given the priority of the previous government to applying market forces to education, it is perhaps surprising that few HTs or HoDs placed a strong emphasis on either parent/community satisfaction, or student satisfaction, as factors which ought to be taken into account in judging the effectiveness of any school. Nonetheless, HoDs gave more weight to the maintenance of a caring pastoral environment and parent/community satisfaction than did HTs.

As we have shown, for both HTs and HoDs, good progress was seen to be the single most appropriate criteria for judging school effectiveness.[2] It is interesting to note that although both HTs and HoDs clearly indicated that good progress was the most important criterion for judging school effectiveness – and less than a third cited a high level of achievement in public examinations as important – promoting student progress was only infrequently reported as being one of the school's principal educational goals as shown earlier in Table 6.1. Our findings suggest, therefore, that although both HTs and HoDs viewed student progress as essential for judging school effectiveness, the majority still attached much greater importance to more visible goals, such as absolute achievement in public examination results. Again this is likely to

Table 6.3

Factors which contribute most to the effectiveness of your school*	HTs		HoDs	
	Rank	per cent	Rank	per cent
Strong support from parents/community	21	21.3	19	20.3
Teachers feel valued	15.5	25.5	20	19.0
A strong emphasis on academic matters	18.5	23.4	17.5	22.8
A good staff development programme	15.5	25.5	22	7.6
Students feel valued as people	8	53.2	3.5	49.4
Careful monitoring of attendance	12.5	38.2	16	25.3
Staff stability in post	14	34.0	5	48.1
Good leadership by heads of departments	11	42.6	2	69.6
A strong and cohesive senior management team	1	78.7	15	32.9
Quality of leadership provided by headteacher	3	63.8	8	43.0
Commitment and enthusiasm of teaching staff	7	57.4	1	70.9
High quality teaching in all/most departments	4.5	59.6	3.5	49.4
Considerable teacher involvement in decision-making	18.5	23.4	17.5	22.8
The creation of an orderly and secure working environment	4.5	59.6	11	38.0
Clear and consistently applied whole school approach to student behaviour and discipline	9	51.1	12.5	36.7
Encouragement of student responsibility	18.5	23.4	14	34.2
Regular marking and monitoring of homework in all/most departments	10	44.7	12.5	36.7
School-wide policies on marking/assessment	18.5	23.4	21	17.7
Regular monitoring of student achievement and progress	4.5	59.6	8	43.0
No shortage of experienced and well-qualified staff	22	17.0	10	41.8
Good working relationships amongst staff	12.5	38.3	6	44.3
Staff and students' shared belief that the school is primarily a place for teaching and learning	2	66.0	8	43.0

*Respondents were asked to identify up to 10 factors.

reflect the impact of league table publications and the experience or prospect of a first OFSTED inspection for schools in our sample.

Factors contributing to the effectiveness of a school
Headteachers and HoDs were asked to identify up to ten most important factors which contributed to the effectiveness of their school. The results are presented in Table 6.3.

For HTs, the factor a 'strong and cohesive SMT' was cited most frequently, followed by 'staff and students' shared belief that the school is primarily a place for teaching and learning' in second place. The 'quality of leadership provided by the HT' ranked third. 'High quality teaching in all/most departments' and 'regular monitoring of student achievement and progress' were the next most commonly noted in joint fourth place, closely followed by the 'commitment and enthusiasm of teaching staff'.

For HoDs, by contrast, 'the commitment and enthusiasm of teaching staff' was most frequently noted, followed by 'good leadership by HoDs' in second place. The factors 'students feel valued as people' and 'high quality teaching in all/most departments' were next most frequently noted (joint third), closely followed by 'staff stability in post' (fifth). HoDs placed rather less emphasis than HTs on the factors 'quality of leadership provided by the HT', 43 per cent listed this, and 'a strong cohesive SMT' was mentioned by a third. Interestingly, HTs and HoDs showed much less similarity in their opinions about what actually contributed to their schools' current success (rank correlation = 0.48) than they had about what factors ought to be taken into account when judging school effectiveness, as we showed earlier in Table 6.2. Thus HTs, for example, gave more credit to 'the creation of an orderly and secure working environment' and a 'clear and consistently applied whole school approach to student behaviour and discipline'. This suggests that they attach more importance than HoDs to the creation of a positive behavioural climate in their school.

In terms of which factor was most important, five HTs (11 per cent) and thirteen HoDs (17 per cent) were unable/unwilling to identify any single factor as most influential, suggesting that a combination of different factors was important. Of those who did respond, HTs cited 'staff and students' shared belief that the school is primarily a place for teaching and learning' most frequently (24 per cent) followed by 'the quality of leadership provided by the HT' and 'high quality teaching in all/most departments' (14 per cent each). More HoDs cited 'the commitment and enthusiasm of teaching staff' as most important than any other factor (17 per cent), closely followed by 'the quality of leadership provided by the HT' (15 per cent). 'Staff and students' shared belief that the school is primarily a place for teaching and learning' came in third, cited as most important by 12 per cent of HoDs.

It is notable that relatively few respondents believed that 'a good staff development programme' contributed to their schools' current effectiveness, particularly amongst HoDs – less than 8 per cent cited this. By contrast, HoDs attached more importance than HTs to the factor 'no shortage of experienced and well-qualified staff'. Only a minority of both groups, around one in five, felt that 'strong support from parents/community contributed to their school's current effectiveness'.

Barriers to greater effectiveness

More detailed information was sought from HTs about certain aspects of the school and equivalent information from HoDs about specific departments. HTs were asked to indicate up to ten most important factors in response to the question about what acted as barriers to the effectiveness of their school. Their responses are shown in Table 6.4.

Our results indicate that 'inadequate leadership by some HoDs' and 'too low expectations of students by some staff' were the most commonly cited items – each noted by 72 per cent of HTs. The 'social disadvantage of the student intake' was also very highly rated, identified as a barrier by a similar proportion of HTs. 'Poor quality teaching in some departments' was a source of concern for over 55 per cent of HTs, and an 'inconsistent approach to student

Table 6.4

Factors which are barriers to the effectiveness of your school	HTs Rank	HTs per cent
Social disadvantage of intake	3	70.2
Shortage of qualified staff in key departments	17	10.6
Inadequate leadership by some heads of department	1.5	72.3
Low staff morale	20.5	6.4
Pressures of external change (e.g. NC, LMS)	7	36.2
Lack of resources	6	38.3
Poor physical environment	12	25.5
High staff turnover	22	4.3
Falling student roll	17	10.6
Lack of consensus in staff goals for students	15	19.1
High levels of staff absence	20.5	6.4
Too little emphasis given to homework	13.5	23.4
Inconsistent approach to student assessment by staff	10	29.8
Inconsistent approach to student behaviour and discipline	5	40.4
Insufficient academic emphasis	10	29.8
Little support from parents/community	8	31.9
Too low expectations of students by some staff	1.5	72.3
Poor quality teaching in some departments	4	55.3
Lack of commitment and enthusiasm by some staff	13.5	23.4
Poor student attendance	10	29.8
Poor student behaviour	17	10.6
Conflict within senior management team	19	8.5

behaviour and discipline' was noted by 40 per cent. External factors such as 'lack of resources' and 'pressures of external change' (e.g. NC, LMS) were also noted by over a third. A quarter cited a 'poor physical environment' as a barrier to greater effectiveness.

Five HTs also commented on other specific factors. These included: 'being an all boys school'; 'union activity'; 'low student motivation' and 'low skills of intake at transfer' and 'lack of space'. However, one HT expressed great confidence, commenting that 'nothing' held the school back from being more effective at present. In all, 43 of the 47 HTs made a response concerning which factors were the most important inhibitor of greater school effectiveness. 'Too low expectations of students by some staff' was identified as most important by twelve HTs (29 per cent of respondents). The 'social disadvantage of the student intake' was noted by seven (17 per cent) of respondents, followed by 'inadequate leadership by some HoDs' – cited by five or 12 per cent. 'Lack of resources' was seen as the main barrier by four HTs.

Major successes/achievements of the school over the last five years
HTs were also asked to describe any major successes/achievements of the school over the last five years. Table 6.5 summarizes their responses. It should be remembered that in interpreting their responses, areas of success/achievement may also provide indicators of areas in which the school was

Table 6.5

Major successes/achievements over the last five years in your school	HTs	
[n=47]	Rank	per cent
Improved record-keeping/student profiles	2.5	83.0
Higher expectations for student performance	4	76.6
Improved organization	1	89.4
Greater student motivation	14.5	55.3
More effective leadership by most heads of department	8.5	66.0
Improved monitoring of student performance	2.5	83.0
Improved student behaviour	7	68.1
Better student attendance	8.5	66.0
Helpful OFSTED inspection	19	36.2
Improved staff morale	16	51.1
Reduction in staff shortages	12.5	57.4
More cohesive and effective senior management team	6	72.3
Greater opportunities for student responsibilities in school	17	44.7
Improved homework policy and practice	12.5	57.4
Greater parental and community involvement	18	40.4
Improved examination results	5	74.5
General improvement in quality of teaching in most cases	10.5	61.7
Better relationships between staff and students	10.5	61.7
Focus on equal opportunities	14.5	55.3
Other achievement/success	20	23.4
None	21	6.4

experiencing difficulties five years before, but which were now perceived to have been resolved or substantially improved.

'Improved organization' was the most commonly noted area of success, reported by 89 per cent of HTs. More specifically, better record keeping and monitoring were the most frequently noted areas being indicated by 83 per cent of respondents. Nearly three-quarters of HTs reported improved examination results over the last five years. 'More cohesive and effective senior management' was also noted by 72 per cent, followed by 'more effective leadership by most HoDs' and 'better student attendance' – both reported by two-thirds of HTs. Areas least frequently noted were a helpful OFSTED inspection (36 per cent),[3] greater parental involvement (40 per cent) and greater opportunities (45 per cent). Fourteen HTs gave extra details of other areas of success over the last five years. These included a policy for more able students, a better SEN focus, an improved school ethos, improved school facilities, more finance under LMS and more students applying. Only three HTs commented that there had been *no* areas of successes/achievement over the preceding five years and one by contrast stated that many areas had already been good and this remained unchanged.

Major problems/challenges faced by the school over the last five years
A positive finding of the survey was that most HTs identified substantially fewer problems/challenges than areas of success/achievement. Table 6.6 summarizes HTs' responses to this item.

Table 6.6

Major problems and major challenges over the last five years in your school	[n=47] Rank	HTs per cent
Creaming of high ability/middle-class students by other schools	4	66.0
Falling student roll	23	17.0
High staff turnover	23	17.0
Shortage of qualified/experienced staff	19	23.4
Lack of cohesion in senior management team	16	34.0
Poor leadership by some heads of department	2	78.7
Low expectations of students by many teachers	11	46.8
Inconsistent approach to student behaviour and discipline	6.5	55.3
Threat of school closure	26	10.6
Low staff morale	11	46.8
External pressures (e.g. NC, LMS)	3	74.5
Difficult OFSTED inspection	25	12.8
Lack of commitment/motivation from significant minority of staff	17	31.9
High staff stress levels	1	80.9
Inadequate buildings/building problems (e.g. fire, asbestos etc.)	9	51.1
General lack of parental and community support/interest	14	42.6
Inadequate resources	11	46.8
Major discipline problems (students)	21	19.1
Lack of coherent policies throughout school	20	21.3
Serious social problems outside school (drugs, racism, unemployment)	5	63.8
Insufficient academic ethos in school	8	53.2
Lacked of shared vision and goals	15	36.2
Disparity in achievements for some student groups (e.g. related to gender, ethnicity)	6.5	55.3
High levels of staff absence	23	17.0
Too great a variation in quality of teaching (lack of interest, poor differentiation, unclear goals, poor organization evident in too many classes)	13	44.7
Inadequate leadership by previous headteacher(s)*	18	29.8

* For 25 HTs this item was not applicable because there had been no change of HT over the previous five years

The most commonly noted major problems/challenges were 'high staff stress levels', 'poor leadership by some HoDs' and 'external pressures' reported by 75 per cent. 'Creaming' of middle class or high ability students was also identified as a problem by almost two-thirds. It should be remembered in this context that all schools in the sample were nominally comprehensives, but located within inner London LEAs. By contrast, threat of school closure, a difficult OFSTED, falling student roll, high staff turnover, high levels of staff absence and major discipline problems were reported much less frequently. Insufficient academic ethos, inadequate buildings, low staff morale, low teacher expectations and lack of parental support were also factors identified as problem areas by between 40 to 50 per cent of HTs.

Departments

In this section we turn to examine the HoDs' perceptions of departmental effectiveness and its influences in more detail.

Table 6.7

Factors which ought to be taken into account in judging the effectiveness of any department*	HoD English [n=39]		HoD Maths [n=40]	
	Rank	per cent	Rank	per cent
Enjoyment/interest of students	4.5	59.0	2.5	62.5
Uptake at GCSE and A-level	14	23.1	12.5	25.0
Quality of teaching in the department	1	94.9	1	85.0
Prior attainment of students (at intake to school)	9	43.6	4.5	60.0
Extent to which independent student learning is fostered	8	46.2	9.5	47.5
Development of students' study skills	14	23.1	17	15.0
Development of students' social skills	18	7.7	18	5.0
Visible student progress	10	38.5	6.5	55.0
Student motivation	4.5	59.0	6.5	55.0
Student behaviour	14	23.1	16	17.5
Student self-confidence	12	25.6	9.5	47.5
Extent to which departmental staff work together as a team	2	74.4	2.5	62.5
Personal effectiveness of teaching staff	11	35.9	12.5	25.0
Examination results	7	48.7	11	45.0
High expectations of students	6	56.4	4.5	60.0
Commitment/enthusiasm of teaching staff	3	71.8	8	52.5
Stability of teaching staff	16.5	15.4	12.5	25.0
Experience of teaching staff	16.5	15.4	15	22.5
Other	19	0.0	19	2.5

* HoDs were asked to indicate up to eight important factors

Judging departmental effectiveness

The HoDs were asked to identify which factors they thought should be taken into account in judging the effectiveness of any department. Table 6.7 compares English and mathematics HoDs' responses.

As a group, HoDs of English and mathematics gave a fairly similar pattern of responses. Both groups noted quality of teaching in the department most frequently – over 85 per cent. For English HoDs, the next most commonly cited factors were the extent to which departmental staff worked together as a team and the commitment/enthusiasm of teaching staff, each noted by over 70 per cent. For mathematics, HoDs gave equal stress to departmental staff team work and the enjoyment/interest of students, which were both noted by 63 per cent. Mathematics HoDs gave more stress to the prior attainment of students at intake to school, which was noted as important by 60 per cent compared with 44 per cent of English HoDs, and visible student progress (55 per cent compared with 39 per cent). Factors less frequently noted as important in judging the effectiveness of any department by both groups included the development of students' social skills and student behaviour. Around a quarter of HoDs thought that the development of students' study skills, the stability and experience of teaching staff, and uptake at GCSE and A-level should be used to judge departmental effectiveness – but nearly half cited examination results.

Table 6.8

Major successes/achievements of the department over the last five years	HoD English [n=39]		HoD Maths [n=40]	
	Rank	per cent	Rank	per cent
Improved record-keeping/student profiles	5	82.1	1.5	85.0
Better staff	17	41.0	12	57.9
Greater departmental cohesiveness	3.5	87.2	4	80.0
Greater incidence of high quality teaching in the department	6.5	71.8	7	75.0
Keeping up with NC changes	2	89.2	3	82.5
Better preparation of students for examinations	6.5	71.8	5.5	77.5
Better preparation of students to manage coursework for GCSE	8.5	66.7	8	72.5
Student enjoyment of subject has increased	12.5	48.7	13	57.5
Greater emphasis given to student independent learning	14.5	46.2	17	40.0
Student attitudes/motivation has improved	12.5	48.7	15	50.0
Examination results have improved	10	61.5	10	62.5
Student behaviour has improved	16	43.6	16	47.5
Department has instituted more extra-curricular activities for students	18	40.0	19	35.0
Greater teamwork in department	3.5	87.2	1.5	85.0
Curriculum development	1	92.3	5.5	77.5
Staff commitment and motivation has risen	11	56.4	11	60.0
Teacher expectations for student achievement have risen	8.5	66.7	9	67.5
Improved homework policy and practice	14.5	46.2	14	55.0
Greater parental/community support	21	7.7	20.5	10.0
Take up of subject at A-level has increased	19	33.3	18	37.5
Other	20	15.4	20.5	10.0

Of the thirty-four mathematics HoDs who identified one factor as most important, a third (eleven) chose the quality of teaching in the department, and five nominated the enjoyment/interest of students. Four noted visible student progress. For English HoDs a similar pattern emerged. Of thirty-five who responded to the same question, ten rated the quality of teaching as most important, five the enjoyment/interest of students and another five visible student progress. Overall, English and mathematics HoDs were broadly in agreement, with a rank correlation of 0.87, although mathematics HoDs attached relatively less importance to the commitment/enthusiasm of teaching staff and rather more to developing student self-confidence than their English counterparts did.

Major successes/achievements of the department

The HoDs' views about any major successes/achievements of their departments over the last five years were also sought. Table 6.8 indicates that HoDs' views were generally positive and identified a number of areas of improvement during this period. The results for English and mathematics HoDs are again broadly similar.

Keeping up with NC changes was identified as a major success (perhaps unsurprisingly!) by a very high percentage of HoDs. Better teamwork in their department was also frequently noted, as was greater departmental

cohesiveness – by 80 per cent or more of respondents from each group. Curriculum development was also identified as a major success area by 92 per cent of
English and 78 per cent of mathematics HoDs. It is possible that the implementation of the NC had encouraged both curriculum development and greater
cohesiveness and teamworking in departments as staff sought to cope with the
pressures of external change.

Better preparation of students for examinations and better preparation of
students to manage coursework for GCSE were also reported. As we discussed
in Chapter 4, overall an upward trend in GCSE results was identified in project
schools over the three years 1990–92, which is in line with national trends. A
greater incidence of high quality teaching was perceived to occur in over 70 per
cent of departments and, in the HoDs' views, staff commitment and motivation had also risen in over half. A similar proportion (around 50 per cent) of
the HoDs from both groups reported that student attitudes/motivation had
also improved.

By contrast, few HoDs felt that parental/community support had increased
during this period, and a third reported that the take-up of their subject at
A-level had increased – although it must be remembered that many schools did
not offer A-level studies. The provision of more extra curricular activities was
noted by a substantial minority.

Table 6.9

Major problems/challenges which faced the department over the last five years	HoD English [n=39]		HoD Maths [n=40]	
	Rank	per cent	Rank	per cent
Changes in student intake	13.5	28.2	17	35.0
Shortages of teaching staff	15	23.1	8.5	47.5
Difficulties getting parental/community support	9	35.9	13	40.0
Implementation of NC changes	1	92.3	1	87.5
Implementation of GCSE changes	2	89.7	2	77.5
Inconsistency in implementation of homework policy	11	30.8	15	37.5
Low expectations of students by some teachers	6	41.0	5.5	57.5
Inflexibility of approach by some teachers	6	41.0	7	50.0
Poor quality teaching in some classes	3	48.7	3	70.0
Low student motivation	6	41.0	5.5	57.5
Significant student behaviour problems	13.5	28.2	15	37.5
Disagreement amongst staff about student grouping policy	16.5	20.5	19	27.5
Low staff morale	8	38.5	11.5	42.5
Insufficient emphasis on homework by some staff	11	30.8	10	45.0
Department has little support from headteacher/previous headteacher	18	17.9	20	25.0
Profile given to department in school too low	16.5	20.5	11.5	42.5
Inadequate student feedback on work	21	12.8	15	37.5
Under resourcing	4	43.6	4	62.5
Inadequate student assessment	19.5	15.4	8.5	47.5
Poor leadership by previous HoD	11	30.8	18	30.0
Difficult OFSTED inspection	19.5	15.4	21	20.0
Other	22	10.3	22	7.5

Major problems/challenges faced by the departments

In line with HoDs' responses concerning major achievements, the implementation of NC changes was seen to have been a major challenge/problem by nearly all respondents (nine out of ten for both English and mathematics HoDs). This was closely followed by implementation of GCSE changes (noted by 90 per cent and 78 per cent respectively). Table 6.9 gives details of their responses.

Some differences between HoDs of English and mathematics in the incidence of other problems/challenges emerged, in contrast to findings concerning successes and achievements. For example, 70 per cent of mathematics HoDs commented on poor quality teaching in some classes, compared with only 49 per cent of English HoDs, and nearly half reported shortages of teaching staff compared with 23 per cent of English HoDs. Insufficient emphasis on homework by some staff was also noted more frequently by mathematics than English HoDs (45 per cent compared with 31 per cent). In addition, inadequate student assessment was reported by 48 per cent of the mathematics but only 15 per cent of the English HoDs. HoDs of mathematics were also more likely to feel that the profile given to their department within the school was too low (42 per cent against 21 per cent). A similar proportion of the two groups cited difficulties in getting parental/community support indicating that this was seen as a problem area in over a third of departments.

Table 6.10

Factors which contribute most to the effectiveness of your department*	HoD English [n=39] Rank	per cent	HoD Maths [n=40] Rank	per cent
Quality of staff	4.5	61.5	10	42.5
Curriculum enabling students to work to their strengths	7	46.2	2.5	62.5
Building students' self-confidence	17	17.9	17.5	15.0
Careful record keeping and marking for GCSE coursework	14	23.1	11	40.0
Departmental staff working as a team	2	71.8	1	77.5
Teaching staff stability	15	20.5	6.5	50.0
Experienced senior staff	12.5	25.6	19	10.0
Teacher commitment/effort	6	59.0	4	60.0
Collective running of department/teacher involvement	10	35.9	8.5	45.0
Congruence of educational views and goals amongst teaching staff	10	35.9	17.5	15.0
Good organization of resources	8	43.6	6.5	50.0
High quality teaching in most lessons	2	71.8	8.5	45.0
Strong academic emphasis in department	17	17.9	15.5	17.5
High expectations of students by most staff	1.5	71.8	5	55.0
Strong emphasis on homework by most staff	19	12.8	13.5	20.0
Good classroom management in most lessons	4.5	61.5	2.5	62.5
Effective assessment by most staff	10	35.9	15.5	17.5
Strong emphasis on examination entry	17	17.9	13.5	20.0
Encouragement of independent learning by students	12.5	25.6	12	32.5
Other	20	5.1	20	0.0

* HoDs were asked to indicate up to eight factors

Factors contributing to departmental effectiveness
The HoDs were asked to indicate up to eight most important factors which they felt contributed to their department's effectiveness (see Table 6.10).

For both groups of HoDs, 'departmental staff working as a team' was cited most frequently as contributing to effectiveness, being indicated by 72 per cent or more. However, 'high quality teaching in most lessons' was identified less commonly by mathematics HoDs, only 45 per cent compared with 72 per cent for English. 'Good classroom management in most lessons' was reported by very similar numbers of HoDs in each group, as was 'teacher commitment/ effort' – 60 per cent. By contrast, 'high expectations of students by most staff' was noted more frequently by English HoDs (72 per cent compared with 55 per cent). The 'quality of staff' was seen to be more important by English (62 per cent) than mathematics HoDs (43 per cent), whereas more weight was attached to a 'curriculum enabling students to work to their strengths' by mathematics HoDs.

In terms of factors seen as less influential, 'a strong emphasis on homework', 'on examination entry' and 'building students' self-confidence' were infrequently cited as contributing to success by both English and mathematics HoDs. English HoDs also gave much less weight to 'teaching staff stability' than their mathematics counterparts, one in five compared with half. However, for English HoDs 'effective assessment by most staff' was more commonly seen to have a positive impact on effectiveness, more than a third of English HoDs compared with less than one in five mathematics HoDs noting this.

In all 35 English and 38 mathematics HoDs made a response about which factor was most important. For English HoDs, 'high expectations of students' and 'high quality teaching' in most lessons were identified as most influential in their department (by 23 per cent of English respondents, followed by teacher commitment/effort at 11 per cent). For mathematics HoDs, 'teamwork' was seen to be most important by almost a third of respondents followed by 'teacher commitment/effort, high quality teaching' and 'high expectations' – each being cited by 13 per cent as most influential).

English and mathematics HoDs shared a fair degree of similarity in their views regarding factors which contributed to departmental effectiveness, with a rank correlation of 0.70. English HoDs were likely to cite the following: 'high quality teaching', 'effective assessment by staff', 'congruence of views and goals' and 'high expectations of students'. By comparison mathematics HoDs gave rather more emphasis to a 'curriculum geared to students' strengths', 'careful record-keeping and marking' and 'staff stability'.

Barriers to greater departmental effectiveness
The HoDs were also questioned about 'what, if anything, holds your department back from being more effective?'. It is clear that, for the vast majority of both groups of HoDs, heavy workload was perceived as a significant barrier to greater effectiveness (see Table 6.11). Large classes were also noted by a

Table 6.11

Factors which hold your department back from being more effective*	HoD English [n=39]		HoD Maths [n=40]	
	Rank	per cent	Rank	per cent
Differences between this department and other departments in school in teaching style	7	25.6	7.5	27.5
SMT support not always present	9.5	20.5	10.5	22.5
Inadequate resources	4	38.5	4	50.0
Heavy workload	1	82.1	1	85.0
Large classes	3	43.6	2	55.0
Insufficient high quality teaching in some classes	6	28.2	6	35.0
Low staff morale	12.5	10.3	16	10.0
Low expectations of students by some teachers	8	23.1	5	37.5
Lack of fresh ideas (static department)	21.5	5.1	12	17.5
Lack of stability in teaching staff	16.5	7.7	18.5	5.0
Lack of consensus in educational philosophy and goals in departments	12.5	10.3	13.5	15.0
Too much teacher autonomy	21.5	5.1	20.5	2.5
Excess administration	2	51.3	3	52.5
High teaching staff absence rates	16.5	7.7	22.5	0.0
Too little emphasis on examination entry by some staff	21.5	5.1	22.5	0.0
Too little emphasis on homework by staff	14.5	7.7	18.5	5.0
Insufficient challenge for high ability students	9.5	20.5	10.5	22.5
Insufficient challenge for low ability students	16.5	7.7	17	7.5
Poor organization of resources	16.5	7.7	13.5	15.0
Insufficient feedback on work to students	21.5	5.1	9	25.0
Inadequate emphasis on student assessment	16.5	7.7	13.5	15.0
Little parental/community support for school	5	30.8	7	27.5
Other	11	11.3	20.5	2.5

* HoDs were asked to indicate up to eight factors

substantial proportion (44 per cent of English HoDs and 55 per cent of the mathematics HoDs). Excess administration was also reported by over half of each group. Rather more of the mathematics than the English HoDs noted 'inadequate resources' as a barrier to greater effectiveness (50 per cent compared with 39 per cent). By contrast, 'Too much teacher autonomy' was identified by very few HoDs as a problem area, as were 'high teaching staff absence rates' and 'low staff morale', this last despite the heavy workload. 'Insufficient challenge for low ability students' was likewise rarely rated, although just over one in five from each group identified 'insufficient challenge for high ability students' as a barrier to greater effectiveness.

'Insufficient feedback on work to students' was noted by a quarter of mathematics HoDs, but only two out of thirty-nine English HoDs highlighted this area. Very few in either group of HoDs identified too little emphasis on examination entry or on homework as factors holding back their department from greater effectiveness.

HoDs' views about barriers to departmental effectiveness were in somewhat greater agreement than regarding factors contributing to greater effectiveness, with a rank correlation of 0.83 vs 0.70. The chief barriers to greater departmental effectiveness were seen to be 'heavy workload', 'excess administration', 'large classes' and 'inadequate resources' (see Table 6.11). 'Inadequate emphasis on student assessment' and 'insufficient high quality teaching' in some classes were also noted by a sizeable minority. However, 'low expectations of students by some teachers' and 'insufficient feedback on work for students' were more likely to be cited by heads of mathematics than their English counterparts.

CONCLUSIONS

Schools

Broadly speaking, as far as HTs were concerned, five years previously the five main educational objectives of their school were centred around personal qualities or social mores, rather than overall academic achievement, but by 1995 both curriculum and examination results were included in the top five objectives, which was not perceived to be the case in 1990. Nonetheless, promoting a sense of achievement, good behaviour and a pleasant environment were still seen as vital to the effectiveness of the school. Perhaps predictably, unlike the HTs, HoDs laid less weight on behaviour and more on curriculum.

Although not rated highly amongst their school's principal goals with regard to judging school effectiveness, good progress or value added by the students was considered by HTs to be the single most important factor. This was also the opinion of the HoDs.

Asked about factors contributing to effectiveness, HTs most frequently mentioned a strong SMT, closely followed by the comment that the school is essentially a place for learning. On the other hand, HoDs were more likely to cite commitment by staff and strong leadership from themselves.

Regarding barriers to effectiveness, HTs were asked to identify the ten most important in their school. Inadequate leadership by some HoDs and low expectations of the students by some staff were the factors most mentioned, although a socially disadvantaged intake was also identified as a major problem by many in our sample.

Almost nine out of ten HTs regarded improved organization as the main achievement by the school over the past five years, with better record-keeping and monitoring also being viewed as important by eight out of ten respondents and many citing better examination results also. Asked about problems and challenges encountered in the previous five years, HTs underlined the high level of stress among staff, poor leadership by some HoDs and external pressures from LMS, NC etc., these factors being mentioned by eight out of every ten HTs.

Departments

In connection with criteria which should be used to judge departmental effectiveness, heads of English and mathematics respectively displayed a fairly high level of agreement – 'quality of teaching' being the factor noted most frequently by both groups, followed by the 'extent to which departmental staff work together as a team'.

Asked about the successes and achievements over the last five years of their own departments, HoDs of English and mathematics were again broadly in agreement, with very nearly nine out of every ten citing 'keeping up with the NC change' as a major triumph! 'Departmental teamwork/cohesiveness' and 'curriculum development' were also seen as important success areas.

As a kind of mirror image of this, the implementation of these changes was viewed as a major problem by almost all respondents, as were changes linked with GCSE syllabi and assessment. High levels of staff stress may be seen as related to the pressures of external change in the education system of the early to mid 1990s.

Of the factors contributing to departmental effectiveness, teamwork was the most mentioned element, with a fair degree of similarity of views between heads of English and mathematics.

A heavy workload was seen as the most unyielding barrier to departmental effectiveness, with a close correlation between English and mathematics HoDs regarding this and indeed on other less important factors. Again, this is likely to reflect the impact of implementing the NC and its subsequent revisions, compounded simultaneously by LMS and GCSE changes.

By and large, these results for both schools and departments indicate that HTs and HoDs tend to hold broadly similar views, as do the heads of English and mathematics departments. There were indications that the HTs laid somewhat more emphasis on aspects which may be viewed as highly visible criteria – academic achievement levels, behaviour and attendance – which tend to affect a school's public image. In the light of current policy emphasis on applying market mechanisms in education, it is notable that student and parent satisfaction were not rated highly by most of the sample in connection with judging school effectiveness.

The chapter that follows presents a non-technical account of the results obtained from the questionnaires analysed above, using multilevel analyses to establish the extent to which it is possible to explain statistically differences between schools in their academic effectiveness. From this it will be possible to examine the links between practitioners' perspectives and understanding with that derived from empirical analyses of the links between students' GCSE outcomes and factors concerning school and department processes.

NOTES

1. Two HTs were unwilling to specify a single goal as most important.
2. In all, around a quarter of HTs (12) and a quarter of HoDs (18) were unable/unwilling to specify one most important factor.
3. However, in terms of the numbers of schools (31) which had been inspected, it is important to note that this represents a majority.

7

Understanding Academic Effectiveness

INTRODUCTION

In this chapter the relationships between measures of school and departmental processes and findings from our value added analyses of GCSE results are explored in an attempt to uncover potential mechanisms which underlie greater school and departmental academic effectiveness.

The Phase 2 case studies, described in Chapter 5, have already provided evidence of the importance of individual institutional and departmental histories. They also offer insights into the extent of similarities and differences between schools and departments which varied markedly in their success in promoting students' GCSE performance over three consecutive years. A number of common patterns and themes emerged from our qualitative analyses, providing pointers towards explanations for differences in academic effectiveness.

We sought to test out, empirically, the findings and hypotheses we developed on the basis of the case studies during the third phase of the study using a larger sample of schools. Practitioners' views and perceptions of the constituents and barriers to effectiveness were reported in the last chapter. Here, information obtained from the same sample of HTs and HoDs is used to establish the strength of statistical associations (correlations) between measures of current and past school and departmental processes and school and subject effects on GCSE performance over three years.[1] Questionnaires were used to obtain process information about schools and departments from HTs and HoDs of English and mathematics departments. Our analyses tested the relationships between their responses and value added measures of effectiveness in terms of total GCSE performance (tscore) and also subject results in two core areas of the curriculum, English and mathematics. Items identified as potentially important in these preliminary analyses were then tested more rigorously, using the multilevel approach described in Chapters 3 and 4. This was done to establish the extent to which it is possible to account statistically for variations between schools and departments in their value added results at GCSE.

The results of Phase 3 of the research enabled us to establish whether the insights obtained from the qualitative case studies of outlier schools and departments could be confirmed amongst a larger sample of schools. The findings which we report in the next section reveal a pattern of significant associations which both supports and extends the qualitative results. It is notable that, in general, the associations between items concerning policy and practice in the past show stronger relationships with the value added measures of academic effectiveness than with items concerning current practice, although relationships are in the same direction. This is as would be expected, because examination results can only be indicators of past performance and will have been influenced by school and classroom processes operating in schools at an earlier period, as well as by students' prior achievement and background. The decision to use an explicitly retrospective focus in both the case studies and questionnaire survey – comparing current policy and practice with that five years before – is supported by this finding. This approach also provides valuable information about HTs and HODs' experiences of substantial educational change – both national and at the school level – during the period (1990–1995).

In the next section we describe the strength of statistical associations in the form of correlations or mean differences. As noted in Chapter 3, a correlation can range from +1 to –1 showing either a perfect positive or a perfect negative relationship. In practice, weaker correlations are commonly found in educational research. All the correlations we report are significant at the 95 per cent confidence limit ($p<0.05$), unless indicated otherwise. This means that a relationship would arise by chance in only one case in 20. Correlations are reported for all questionnaire items which form a scale, for example where an HT or HoD rated their school's academic emphasis from 1 (very strong) to 5 (weak). For other items where respondents indicated the presence or absence of a factor (e.g. in relation to a key factor promoting effectiveness), mean differences in value added results for the two groups are shown. As with the correlations, the 95 per cent confidence limit is used unless otherwise stated.

HTs' and HoDs' judgements of performance

Students' academic performance

Headteachers' and HoDs' assessments of students' academic achievement were analysed to establish their relationship with the quantitative value added measures of effectiveness at GCSE. HTs and HoDs were asked to rate their satisfaction with the school in terms of current and past levels of academic achievement on a scale of 1 (very satisfied) to 5 (very dissatisfied). The results showed that both English and, to a lesser extent, mathematics HoDs' satisfaction levels with their schools in terms of students' past academic achievement were strongly related to the value measure of effectiveness in promoting overall GCSE results (r=–0.75 English HoDs; r=–0.60 mathematics HoDs).[2] Current satisfaction levels were also significantly correlated, but less strongly.

In addition, HTs' past satisfaction with their school in terms of student

Table 7.1   HTs' and HoDs' current and past levels of satisfaction with student academic achievement in the school*

	HT [n=47]	English HoD [n=38]	Mathematics HoD [n=39]
a] Present	%	%	%
Very satisfied	2.1	13.2	10.3
Quite satisfied	25.5	18.4	23.1
Variable	34.0	57.9	43.6
Not very satisfied	36.2	7.9	20.5
Very dissatisfied	2.1	2.6	2.6
b] Past			
Very satisfied	4.7	10.8	2.6
Quite satisfied	7.0	21.6	10.5
Variable	27.9	40.5	50.0
Not very satisfied	34.9	27.0	28.9
Very dissatisfied	25.6	–	7.9

* Non-responses excluded

academic achievements was also significantly correlated with effectiveness in promoting overall GCSE performance (r=–0.47). Overall HTs' perceptions were much less positive about overall academic achievement in the past than were HoDs, as we show in Table 7.1. This is likely to be at least, in part, a reflection of the impact of raw league tables from 1992 onwards (in which this sample of inner London schools had fared badly) and an indicator of concern about absolute levels of student achievement in public examinations. Value added results, by contrast, provide a more realistic picture of a school's relative performance. Our results suggest that subject HoDs' satisfaction levels with students' overall academic achievement in the school were more closely related to their school's impact on student progress than were HTs'.

The middle managers' assessments of the GCSE examination performance of their department, compared with other departments in their school, indicated that mathematics HoDs' views were more negative than their English counterparts. For example, only 8 per cent of English HoDs thought their department was below the average for their school in the past, compared with over 47 per cent of mathematics HoDs. Headteachers' views of the relative performance of English and mathematics performance were in line with this trend. Thus, just over two-thirds of HTs thought their mathematics departments' past examination performance was below the average of other departments in their school; for English the equivalent proportion was less than one in ten.

HTs' assessments of the past examination performance of mathematics departments were more strongly correlated with the value added estimate of effectiveness for mathematics (r=–0.50) than for other subjects. By contrast, mathematics HoDs' assessments of their own department's examination performance in relation to others in their school showed very little association with this effectiveness measure. For English HoDs, the assessment of their department's past examination performance was significantly correlated with their value added results (r=−0.49).[3]

Our results show that practitioners' assessments of departments' subject performance are not perfectly correlated with value added measures of GCSE performance. Relationships were generally strongest for the assessment of overall student achievement in the school in the past and the total GCSE performance measure.

Other student outcomes

Also of relevance are practitioners' perceptions of other non-academic outcomes. Our case studies (Chapter 5) drew attention to the fact that HTs and HoDs reported that improvements in social aspects such as attendance, attitudes/motivation and behaviour are related to, and often precede, a rise in examination results. Table 7.2 shows the satisfaction levels of HTs and HoDs with student attendance behaviour and motivation currently (1995) and for five years before.

Proportionally, English HoDs expressed greater satisfaction with student attendance, behaviour and motivation than either HTs or HoDs of mathematics. In general, respondents reported some improvements in these three areas when comparing the situation in their school in the past with that obtaining in 1995. For HoDs of mathematics, however, the increase in satisfaction was fairly modest, whereas for HTs it was marked. At the time of our research, fewer than one in ten HTs were dissatisfied with behaviour in their school, down from nearly 47 per cent five years before. Attendance now was rated much less positively than student behaviour or motivation by HTs, with over a third expressing a negative view. Five years before, however, more than 58 per cent of HTs were dissatisfied with student attendance.

The relationships between HTs' and HoDs' perception of these three social outcomes and our value added measures of schools' academic effectiveness were also investigated. In Table 7.3 we show that the correlations between these are fairly strong though not perfect. This finding suggests that, as would be expected, secondary schools' effectiveness in promoting academic outcomes is likely to influence and be influenced by student attendance, behaviour and attitudes.

An improvement in interim outcomes, such as attendance, behaviour and motivation, may occur more rapidly than achieving success in raising academic results. At the student-level such outcomes are generally closely related. Therefore, a focus on these social and affective outcomes can be seen as a necessary prerequisite, though not a sufficient condition, for academic effectiveness (a point we return to in Chapters 8 and 9).

MECHANISMS OF EFFECTIVENESS

A large number of questionnaire items for both HoDs and HTs were found to be linked with our value added measures of schools' and departments'

Table 7.2   HTs' and HoDs' current and past levels of satisfaction with students' non-academic outcomes*

	HT [n=47]	English HoD [n=39]	Mathematics HoD [n=40]
i) Attendance	%	%	%
a] Present			
Very satisfied	4.3	5.1	10.0
Quite satisfied	32.6	46.2	32.5
Variable	28.3	33.3	25.0
Not very satisfied	30.4	15.4	20.0
Very dissatisfied	4.3	–	12.5
b] Past			
Very satisfied	2.3	8.1	2.6
Quite satisfied	16.3	27.0	23.7
Variable	23.3	32.4	39.5
Not very satisfied	32.6	32.4	23.7
Very dissatisfied	25.6	–	10.5
ii) Behaviour			
a] Present			
Very satisfied	6.4	12.8	5.0
Quite satisfied	38.3	35.9	35.0
Variable	46.8	38.5	35.0
Not very satisfied	8.5	10.3	17.5
Very dissatisfied	–	2.6	7.5
b] Past			
Very satisfied	4.7	5.4	–
Quite satisfied	14.0	37.8	37.8
Variable	34.9	27.0	27.0
Not very satisfied	32.6	29.7	20.7
Very dissatisfied	14.0	–	5.4
iii) Motivation			
a] Present			
Very satisfied	4.3	5.1	5.0
Quite satisfied	27.7	35.9	32.5
Variable	48.9	46.2	25.0
Not very satisfied	17.0	10.3	32.5
Very dissatisfied	2.1	2.6	5.0
b] Past			
Very satisfied	4.7	5.4	2.7
Quite satisfied	4.7	29.7	21.6
Variable	41.9	48.6	45.9
Not very satisfied	37.2	16.2	27.0
Very dissatisfied	11.6	–	2.7

* Non-responses excluded

Table 7.3 Correlations between school effects on total GCSE performance score (shrunken residuals) and HTs' and HoDs' satisfaction with student attendance, behaviour and motivation five years before*

Level of satisfaction with non-cognitive outcomes (past)+	HT [n=47] r	HoD English [n=39] r	HoD Mathematics [n=40] r
Student attendance	−0.51	−0.69	−0.52
Student behaviour	−0.48	−0.57	−0.43
Student motivation	−0.58	−0.62	−0.53

* Non-responses excluded   + Where 1 = very satisfied; 5 = very dissatisfied

Table 7.4 Features associated with greater academic effectiveness at GCSE

1	High expectations	
2	Strong academic emphasis	– goals – homework – assessment
3	Shared vision/goals	– school wide – with individual departments
4	Clear leadership	– school – departmental
5	An effective SMT	– team work – staff morale
6	Consistency in approach	– school policies and practice – departmental policies and practice
7	Quality of teaching	– for all ability groups – work focus – effective control – enthusiasm – student feedback – student grouping – staff absence/shortages
8	Student-focused approach	– pastoral environment – staff/student relationships
9	Parental support/involvement	

academic effectiveness at GCSE. The patterns of associations provide additional evidence concerning probable underlying mechanisms of effectiveness at the school and departmental level. We do not use the term mechanisms in a deterministic sense, but rather as a way of understanding the patterns of interconnections between different aspects of policy and practice. Our results point to the importance of nine inter-dependent features. These affect the functioning of the school as a whole and that of individual departments, the vehicle through which effective teaching and learning is delivered. Table 7.4 summarizes these nine features.

Table 7.5 HTs' assessments of staff performance in English and mathematics departments

n = 47	Present	Past*
English	%	%
i] Expectations for student performance		
Good	34.0	20.5
Fairly good	42.6	27.3
About average	23.4	34.1
Not very good	–	13.6
Poor	–	4.6
ii] Expectations for student behaviour		
Good	44.7	20.5
Fairly good	34.0	40.9
About average	21.3	20.5
Not very good	–	11.4
Poor	–	6.8
Mathematics		
i] Expectations for student performance		
Good	21.7	6.8
Fairly good	23.9	9.1
About average	34.8	25.0
Not very good	15.2	36.4
Poor	4.4	22.7
ii] Expectations for student behaviour		
Good	23.9	9.1
Fairly good	37.0	22.7
About average	23.9	27.3
Not very good	6.5	18.2
Poor	8.6	22.8

* Non-responses excluded

1   High expectations

In line with findings from the case studies, the results of the quantitative analyses of questionnaire data emphasize the importance of high teacher expectations of student performance. The HTs rated teaching staff in English and mathematics departments separately in terms of expectations for student performance and expectations for student behaviour. Perceptions of staff expectations in English departments were notably more positive than in mathematics departments (see Table 7.5). Also HTs' views of the present level of staff expectations were much more favourable than in the past. For example, the majority (over 61 per cent) rated expectations for student performance in their mathematics departments five years before as not very good or poor.

The HTs' ratings of staff expectations for both student performance and behaviour were significantly correlated with the value added measures of school and departmental effectiveness. Relationships were stronger for English staff expectations of student performance in the past and overall GCSE performance (r=–0.41), although weak correlations were also found with English subject results. For mathematics, the HTs' assessments of current staff expectations were related to both overall GCSE performance (r=–0.41) and mathematics results (r=–0.37); correlations with past expectations for student behaviour (r=–0.48) and student performance (r=–0.32) were also significant for mathematics.

The English HoDs' responses also drew attention to the link with high teacher expectations in the past, although the equivalent results were not significant for the survey of mathematics HoDs. For example, the correlations between English HoDs' assessments of English teachers' expectations of student performance in the past and value added measures for total GCSE score and English were strong and significant (r=–0.52, r=–0.62 respectively).

Our findings show similarity between HTs' and English HoDs' responses on the relationships between teacher expectations and value added measures of GCSE performance. The picture is less clear, however, for mathematics departments. It may be that mathematics HoDs' perceptions of teacher expectations were less accurate than those of HTs or English HoDs. Alternatively, teacher expectations may play a more important role in influencing student views and performance in subjects other than mathematics.

Another, though indirect, indicator of expectations is provided by HTs' and HoDs' ratings of the academic balance of their intake. Because our value added measures controlled for prior attainment and also for student background influences – such as gender and free school meals – it would be expected that staff ratings of academic balance would not be related to the value added measures of GCSE effectiveness. Of course, they would be expected to show a strong relationship with raw (unadjusted) GCSE results. In fact, despite controls for prior attainment and background, we found that HoDs' perceptions of the academic balance of their intakes were significantly correlated with our academic effectiveness measures.[4]

Again, mathematics HoDs' perceptions of the proportion of low ability students at intake were more negative than English HoDs. In both cases the ratings showed a similar relationship (r=0.36 for mathematics HoDs' rating of intake ability in the past and total GCSE score; r=0.33 for English HoDs' ratings and total GCSE score; r=0.36 for English HoDs' ratings and English results). These results provide some indications that negative staff perceptions of student ability at intake may depress schools' overall academic effectiveness. By contrast, more positive views were related to greater effectiveness, even after controlling for actual differences in student intake.

2   Academic emphasis

Allied to the findings on expectations, both HTs' and HoDs' responses highlighted the importance of a strong academic emphasis in the school and in individual departments. Schools where the HT identified an inadequate academic ethos as a major challenge/problem faced by the school over the last five years exhibited significantly lower value added effects in terms of total GCSE performance (mean residual difference −1.84). This problem was reported by 53 per cent of HTs. The value added measures for English were also significantly lower in these schools. Differences were also found in relation to principal educational goals – positive effects in mathematics or English being associated with a goal of improving examination results (in the past) and 'ensuring each student obtains the highest qualifications possible'.

Headteachers were asked to rate the current and past emphasis placed on academic achievement in their English and mathematics departments. Again, views of English departments were the more positive, and views of the present situation in the school more favourable than the past. For example, over a third of HTs reported that their mathematics departments suffered from a 'fairly or very weak' emphasis on academic achievement five years before, whereas only 15 per cent reported this for English. Currently none rated their English departments as 'fairly or very weak', but just under one in ten thought this was still a problem for the mathematics department. The HTs' assessments of emphasis on academic achievement in the past and currently were significantly correlated with value added effects on total GCSE performance ($r=-0.35$ for English departments' past emphasis, $r=-0.32$ for mathematics departments' past emphasis). They were also related to subject effects in mathematics ($r=-0.40$ for present emphasis) and English ($r=-0.30$ for past emphasis).

In line with HTs, the HoDs' questionnaire responses drew attention to the benefits of having a strong academic focus. The emphasis placed on evaluating examination results by the English department was significantly related to value added measures of effectiveness ($r=-0.48$ [total GCSE score], $r=-0.34$ [English]). Similarly, in schools where English HoDs stated that a strong academic emphasis contributed to their department's effectiveness, value added effects on total GCSE performance and English were positive. By contrast, where English HoDs noted 'insufficient challenge for high ability students' as something which held their department back from being more effective (reported by just over one in five), value added results in terms of overall GCSE performance were poorer. The extent of past emphasis on teaching and learning also showed a strong correlation ($r=-0.53$ [English], $r=-0.49$ [tscore]) was likewise important ($r=-0.38$ for total GCSE score).

Schools where mathematics HoDs indicated that 'ensuring each student obtains the highest qualifications possible' was a principal educational goal in the past, recorded positive value added effects on total GCSE performance (mean residual difference 2.24). This was cited by a third. Also in line with English HoDs, where mathematics HoDs thought that examination results ought to be taken into account in judging school effectiveness, value added effects on total GCSE performance were significantly better (mean residual difference 2.14). Nonetheless, fewer items relating to academic emphasis from

Table 7.6 HTs' ratings of the past and present overall emphasis (quality and quantity) on homework for English and mathematics departments

n = 47	Present	Past*
a] English	%	%
Very high	14.9	2.1
Quite high	53.2	36.2
About average	31.9	42.6
Quite low	–	12.8
Very low	–	6.4
b] Mathematics		
Very high	12.8	6.7
Quite high	27.7	8.9
About average	55.3	48.9
Quite low	2.1	20.0
Very low	2.1	15.6

* Non-responses excluded

the HoDs' questionnaire were found to relate to departmental differences in value added results for mathematics than for English.

Homework

Homework was reported to be given a higher priority by both HTs and HoDs of more academically effective schools and departments. Homework provides an additional important indicator of academic emphasis at the secondary level. Table 7.6 shows HTs' ratings of past and present emphasis placed on homework in English and mathematics departments. Marked differences in practice can be inferred from the HTs' responses, with less than 16 per cent of mathematics departments rated highly in this area five years previously, compared with 38 per cent of English departments. The HTs' assessments of the overall emphasis – quality and quantity – of homework set by the mathematics department were significantly correlated with the value added measure for mathematics ($r=-0.44$ [present], $r=-0.46$ [past] emphasis). However, the HTs' ratings of emphasis on homework in English showed little relationship with value added measures, although there was a weak but significant association ($r=-0.29$) with the total GCSE performance. This may reflect the generally positive nature of these ratings which varied much less than for mathematics.

The HoDs' responses, in line with HTs, showed a great change in emphasis given to homework in the last five years. The applicability of the statement 'homework given a high priority' revealed that, in the past, nearly 37 per cent of English HoDs felt this was not very or not at all applicable to their department. For mathematics the figure was even higher at 51 per cent. However, only 15 per cent of English and less than 13 per cent of mathematics HoDs felt this description was not very applicable at present, supporting HTs' views of significant improvements in this area.

From the subject leaders' perspective, mathematics HoDs' rating of the current applicability of the statement 'homework given a high priority' showed a significant relationship with value added effects on total GCSE performance ($r=-0.48$). Likewise, for English HoDs, the applicability of this statement to their department in the past was strongly correlated with the total GCSE measure ($r=-0.53$) and English results ($r=-0.39$). Moreover, improved homework policy and practice – reported by the HoDs as a major success/ achievement of the mathematics department over the last five years – was also found to be significantly related to positive value added effects on total GCSE scores (mean residual difference 1.94). This was cited in 22 cases (over half of the sample).

Assessment

As was the case with homework, the analysis of links between HTs' and HoDs' questionnaire responses and our value added measures of academic effectiveness confirm the importance of student assessment. Thus HTs' ratings of the frequency of student assessment by teachers in the English and mathematics departments were correlated with the value added measures. The correlation with value added mathematics results and frequency of assessment by mathematics teachers in the past was strongest ($r=-0.48$), while frequency of student assessment by English teachers (past) was related to value added results for total GCSE score ($r=-0.38$).

Heads of department rated their satisfaction with their school's student assessment/monitoring system. For both English and mathematics respondents their level of satisfaction was correlated significantly with overall academic effectiveness. For English HoDs, satisfaction with the school's student assessment/monitoring system was also related to the value added subject performance measure for English ($r=-0.44$). In 47 per cent of English departments HoDs indicated that the statement 'strong emphasis on student assessment' was very applicable as a description of past practice in their department. In these schools value added results in terms of total GCSE performance were better ($r=-0.38$). For mathematics HoDs, their level of satisfaction with their school's past student assessment/monitoring system was also correlated with value added effects on total GCSE performance ($r=-0.34$).

As might be expected, a stronger focus on assessment was found in schools and departments which laid more emphasis on homework, both aspects contributing to the overall academic emphasis of both individual departments and the institution as a whole. This supports the findings of the earlier case studies (reported in Chapter 5).

3   Shared vision/goals

Additional evidence concerning the positive relationship between shared vision/goals and secondary schools' academic effectiveness was found from the analyses of both HTs' and HoDs' questionnaire responses. Two-thirds of HTs indicated that a shared belief by 'staff and students' that the school is primarily a place for teaching and learning' was an important factor contributing to their school's effectiveness. The value added measures for these schools were significantly different (mean residual difference 2.29, [total GCSE score]; mean residual difference 0.22, [English]). In nine cases, nearly a fifth of responses, the HT perceived that a 'lack of shared vision/goals' had been a major problem or challenge faced by their school during the last five years. The value added measures for total GCSE score and mathematics were somewhat lower in these institutions (p<0.06).

Findings from the HoDs' questionnaire survey also point to the importance of a shared vision/goals for specific subject results as well as for overall GCSE performance. This indicates that congruence in views and goals is likely to be very important for the effective functioning of individual departments and can also help to foster a more supportive school climate.

For both English and mathematics HoDs, the extent to which they felt the statement 'clear sense of direction' applied to their department was significantly correlated with the value added measures of academic effectiveness. In all, 35 per cent of English HoDs felt a clear sense of direction had been lacking in the past in their departments, compared with only 5 per cent at present. The link between a lack of clear direction in the past was strongest for English HoDs' responses (r=−0.49 [total GCSE score], r=−0.54 [English]). By contrast, mathematics HoDs were less likely than their English counterparts to indicate that their department had lacked a clear sense of direction five years ago (18.4 per cent reported this for the past and 7.5 per cent currently). The correlation for this item was significant in relation to current lack of clear direction (r=−0.33 [total GCSE score], r=−0.32 [mathematics]).

Closely related to a sense of direction was the item concerning teaching staff unity in the department. Disunity was reported as a feature of their department by over 40 per cent of English HoDs in the past and 36 per cent of mathematics HoDs. Currently, however, only 10 per cent of each group felt this was still the case. The extent to which the statement 'disunited teaching staff' was seen as applicable correlated with effectiveness in terms of total GCSE score for both English and mathematics HoDs (r=0.39 and r=0.33 respectively). The relationships with subject results were in the same direction but weaker (p<0.08) for mathematics.

The extent of 'shared values/goals by all/most teaching staff in the department' was seen to have altered markedly over the last five years by both English and mathematics HoDs. In all, 50 per cent of English and 58 per cent of mathematics HoDs felt this statement was not very applicable to their department in the past compared with current figures of only 10 and 13 per cent. This item correlated with value added subject results (r=−0.42 for English [HoDs' rating of past] and r=−0.37 for mathematics [HoDs' rating of present]).

In the six schools (15 per cent) where mathematics HoDs indicated that 'congruence of educational views and goals amongst teaching staff' was an important factor contributing to the effectiveness of their department, value added mathematics results were better. By contrast, in another six schools where 'lack of consensus in educational philosophy/goals in the department' was seen as holding the department back from greater effectiveness, both total GCSE performance and mathematics results were poorer (mean residual difference −2.84 [total GCSE performance], −0.37 [mathematics]).

In schools where mathematics HoDs reported that 'staff and students shared belief that the school is primarily a place for teaching and learning' was one of the factors which contributed most to the effectiveness of their school, value added effects on total GCSE performance were significantly higher (mean residual difference 2.11, p<0.05), in line with the results for HTs.

For English HoDs, the extent to which the item 'full involvement with whole school policies' applied to their department was weakly correlated with effects on total GCSE performance (p<0.08). By contrast, where they indicated that greater 'departmental cohesiveness' was an area in which there had been success over the last five years, value added effects on total GCSE were significantly poorer (mean residual difference −2.54). This probably reflects a problem of lack of cohesiveness in the past. It should be remembered that our value added measures were also retrospective − based on the 1990–92 GCSE cohorts. Similarly, where English HoDs reported that 'disagreement amongst staff about student grouping policy' had been a major problem/challenge for their department over the last five years, those departments recorded significantly poorer effects on total GCSE performance (mean residual difference −2.18). A similar pattern emerged where English HoDs indicated that differences between individual departments' teaching style within their school was a major factor holding their department back from being more effective, with poorer GCSE performance evident.

Items which provide indicators of the existence of shared vision/goals were also related to those which indicate the extent of consistency in approach, and the two can be seen to be inextricably linked − consistency in practice being dependent in large part upon the existence of shared vision/goals. The creation of shared vision/goals is also a feature of positive leadership by senior as well as middle managers, as we discuss below.

4   Clear leadership

The importance of both HTs' and HoDs' leadership for the effective delivery of teaching and learning in schools and individual departments was highlighted by the case study data (Chapter 5). The questionnaire results support this conclusion. Overall, HTs were far more satisfied with the current than the past leadership of HoDs of both mathematics and English, although, in line with earlier findings, their views of mathematics were less positive. It should be remembered that a substantial minority of departments had undergone a change of HoD in the last five years and this is likely to have influenced respondents' views. In all nearly 46 per cent of mathematics HoDs' leadership was rated as 'not very good or poor' in the past, compared with only 22 per cent of English HoDs, as can be seen in Table 7.7.

Table 7.7   HTs' assessments of leadership of HoDs of English and mathematics

n = 47	Present	Past*
a] English	%	%
Good	26.1	31.1
Fairly good	34.8	20.0
About average	23.9	26.7
Not very good	13.0	13.3
Poor	2.2	8.9
b] Mathematics		
Good	23.9	15.2
Fairly good	21.7	10.9
About average	26.1	28.3
Not very good	19.6	21.7
Poor	8.7	23.9

* Non-responses excluded

The HTs' assessment of mathematics HoDs' leadership was correlated with effectiveness in promoting mathematics performance (r=–0.50, [now]; r=–0.45, [past]. Similar results were found for the HTs' rating of mathematics HoDs' effectiveness and, to a lesser extent, commitment. These three aspects were closely related, as would be expected. The HTs' ratings of English HoDs, though in the same direction, were weakly and not significantly related to effects on English.

In many schools (79 per cent), HTs reported that 'poor leadership by some HoDs' was one of the major problems/challenges faced by their school over the last five years. This item was weakly associated with poorer English results (p<0.08). Likewise, where HTs perceived that poor leadership by some HoDs was a major factor holding their school back from being more effective (reported by 72 per cent), performance in mathematics was lower (mean residual difference –0.14). Nearly 30 per cent of HTs, all of whom had taken up post within the last five years, indicated that inadequate leadership by their own predecessor had been a major weakness/challenge which had to be faced by their school in the past. In these schools poorer effects in English were identified (mean residual difference –0.28).

The HoDs' questionnaire responses revealed a significant relationship between their overall satisfaction with the performance of HoDs in their school in the past and the value added measures of academic effectiveness, particularly total GCSE performance score (r=–0.42 [mathematics HoDs]). In addition, for HoDs of English departments, where poor leadership of the previous HoD had been identified as a major problem/challenge faced by the department in the last five years, poorer effects on English were found (mean residual difference –0.26).

Introducing new ideas was an aspect of their leadership identified as important for English HoDs (mean residual difference 1.54, [tscore]). By contrast, in schools where English HoDs indicated that supporting staff was an important

Table 7.8 HoDs' satisfaction with leadership of their school

		Present	Past*
a] **English**	[n = 39]	%	%
Very satisfied		33.3	21.1
Quite satisfied		28.3	23.7
Varies		33.3	36.8
Not very satisfied		5.1	15.8
Very dissatisfied		–	2.6
b] **Mathematics**	[n = 40]		
Very satisfied		17.9	10.8
Quite satisfied		46.2	27.8
Varies		25.6	48.6
Not very satisfied		5.1	10.8
Very dissatisfied		5.1	2.7

* Non-responses excluded

aspect of their work, effects were negative (mean residual difference -1.56, [tscore]; -0.15 [English]). This may possibly be an indication that staff who were weak were seen to need more support.

Schools where mathematics HoDs indicated that considerable involvement in 'curriculum planning' was an important feature of their role had better effects on total GCSE performance score (mean residual difference 1.85). Where mathematics HoDs described their leadership approach as 'persuasion rather than coercion', however, negative effects on mathematics performance (mean residual difference -0.23) were recorded. In all, 37 per cent of mathematics HoDs chose this description.

The impact of the HT leadership in relation to the academic effectiveness of the school was also supported by HoDs' responses. Over 60 per cent of English and mathematics HoDs were satisfied with the quality of HT leadership now, a higher proportion than five years before, as can be seen in Table 7.8.

Schools where English HoDs were more satisfied with leadership both now and in the past had better effects on total GCSE performance ($r=-0.40$) and somewhat higher English results [p<0.08]. Similarly, schools where mathematics HoDs drew attention to the quality of the HT's leadership as a major factor contributing to the effectiveness of their school – noted by over 47 per cent of respondents – recorded slightly better effects on total GCSE performance (p<0.08).

In connection with the HT's leadership approach, it is interesting to note that in the eight cases (20 per cent) where 'considerable teacher involvement in decision making' was cited by mathematics HoDs as a key factor contributing to their school effectiveness, there was a significantly *lower* effect on students' total GCSE performance (mean residual difference -1.94).

There was also evidence that schools where HTs had spent more time as a DHT exhibited a more positive impact in terms of our value added measures of total GCSE performance (r=0.38), suggesting that experience gained as a DHT is likely to have assisted HTs in developing leadership and management skills.

5 An effective SMT

Our case studies drew attention to the impact of the SMT in relation to schools' academic effectiveness and the questionnaire analyses support this conclusion. In four schools (9 per cent) HTs indicated that conflict within their school's SMT was a major factor holding back their school. The value added measure of total GCSE performance for these schools were significantly lower (mean residual difference –2.39).

Responses by HoDs likewise drew attention to the impact of the SMT. For example, schools where English HoDs highlighted 'a strong cohesive SMT' as one of the most important factors contributing to the effectiveness of their school (noted by 41 per cent) were more effective in promoting total GCSE performance (mean residual difference 1.87, [tscore]; 0.16, [English]). By contrast, in eight cases (20.5 per cent) English HoDs indicated that 'SMT support not always present' was a major factor holding their department back from being more effective. This was associated with a negative value added impact on total GCSE performance (mean residual difference –1.90).

Nearly half of English HoDs were quite or very satisfied with the SMT, a higher figure than their mathematics counterparts (nearly 37 per cent). Both groups' views of the present were rather more favourable than of their SMT five years before. English and mathematics HoDs' levels of satisfaction with the current and past performance of their school's SMT were significantly correlated with the value added measures of academic effectiveness (r=–0.50, [English HoDs' past satisfaction with the SMT and tscore]; r=–0.41 [mathematics HoDs' past satisfaction with the SMT and tscore]). In addition, satisfaction with their school's organization in the past was also related to value added effects on total GCSE performance score (r=–0.45, [English HoDs]). As would be expected, middle managers' satisfaction with the performance of the SMT and with their school's organization were themselves also closely related.

6 Consistency in approach

The importance of shared vision/goals, high expectations and an academic emphasis have already been noted. Our case studies suggested that greater consistency in policy and practice was also a feature of more effective schools and more effective departments (see Chapter 5). Of course, consistency in approach is also more likely where the SMT and staff have a shared vision/goals and will be influenced by the leadership of the HT and SMT, as well as by HoDs at the departmental level. The questionnaire survey also indicates that a consistent whole school approach to student behaviour and discipline was very important for academic success. For example, in the twenty-six schools (55 per cent) where HTs indicated that an 'inconsistent approach to student behaviour and discipline matters' had been a major problem/challenge faced by their school over the last five years, value added effects were lower (mean residual difference of –1.87, [tscore]; –0.13, p<0.08 [English]; –0.17, [mathematics]).

In all, 40 per cent of HTs identified an 'inconsistent approach to student behaviour/discipline' as a major factor holding their school back from being more effective. In these schools effects on mathematics were poorer (mean residual difference of –0.21). A similar association was found where an 'inconsistent approach to student assessment' was cited as a major factor holding the school back from being more effective, a problem noted by 30 per cent of HTs.

English HoDs' responses also drew attention to the importance of consistency in homework and marking policies at the departmental level, especially in relation to past practice. The correlation with value added effects on English was significant (r=–0.48 for marking and –0.38 for homework). The relationship between past consistency in approaches to homework and marking in the English department and schools' general academic effectiveness was even stronger (r=–0.61 [homework] and r=–0.57 [marking]). Consistency in practice in these areas currently was also identified as having a significant correlation with the value added measures of academic effectiveness from the mathematics HoDs' responses. The correlation between consistently applied marking policy and mathematics results was strong (r=–0.51).

The extent of consistency in homework and marking practice was reported to have changed markedly over the last five years. In all, over two-thirds of mathematics HODs said consistency was not very or not at all applicable as a description of past practice in these areas in their department compared with 15 per cent (homework) and 28 per cent (marking) now. For English, over 50 per cent of HoDs reported consistency was not applicable in relation to either area in the past, compared with current figures of 18 per cent (homework) and 13 per cent (marking). This may represent the impact of the introduction of the NC and NA.

7   Quality of teaching

Headteachers' views

Academic emphasis, teacher expectations and consistency in practice can be seen as influences on the quality of teaching in a school and in specific departments. Our analysis of associations between HTs' and HoDs' questionnaire responses and the value added measures of school effectiveness, however, draw strong attention to the quality of teaching in the school as a whole and in individual departments in their own right. For example, in schools where HTs indicated that 'poor quality teaching in some departments' was a key factor holding their school back from being more effective – noted by just over half of the respondents – effects on students' total GCSE performance were poorer than in other schools (mean residual difference = –1.49). Table 7.9 shows HTs' assessments of the past and present quality of teaching in their schools' English

Table 7.9 HTs' assessments of the quality of teaching in English and mathematics departments

n = 47	Present	Past*
a] English	%	%
Good	42.6	13.6
Fairly good	40.4	40.9
About average	10.6	25.0
Not very good	2.1	15.9
Poor/very variable	4.3	4.5
b] Mathematics		
Good	13.0	–
Fairly good	23.9	15.9
About average	41.3	29.5
Not very good	15.2	31.8
Poor/very variable	6.5	22.7

* Non-responses excluded

and mathematics departments. The quality of teaching was seen to have improved over the last five years and English was again rated more favourably than mathematics in terms of quality of teaching. HTs' assessments of the past and present quality of teaching in the English and mathematics departments were significantly correlated with our value added measures of GCSE. The HT's assessment of the quality of teaching in the English department in the past was significantly correlated with the value added measures of effectiveness (r=–0.31 [tscore], r=–0.28, p<0.08 [English]. For mathematics, the relationship was similar for both the current and past assessment of teaching quality and effects on mathematics (e.g. r=–0.37 [present], r=–0.34 [past]).

The HT's assessment of English and mathematics staff's past performance in terms of 'exercise effective control over students (firm but friendly relations)' was also associated with the effectiveness measures. For example, the correlation with HTs' assessment of effective control was r=–0.31 (tscore) and r=–0.34, (English) for English. For mathematics, the correlation was r=–0.27, p<0.08 (tscore), r=–0.43 (mathematics). The associations with the HTs' assessment of teacher enthusiasm in these departments were also significant for mathematics staff (r =–0.45 [mathematics]) though weaker for English staff (r =–0.29, [tscore]).

Table 7.10 shows HTs' reports of the use of student grouping policies in English and mathematics departments. It can be seen that mixed ability approaches were more common in the past. Mixed ability approaches remained the predominant approach to student grouping for English departments currently (1995) but only one in five of mathematics departments remained mixed ability throughout.

In terms of student grouping practices, the HT questionnaires indicated that a wider use of setting rather than mixed ability teaching by the English department in the past was associated with positive value added effects on total

Table 7.10   HTs' reports of the use of different student grouping policies

n = 47	Present	Past*
a] English	%	%
Mixed ability throughout	66.0	70.2
Mixed ability (set Y10 & 11)	17.0	12.8
Mixed ability (set Y9, 10 & 11)	4.3	4.3
Set by ability (except Y7)	10.6	4.3
Set by ability throughout	2.1	4.3
Other	–	4.3
b] Mathematics		
Mixed ability throughout	21.3	48.9
Mixed ability (set Y10 & 11)	14.9	14.9
Mixed ability (set Y9, 10 & 11)	29.8	10.6
Set by ability (except Y7)	27.7	12.8
Set by ability throughout	4.3	4.3
Other	2.1	6.4

* Non-responses excluded

GCSE performance and on English (r=–0.33 [tscore], r=–0.32 [English]). A greater emphasis on setting by mathematics department as reported by the HT was also correlated with better value added results in terms of overall GCSE scores (r=–0.31), but was unrelated to effectiveness in mathematics results.

HoDs' views

As might be expected, the HoDs' assessments of teaching quality and practices were significantly associated with value added effects on their department's subject results. In addition, the English HoDs' assessments of aspects of teaching in the English department were also found to be significantly related to the school's effects on total GCSE performance – again indicating the importance of this department as an influence on the school's general academic effectiveness at GCSE.

The English HoDs' overall assessments of the quality of teaching in the English department in the past was significantly correlated with value added measures of performance (r=–0.45, [tscore], r=–0.49, [English]). Likewise, their general satisfaction with their school's teaching staff in the past was also correlated, particularly for total GCSE performance (r=–0.67). In schools where English HoDs cited 'better staff' as a major success/achievement of their department over the last five years, effectiveness in terms of total GCSE and English results was poorer, presumably reflecting the existence of major staff problems in the past (mean residual difference –1.49, [tscore], –0.17 [English]).

The English HoDs' responses also provide guidance regarding particular features of more effective teaching practices. For example, in line with the HT analysis, the importance of effective control – firm, but friendly relations – particularly in the past is evident (r=0.51, [English]. A 'strong emphasis on

Table 7.11 Aspects of teacher performance correlated with value added effects total GCSE performance and English scores: English HoDs' judgements*

n = 39		tscore	English
Work focus of lessons (keep most students on task most of the time)	past	−0.34	−0.46
Making subject interesting/relevant	past	−0.30+	ns
Clarity of goals for student learning	past	−0.40	−0.47
Promptness starting/finishing lessons	past	−0.53	−0.39
Student responsibility/independent learning is encouraged	past	ns	−0.38
Planning of lesson material	past	−0.36	−0.41
Lessons generally challenge students of *all* ability levels	past	−0.47	−0.51
Staff qualifications for teaching the subject	past	−0.39	−0.42
Knowledge of content of subject	past	−0.36	−0.49
Knowledge of content of GCSE exam syllabus	past	−0.43	−0.39
Staff experience of teaching the subject	past	−0.40	−0.48
Teacher enthusiasm	past	ns	−0.46
Hard working teaching staff	past	−0.51	−0.39

All items were rated from 1 'good' to 5 'poor'
+ p<0.08 – all other p<0.05
* Non-responses excluded

giving students constructive feedback' was also significantly associated with positive value added effects on tscore and English (r=−0.37, r=−0.35). The quality of teacher-student relationships is also relevant. The HoDs' assessment of these in the past was associated with both effectiveness measures (r=−0.33 [tscore], r=-0.46 [English]). Likewise, strong emphasis on student assessment in the English department in the past was also related to school effects on total GCSE performance score (r=−0.38).

Aspects of teacher organization such as planning of lessons and punctuality in starting and finishing lessons then were also correlated with our value added measures of academic effectiveness, as was attention to ensure that lessons challenge students of all ability levels. A strong work focus to lessons and clarity in goals for student learning were also associated with better value added results at GCSE, as can be seen in Table 7.11.

Unsurprisingly, indicators of the quality of teaching staff were found to be relevant. The HoDs' assessment of staff experience of teaching their subject, their qualifications for teaching the subject and knowledge of the content of the subject and of the GCSE examination syllabus were all significantly associated with value added effects on total GCSE performance and English. Likewise, teacher enthusiasm and a 'hard working' teaching staff were also related to our measures of academic effectiveness at GCSE.

Other factors identified as significant from the English HoDs' interviews were low levels of staff shortages in the English department in the past (r=0.36, [tscore], r=0.32 [English]) and, more strongly, low levels of teacher absence in the past (r=0.62, [tscore], r=0.40 [English]).

Fewer items from the HoDs of mathematics than the English HoDs' questionnaire were found to be significantly associated with schools' effects on total GCSE performance score or mathematics. Nonetheless, the results suggest the importance of quality of teaching. For example, the mathematics HoDs' level of past satisfaction with their schools' teaching staff was correlated with the effects on total GCSE performance (r=−0.39). Mathematics HoDs' assessment of the extent to which the descriptive statement 'high quality teaching in all/most cases' applied to their department five years before was also related to school effects on mathematics (r=−0.43). In the fourteen schools (35 per cent) where mathematics HoDs identified 'insufficient high quality teaching in some cases' as a key factor holding their department back from being more effective, value added effects on mathematics were depressed (mean residual difference −0.28).

Teachers' use of student feedback was also found to be associated with effectiveness. In the ten cases (25 per cent) where the HoD identified 'insufficient feedback on work to students' as a key factor holding their department back, poorer value added effects on both overall GCSE (p<0.08) and mathematics results were identified (−0.23, [mathematics]). In addition, the applicability of the statement 'strong emphasis on giving students constructive feedback' was correlated with the overall academic effectiveness (r=−0.31, [tscore]), in line with findings for English.

Promptness in starting and finishing lessons by mathematics department staff in the past was correlated with the school's academic effectiveness (r=−0.43, [tscore]), but not with mathematics results specifically, suggesting this factor may simply operate more generally as an aspect of the school's climate.

A small number (from six schools or 15 per cent) of mathematics HoDs identified 'insufficient emphasis on student assessment' as a key factor preventing greater effectiveness. In these cases value added effects on mathematics were poorer (mean residual difference −0.34). Likewise, the extent of emphasis on 'achievement for all ability levels' (now) was associated with better effects on mathematics performance (r=−0.34). The HoD of mathematics assessment of the current work focus of lessons was also found to be important (r=−0.35, [mathematics]).

Where HoDs of mathematics identified curriculum planning as an important feature of their role, total GCSE performance (as measure by value added residuals) was better (mean residual difference 1.85) but no clear association with mathematics performance was found. Moreover, in departments where teaching and learning was said to be regularly discussed, poorer mathematics effects were currently to be found (r=−0.34). This item referred to current practice, the equivalent item concerning the situation five years before was not associated with any effectiveness measure. It is possible that the relationship may indicate that teaching and learning were regularly discussed because of awareness of low past performance and may be linked with a need to develop shared vision/goals.

The HoD of mathematics' responses indicated only a weak relationship between the extent to which 'student responsibility/independent learning is encouraged', in the past and effects on mathematics performance (p<0.08). However, in schools where mathematics HoDs indicated that 'promoting students ability to learn independently' was a principal goal of the school in the past, poorer effects on mathematics were found (mean residual difference – 0.28). In this case, however, it was associated with a lower emphasis on qualifications as a principal goal of the school.

As with English HoDs, low levels of staff shortage in the mathematics department – both now and five years before – were associated positively with effects on mathematics (r=0.36 [now], r=0.35 [past]). Likewise, low levels of staff absence in the past in the school as a whole (as reported by the HoD of mathematics) were correlated with greater effectiveness (r=0.40, [tscore]) and in the mathematics department in the past were also associated with better effects on mathematics (r=0.30). In contrast to results for English, however, HoDs' ratings of staff experience of teaching the subject and their qualifications were not correlated with effectiveness in promoting students' subject performance in mathematics. Nonetheless, a weak relationship with the item 'teachers' knowledge of the content of the subject' were found.

High staff morale can be seen as an indicator of an effective and well-managed school. Conversely lower staff morale may be a reflection of ineffectiveness in organization as much as a factor which can influence teaching quality, students' motivation and academic performance directly. The case studies had shown that low staff morale was a feature of less academically effective schools and the questionnaire results likewise revealed a significant association, particularly in the past. For example, the HTs' satisfaction with staff morale in the past was significantly related to effects on total GCSE performance (r=–0.31). The HoDs' satisfaction levels also demonstrated a significant association with this outcome (r =–0.48 [HoDs English]; r=–0.48 [HoDs mathematics]). In addition, HoDs' satisfaction levels with staff morale were also significantly correlated with effects on their departments' subject performance, although more weakly.

Student grouping
Student grouping policy in the English department, as reported by the HoD, was not significantly correlated with effectiveness in promoting English, but was associated with better effects on total GCSE performance score. A greater use of setting in English, especially in the past, was linked with positive value added effects on overall GCSE results (r=0.55). This is in line with the findings from the HT questionnaire. It should be noted that schools which set for English are more likely to set for other subjects also. This factor may therefore be indicative of greater consistency in approach at this school level.

Although a greater use of setting in the past was found to be associated with greater effectiveness for total GCSE performance score and English (in the HT and English HoDs analysis), the correlation for mathematics was weakly negative (p<0.08). It should be noted that, overall, setting was more common in mathematics than English departments.

On the whole, our results demonstrate the importance of high quality teaching for overall GCSE performance and performance in specific subjects. However, the associations between specific aspects of teaching behaviour and value added effects were somewhat closer for past practice in English departments and both total GCSE performance and subject performance in English than was the case for mathematics. Our case studies suggested that student grouping practices were not a major factor in accounting for differences in effectiveness (Chapter 5), however, the questionnaire results for a larger sample of schools indicate that setting may be important for overall GCSE results. The findings for mathematics were not in line with this trend, however, and therefore firm conclusions should not be drawn.

8   Student-focused approach

A student-focused approach, in terms of an academic emphasis and high teacher expectations for student performance, has already been highlighted. Other results pointed to the importance of focusing on students and their experiences of schooling. For example, the quality of teacher-student relationships was associated with the value added measures of schools' academic effectiveness. Good relationships in the past (as assessed by English HoDs) were associated with significantly better value added results on total GCSE performance and English ($r=-0.33$ [tscore], $r=-0.46$ [English]).

The primacy of promoting academic goals for students has been discussed in connection with Factor 2 (Academic Emphasis), and also the value of shared vision and goals, including a shared belief by staff and students alike that the school is primarily a place for teaching and learning. Other goals were also associated with the academic effectiveness measures. For example, where HTs reported that 'a caring pastoral environment' ought to be taken into account in judging any school's effectiveness, significantly better effects on GCSE performance were identified (mean residual difference 1.83). This was cited by fourteen (30 per cent) of HTs. Also in the eighteen cases (46 per cent of responses) where HoDs of English thought that a caring pastoral environment ought to be taken into account in judging the effectiveness of any secondary school, value added effects on English and overall GCSE results were also found to be weakly positive ($p<0.08$).

The HoDs' satisfaction with the school's pastoral staff both past and present was associated with greater academic effectiveness. For mathematics HoDs, the extent of satisfaction in the past was associated with effects on total GCSE performance ($r=-0.32$). For English HoDs the correlations with this item were stronger for current than past satisfaction ($r=-0.42$ [tscore], $r=-0.31$ [English]).

In all, twenty-five (63 per cent) of HoDs of mathematics felt that the 'enjoyment/interest of students' was an important factor which ought to be taken into account in judging the effectiveness of any department. In these schools value added effects on total GCSE performance score were also higher (mean residual difference 1.35). Also, where the HT stressed 'students feel valued as people' as one of the key factors which contributed to the effectiveness of their school, effects on total GCSE performance were positive (mean residual difference 1.73). This was noted by twenty-five HTs or 53 per cent of respondents. Currently, nearly 43 per cent of HTs stressed promoting student responsibility as a principal educational goal of their school and value added effects on students' mathematics performance were higher (mean residual difference 0.19) in these schools. 'The encouragement of a positive attitude to school' identified by HoDs of mathematics as a factor which ought to be taken into account in judging the effectiveness of any school, was also weakly associated with positive effects on mathematics ($p<0.08$).

Two-thirds of HTs reported that 'maintaining good standards of behaviour and attendance' was a principal educational goal in the past, but more than eight in ten emphasized this currently. Positive effects on mathematics were identified in schools where this factor was indicated as a principal educational goal five years ago (mean residual difference 0.20), and likewise, where HoDs of mathematics stressed this item as a principal educational goal in the past, weak ($p<0.08$) but positive effects on total GCSE performance score were found.

By contrast, other items showed a less clear pattern. For example, where 'emphasizing equal opportunities' was identified as a principal educational goal of the school by HoDs of English currently (reported by 64 per cent of respondents), the association with value added effects on total GCSE performance score was negative (mean residual difference past –1.98, [tscore], –1.69, [English]). A similar result emerged for mathematics HoDs, although the association was weaker ($p<0.08$). It is possible that this association may reflect a lower emphasis on academic achievement or lower expectations for students' academic achievement. However, it is also possible that an awareness of poor academic results has led schools to focus on equal opportunities now. Thus, it is not possible to say whether the current attention paid to this factor distracted from academic aims, or was a response to problems in the past.

By contrast, in schools where mathematics HoDs identified 'increasing student self confidence' and 'promoting student progress' as principal educational goals (present), positive school effects on total GCSE performance were found (mean residual difference 1.68, and 1.71 respectively). However, 'developing self-respect' as a principal goal in the past was associated with poorer value added results for mathematics (mean residual difference –0.25). Also in a quarter of cases where English HoDs reported that 'preparing students for the world of work' had been a principal goal of the school in the past (noted by ten respondents) or was currently a goal, effects on total GCSE performance were lower (mean residual difference –1.57, [past], –1.09, $p<0.08$ [present]). These factors tended to be reported by schools where a lower priority was given to student progress and qualifications in terms of principal goals. We can conclude, therefore, that an emphasis on academic matters remains important for all schools, as well as a focus on students' affective development.

9   Parental support/involvement

Our case studies of more and less effective schools indicated the existence of differences between schools in staff perceptions of parental interest and involvement in their children's education and support for the school. All cited examples of ways in which they were attempting to improve home-school relationships, but, in the more effective schools, views of parental support and involvement tended to be much more positive. The analyses of questionnaire responses also drew attention to this factor. For example, in schools where HTs noted greater parental involvement as a major success of the school over the last five years (reported by 40 per cent) positive effects were identified for English (mean residual difference 0.14).

In all, one in five HTs commented on 'strong support from parents/community' as a key factor contributing to their school's effectiveness. This was associated with better effects on total GCSE performance and English (mean residual difference 2.05, [tscore]; 0.17, [English]). Correlations between the HT's level of satisfaction current and past with the school in terms of parent/community support were also significant (r=–0.42 [tscore]; r=–0.32 [English]).

For HoDs of English and mathematics, the findings were similar to those noted in relation to HTs' responses. Correlations between satisfaction levels and value added results were strongest for satisfaction with parental support in the past for both English (r=–0.63 [tscore]; r=–0.37 [English]); and mathematics HoDs (r=–0.47, [tscore]). In addition, an association between the identification of 'strong support from parents/community' as a key factor contributing to the school's effectiveness and better total GCSE performance was noted for both English and mathematics HoDs (mean residual differences of 1.79 and 2.00 respectively). By contrast, where mathematics HoDs identified 'little parental/community support for school' as a key factor holding their department back from being more effective, school effects on total GCSE performance were lower (mean residual difference –1.59).

We can conclude that practitioners' perceptions of parental/community support are significantly related to the value added measures of schools' effectiveness, but the meaning of this relationship is not completely clear. It can be seen to link with low expectations and may provide an indicator of a tendency to lay the blame and responsibility for poor performance on elements outside the school. This was a major problem indicated by some respondents in the case study interviews (Chapter 5) and written comments on some questionnaires. However, it is important to recognize that some schools are more advantaged than others in terms of parental support and involvement. Moreover, some others devote a great deal more energy to promoting such involvement and attach a higher priority to it.

Coleman *et al.* (1994) have drawn particular attention to the interconnectedness of the affective and cognitive domains in the triad of relationships between teacher, parent and student. MacBeath (1994) has also highlighted the benefits derived from the involvement of parents and demands made on them by successful schools.

Other factors

Effective functioning of departments

The questionnaire survey in Phase 3 confirmed the importance of effective departmental functioning in promoting students' academic outcomes, both in terms of total GCSE performance and in specific subjects. In addition to high expectations amongst staff in individual departments, a strong academic emphasis, quality of teaching, the existence of a shared vision/goals and the HoD's leadership – all of which influence the work of individual departments – three further aspects of departmental functioning were found to be relevant. These are teamwork, staff morale and staff absence/shortages.

Most HoDs indicated that improvements in teamwork had been a major success for their department during the last five years (87 per cent of English and 85 per cent of mathematics HoDs). For mathematics departments, this was positively related to the value added measures for that subject (mean residual difference 0.28). Likewise where mathematics HoDs identified teamwork as a major contributing factor for greater effectiveness (noted by over 77 per cent), weak positive effects on performance were found (p<0.08). However, in the case of English HoDs, in schools where greater teamwork over the last five years was noted as a major achievement/success, value added results in terms of GCSE performance were lower (mean residual difference – 3.81). The interpretation of this finding is not clear. It may be related to the retrospective nature of the study. In the five schools where English HODs did not comment on improvements in teamwork, this may have been a positive feature already, whereas for the six mathematics departments which did not report improvements in teamwork, the results may have indicated the continuation of pre-existing severe problems in this area. Our qualitative case studies emphasized the benefits of teamwork and the importance HoDs attached to developing and monitoring this.

Student mobility and falling rolls

High levels of student mobility and falling student rolls were factors which were found to be significantly associated with negative value added school effects on academic outcomes. These factors can be interpreted in two ways: as external factors exerting a direct influence on the learning environment, or as outcomes in their own right. For example, student mobility may be a reflection of parental or student dissatisfaction and it is also possible that this factor may operate in both ways simultaneously in some schools. HTs rated the level of student turnover/mobility in their school on a scale from 1 (very high) to 5 (very low). The correlations between low current mobility levels and the measures of school effects on academic outcomes were stronger than those in the past, in contrast to the pattern for many of the process variables (r=0.42, [tscore], r=0.35, [English]).

A falling roll was also associated with negative effects. Where HTs identified this as a major problem/challenge faced by the school over the last five years (noted by eight HTs or 17 per cent), poorer results in mathematics were found (mean residual difference –0.29). In addition, in the five schools (around 11 per cent) where HTs identified a 'falling student roll' as a key factor holding their school back from being more effective, effects on both total GCSE performance and mathematics were worse (mean residual difference –2.17, [tscore], –0.32, [mathematics]). The threat of school closure, itself closely related to falling rolls, also had an adverse impact. This was associated with poorer effects in terms of total GCSE performance score (mean residual difference –1.97) and mathematics (mean residual difference –0.30).

ACCOUNTING FOR VARIATIONS BETWEEN SCHOOLS IN GCSE PERFORMANCE

Turning from the description of patterns of association between different process items and our value added measures of effectiveness, we give a non-technical account of the way we used multilevel models to test the extent to which these items can be used to explain, in a statistical sense, the differences between schools in students' GCSE outcomes. Sixty-four HT variables, 68 English HoD variables and 68 mathematics HoD variables were selected as strongly significantly associated with our value added estimates of academic effectiveness at GCSE – total performance score (tscore), English and mathematics. These questionnaire items were tested individually using multilevel models to establish whether they had a significant impact in reducing school level variance in the relevant outcome measures (tscore, English, and mathematics).

In order to identify which combination of items provided the best fit in terms of statistical explanation of variance in students' performance at the school level, items identified as significant were then tested jointly. For each item all cases with missing data were excluded. Variables identified as significant for each group of respondents (HT, English HoDs, mathematics HoDs) were then tested separately to maximize the number of schools included in each analysis and to enable the comparison of results for each group. The HT items identified as significant were tested against three outcome measures (tscore, mathematics and English). For the HoD analyses, items identified as significant were tested against tscore and English for English HoDs or tscore and mathematics (for mathematics HoDs).

A total of seven separate models (three for tscore and two each for English and mathematics) were compared. In each model a different number of schools were included in the analyses, reflecting the different response rates for HTs and HoDs to the questionnaire survey. In each case process variables which were found to have a significant impact on the reduction of school level variance were retained in the final models. Tables in Appendix 2 illustrate some of the results of the multilevel models used. For further details of the analysis strategy see Sammons *et al.* (1995a and b). In the next section we describe the key results of the multilevel analysis in terms of the three value added measures in turn.

Total GCSE performance score

Over a third of the HT items tested were found to show statistically significant relationships with students' total GCSE performance score, when included in a multilevel model, which controlled for prior attainment and background. Six were also found to be significant both individually and in combination. Our model, based on 46 schools and 9047 students, accounted for a substantial proportion (over two-thirds) of the school level variation in students' GCSE performance.

Our analyses of models which tested items derived from the HoDs question-naires likewise demonstrated that process items accounted for most – over 85 per cent – of the school level variation in students' total GCSE performance not attributable to intake factors (prior attainment and student background charac-teristics). For English HoDs responses, a total of 24 items were found to have a significant impact on total GCSE performance scores when tested individually, and 6 were found to be significant when tested in combination. The analysis of mathematics HoDs items showed that of the 64, 18 had a significant impact tested individually, and 5 when tested in combination.

It should be remembered that, because most of the process items were them-selves closely interrelated, only a small number were retained in the final multi-level models as making a significant contribution to the explanation of variance.[5]

Headteacher variables
- Strong support from parents/community (+) (identified as a key factor con-tributing to the effectiveness of their school by HT)
- Falling student roll (–) (identified as a key factor holding their school back from being more effective by HT)
- Weak academic emphasis of English department five years before (–) (HT's rating)
- Students feel valued (+) (identified as a key factor contributing to the effec-tiveness of their school by HT)
- Clear and consistently applied whole-school approach to student behaviour and discipline (+) (identified as a key factor contributing to the effectiveness of their school by HT)
- Pressure of external change (e.g. NC, LMS) (+) (identified as a key factor holding their school back from being more effective by HT).

The items identified in this multilevel analysis emphasize the benefits of sup-port from parents/community, affective goals, a strong academic emphasis in the English department and the negative impact of a falling roll. The last factor, pressure of external change, although identified by HTs as a barrier to effective-ness, had a positive impact when tested individually and in combination. However, the impact of this is in line with findings from the case studies (Chapter 5). These indicated that, in the academically more effective schools, outside factors were more likely to be identified as problem areas, whereas in less effective schools major internal difficulties focused the attention of HTs.

English Head of Department variables
In all six items from the English HoDs survey were also found to be significant in accounting for the school level variation in total GCSE performance, both individually and in combination. This model was based on 35 schools and 7,593 students.

- A strong cohesive SMT (+) (identified as a key factor contributing to the effectiveness of their school by HoD English)
- Dissatisfaction with performance of school's teaching staff (–) (HoD English's rating of school's teaching staff five years before)
- Absence of staff shortages in school (+) (HoD English's rating of shortages five years before)
- Introducing new ideas (+) (identified as a key feature of HoD's role by HoD of English)
- Teaching staff expectations for student behaviour poor (–) (HoD English's assessment of English staff's expectations five years before)
- Low level of staff absence (+) (HoD English's rating of level of English teaching staff absence five years before).

The English HoD analyses draws attention to the importance of high teacher expectations and quality. The adverse impact of staff shortages in the school and of staff absence in the English department in the past are highlighted. The SMT is also identified as a significant influence, as was one item concerning the HoDs' role in introducing new ideas.

Mathematics Head of Department variables
Twenty-six questionnaire items were found to be important in the multilevel analyses. Four mathematics HoD items were identified as having a significant effect both singly and in combination. The model was based on 38 schools and 7,587 students.

- Ensuring each student obtains the highest qualifications possible (+) (identified as a principal educational goal of the school five years before by the HoD mathematics)
- Quality of leadership provided by the HT (+) (identified as a key factor contributing to the school's current effectiveness by the HoD mathematics)
- Considerable teacher involvement in decision-making (–) (identified as a key factor contributing to the school's effectiveness by the HoD mathematics)
- Examination results (+) (identified as a factor which ought to be taken into account in judging departmental effectiveness by the HoD mathematics).

The HoD mathematics' responses drew attention to the importance of items which can be seen to relate to the extent of academic emphasis at the school and department level. In addition, the importance of the HT leadership for overall academic effectiveness was highlighted. Considerable teacher involvement in decision-making in the school, however, was associated with low academic effectiveness and this may provide an indication of lack of clear leadership by the SMT as a group or by the HT as an individual.

Our multilevel analyses of the extent to which process items from the HT and HoDs questionnaires account for school level variation in students' total GCSE performance scores indicate that substantial reductions are achieved in each model which incorporated such information.

The majority of the items identified as important in the statistical explanation of variations between schools in their effects on students' total GCSE performance scores cover both aspects to do with the functioning of the school as a whole, as well as specific departments. This indicates that matters reflecting the functioning of the school (e.g. of the SMT and leadership of the HT) have measurable impact on student performance. It suggests that, in some institutions, the school provides a more supportive environment for teaching and learning than in others. Our results also draw attention to the importance of teachers (including aspects such as staff absence levels/shortages and expectations) and the functioning of specific departments. We think that the results of the multilevel analyses presented here, all of which were based on similar but not identical samples of schools, reflecting the different response rates for each questionnaire, generally support the main conclusions concerning the mechanisms of effectiveness outlined earlier in the chapter. Moreover, they demonstrate that it is possible to account statistically for much of the variance in schools' overall academic effectiveness by differences between them in school and departmental processes.

English GCSE Scores

Headteacher variables
The HT analysis of students' English GCSE scores tested a total of 18 items (out of 64) identified as individually statistically significant. The final model was based on 38 schools and 7,529 students. It accounted for over 80 per cent of the remaining school level variance in students' English GCSE performance, after controlling for student prior attainment and background. The five items identified by this model were:

- Reduction in staff shortages in the school over the last five years (–) (identified as a major school success by the HT)
- Student satisfaction (+) (identified by the HT as a key factor which ought to be taken into account in judging school effectiveness)
- Insufficient academic emphasis in the school (–) (identified by the HT as a key factor holding their school back from being more effective)
- A caring pastoral environment (+) (identified by the HT as a key factor which ought to be taken into account in judging school effectiveness)
- A clear and consistently applied whole school approach to student behaviour and discipline (+) (identified by the HT as a key factor contributing to their school's effectiveness).

As with the overall analyses of total GCSE performance, the negative relationship between students' English results with a reduction in past staff shortages can be seen to indicate the existence of a significant problem in the past, during the period to which the examination analysis related. Not unexpectedly it supports the view that school-wide staff shortages have a detrimental impact on achievement in English GCSE. Also important were measures related to a strong student focus, academic emphasis and consistency in school approach to student behaviour and discipline.

English Head of Department variables
The English HoDs' questionnaire responses were also analysed to establish their relationships with effects on English GCSE performance. A total of 24 HoDs of English questionnaire items were tested jointly and 8 were found to exert a significant impact both individually and in combination. The final model was based on 38 schools and 8,006 GCSE candidates and accounted for all the remaining school level variance after taking account of student intake characteristics.[6]
The items found to be important were:

- Promoting students' ability to learn independently (+) (identified as a principal educational goal five years before by HoD English)
- A caring pastoral environment (+) (identified by HoD English as a factor which ought to be taken into account in judging school effectiveness)
- The creation of confident, articulate people (–) (identified by HoD English as a factor which ought to be taken into account in judging school effectiveness)
- A strong cohesive SMT (+) (identified by HoD English as a key factor contributing to their school's effectiveness)
- Low level of staff shortage in school (past) (+)
- Difficulties in getting parental/community support (–) (identified by HoD English as a major challenge/problem for their department over the last five years)
- Uptake at GCSE and A-level (+) (identified by HoD English as a factor which ought to be taken into account in judging
- Too little emphasis on homework by English staff (–) (identified by HoD English as a key factor holding back their department from being more effective).

These findings again draw attention to the importance of an academic emphasis in the department, indicated by the importance of examination entry and homework. As with the HT results, the positive impact of a caring pastoral environment and a strong and cohesive SMT was identified. In line with the findings on total GCSE performance, the importance of parental/community support was again evident.

However, in terms of the school's principal educational goals, promoting students' ability to learn independently had a positive impact, whereas the creation of confident, articulate people did not. This latter goal may indicate a lack of academic emphasis and should be interpreted in conjunction with other items identified as significant in this model, especially the importance attached to uptake at GCSE and A-level and the emphasis on homework.

In line with the HT results, the HoD of English findings draw attention to the importance of staffing; low levels of staff shortages in the past in the school as a whole having a positive impact on English examination performance. The item 'shortages of teaching staff in the English department over the last five years' was also significant, with low levels of shortage related to better GCSE results.

Mathematics GCSE performance

Headteacher variables

The analysis of HT items revealed that 20 items were significantly related to GCSE mathematics performance using multilevel techniques when tested individually. The results revealed that 5 items were significant when tested individually and in combination and accounted for the vast majority of the variance in students' GCSE mathematics scores. The model was based on 39 schools and 7,983 students.

- Promoting student responsibility (+) (identified by the HT as a principal educational goal for the school five years before)
- The creation of a positive climate for learning (+) (identified by the HT as an important factor which ought to be taken into account in judging school effectiveness)
- Inconsistent approach to student assessment (+) (identified by the HT as a key factor holding back their school from being more effective)
- Poor leadership by HoD of mathematics (past) (–) (HT's rating of past performance)
- Inconsistent approach to student behaviour and discipline matters in school (–) (identified by HT as a major problem faced by their school over the last five years).

These results point to the importance of the following: the HoD's leadership, promoting the school goal of student responsibility, a positive climate for learning and consistency in approach to behaviour and discipline within the school. However, the interpretation of one item is unclear. The HT's identification of inconsistency in assessment as a key factor holding back their school from being more effective had a positive sign. It is possible that in this area, assessment for mathematics requires a different approach from other subjects and is not promoted by consistency in practice in the school. By contrast, an inconsistent approach to student behaviour and discipline in the school was identified as having a negative impact on performance in this subject, in line with findings for English.

Mathematics Head of Department variables

For the analysis of HoDs of mathematics' responses, 7 items were found to have a statistically significant impact on students' GCSE mathematics performance, both individually and in combination. The analysis was based on 34 schools and 7,150 students. In combination these items accounted for almost all the variance between schools not already explained by students' prior attainment and background factors.

The items identified as significant in accounting for differences between schools in GCSE mathematics performance in the HoDs analysis are listed below.[7]

- A high level of achievement in examinations (+) (identified by HoD of mathematics as a key factor which ought to be taken into account in judging school effectiveness)
- Staff and students' shared belief that the school is primarily a place for teaching and learning (+) (identified by HoD of mathematics as a key factor which contributes to their school's effectiveness)
- Low student motivation (past) (–) (HoD mathematics level of satisfaction with student motivation five years ago)
- HoD's leadership approach persuasion rather than coercion (–) (HoD mathematics description of their leadership style)
- Low student motivation (–) (identified by HoD mathematics as a major challenge faced by their department over the last five years)
- Insufficient high quality teaching in some classes (–) (identified by HoD mathematics as a key factor holding their department back from greater effectiveness)
- Staff shortages in mathematics department rare (past) (+).

As with findings for total GCSE performance score and for English, the results for mathematics HoDs highlight both factors to do with the school as a whole and aspects of the functioning of individual mathematics departments. The items draw attention to the importance attached to academic achievement in the school and shared beliefs about the school as a place for teaching and learning. The importance of high quality teaching was also underlined, as was the freedom from staff shortages in the past. Only one item describing the HoD's leadership approach was significantly negative in relation to students' mathematics outcomes. This suggests that, on its own, persuasion may not always be an effective strategy. It should be remembered that HTs were far more critical of their mathematics department's performance and mathematics HoDs' leadership in the past than was the case for English. Where there are major problems, sole reliance on persuasion may be an inappropriate response.

Items concerning student motivation and behaviour indicate, as might be expected, that these items are related to mathematics achievement. However, they can also be seen as important student outcomes in themselves and may also be influenced by school and departmental processes. It is interesting to note that these items were not found to be significant in the multilevel analysis of either to English or overall GCSE performance. These aspects may be of particular relevance for mathematics performance.

DISCUSSION AND CONCLUSIONS

The results of our case studies, described in Chapter 5, draw attention to the nature of the whole-school context, including the leadership of the HT and the role of the SMT. This may be a reflection of the selection of case study schools and departments, which covered both more and less effective examples, rather than concentrating solely on more effective departments. While the departmental level was undoubtedly very important, in some schools it was apparently 'easier' for all departments to function effectively, due to a more supportive context, a shared whole-school emphasis on the importance of student learning and achievement, and the apparently mutually beneficial impact of successful departments supporting each others' efforts and spurring each other on to further success. Conversely, in other schools it was 'harder' for departments to be effective due to a lack of overall leadership, shared goals and vision, poor expectations and inconsistent approaches. The results support the view that higher level conditions – school and departmental – facilitate lower level conditions which impact directly on student outcomes, particularly the quality of teaching and learning in the classroom (Scheerens, 1992), a topic we return to in the next chapter.

The third phase of the research was used to investigate, among a larger sample of schools and departments, the applicability of the results of the qualitative case studies. The questionnaire survey provided an analysis of HTs' and HoDs' perceptions of the factors which ought to be taken into account in judging school or departmental effectiveness, as well as those which influenced their school's and department's effectiveness (described in Chapter 6).

In addition to exploring practitioners' perceptions and priorities, the third phase of the research examined the *relationships* between school and departmental processes and value added effects on students' GCSE performance in terms of three value added measures – total GCSE performance score, English, and mathematics. Screening analyses to examine the links between effects on these outcomes and process measures were used to select items for more rigorous testing utilizing multilevel techniques. Our intention was to establish the extent to which information about variations in school and departmental processes was systematically related to schools' effects on specific student outcomes.

The results of Phase 3 – in line with the qualitative findings from Phase 2 – indicate that factors concerning both school and departmental processes are significant predictions of schools' academic effectiveness. Questionnaires completed by HTs and HoDs were analysed and both demonstrated the impact of particular school and departmental processes. It is notable that HTs' assessments of the performance of their mathematics departments were generally much less favourable, especially concerning the situation in the past, than was the case for English. We do not know whether this trend is peculiar to our inner London sample but believe it is a topic worthy of further investigation.

Overall, the findings from the empirical analyses of Phase 3 are broadly in line with those found from the qualitative case studies, although Phase 3 draws more attention to the value of consistency and of a student-focused approach. Our analyses highlight the need to investigate both variations in school and departmental processes and their separate and joint impact upon different measures of academic effectiveness. Nine inter-dependent features which provide pointers concerning the mechanisms of school and departmental effectiveness were derived from an examination of the pattern of associations between process items and schools' effects on GCSE performance.

While we have focused on the topic of academic effectiveness, it is of interest also to note that HTs' and HoDs' evaluation of their school's performance in terms of non-academic outcomes of education – behaviour, attendance and motivation – were significantly related to the value added measures of schools' effects on GCSE results, especially total performance score.

Our findings concerning the mechanisms of effectiveness derived from both the case studies and the questionnaire survey show fairly broad agreement about the importance of particular factors. The case studies, however, inevitably provide a more detailed picture of school and departmental functioning and are of particular interest to those concerned with issues of school change and improvement. They point to the importance of school and departmental histories in the study of effectiveness and of effective management in schools at different levels and this supports the conclusions by Bolam *et al.* (1993); Brown and Rutherford (1995) and Wallace and Hall (1975).

The results of our investigation of process information are also generally in line with those identified in recent reviews of the school effectiveness literature (see Reynolds, 1994a; NWREL, 1995; Sammons Hillman and Mortimore, 1995). However, in contrast to many earlier studies, the linking and testing of school and departmental process information to students' GCSE outcomes, using appropriate multilevel models, demonstrates, statistically, the existence of significant relationships between process variables and student outcomes. The research conducted in Phase 3 also reveals that much of the remaining variation between schools in their effects on subject performance or on overall GCSE results (after control for prior attainment and background factors) can be accounted for by multilevel models including a relatively small number of process indicators. We can thus go beyond mere descriptive analyses in constructing empirically based explanations for differences in secondary schools' academic effectiveness.

The combination of different methodologies – qualitative case studies with a questionnaire survey – regarding school and departmental processes provided a rich database to explore academic effectiveness in detail, and is more illuminating than reliance on either methodology in isolation. The retrospective focus to the data collection, contrasting current with previous practice five years earlier, also proved productive. Scheerens (1995) and Creemers (1994c) have pointed to the importance of relating empirical findings to the development of better theories of educational effectiveness and to help shape and improve the design of future school effectiveness studies. In Chapter 8 we investigate theories of educational effectiveness and examine the contribution the results of our Differential School Effectiveness project can make to their further development. In particular we examine the links between the results of the multilevel analysis of process items for the three outcomes, English, mathematics and total GCSE performance in more detail and relate this to an understanding of an effective school culture. The implications of the study for policy and practice form the subject of Chapter 9.

NOTES

1. As noted in Chapter 6 a questionnaire survey was used during Phase 3 of the study and one or more responses was received from 126 HTs and HoDs drawn from 55 of the 88 secondary schools approached.
2. Correlations are negative because the questionnaire rating scale ranged from 1 'very satisfied' to 5 'very dissatisfied'.
3. HoDs and HTs rated departments from 1 'well above average' to 5 'well below average', given this, correlations with value added measures are negative.
4. HoDs rated the academic balance of their intakes in terms of the proportion of low ability students at entry from 1 'much above average' to 5 'well below average'.
5. In addition, reflecting these complex interrelationships, two factors which changed signs when included in the final models were omitted because the lack of stability means uncertainty in their interpretation. These factors were 'poor work focus of lessons' (English HoDs' rating of the extent to which English teaching staff had a strong work focus in lessons five years before) and 'significant student behaviour problems' (identified as a major challenge faced by their department in the last five years by HoDs of mathematics). Both were found to have a negative impact, as would be predicted, when tested individually but in combination with other items the sign of the relationship proved unstable.
6. The item 'shortages of teaching staff in the English department over the last five years' (rated by HoDs on a scale from 1 – shortages a major problem to 3 – shortages are rare) was also significant but this item changed sign from negative (tested individually) to positive and is therefore difficult to interpret. (It was closely related to the item on low levels of staff shortages in the school which was positively related to English GCSE scores in the multilevel analysis.)
7. One item, 'low student motivation' identified by the HoDs of mathematics as a major challenge faced by their department in the last five years, changed sign when tested in combination. This item was closely related to the HoD's overall level of satisfaction with student motivation in the school as a whole in the past (also included in the model). Given this instability the interpretation of this item is unclear.

PART 3: THEORETICAL AND PRACTICAL IMPLICATIONS

8

Towards a Model of Academic Effectiveness in Schools

INTRODUCTION

The school effectiveness research tradition has been criticized on a variety of grounds – philosophical and moral as well as technical and empirical (e.g. Sirotnik, 1985; Preece, 1989; Ball, 1994; Hamilton, 1996; White, 1997). Indeed Pring (1995) has argued that the field should not be seen as part of educational research at all because, in his view, its context is not 'educational', although this is not an argument we accept! It is beyond the scope of this chapter to discuss all these criticisms (see Mortimore, Sammons and Ecob, 1988; Reynolds, 1995; Sammons, Mortimore and Hillman, 1996; Mortimore and Sammons, 1997; Sammons and Reynolds, 1997 for responses to some of these critiques). However, one of the major weaknesses of school effectiveness research is still seen to be its weak theoretical base (Creemers, 1992; Mortimore, 1991a; Scheerens, 1992) and it is the criticism of a-theorism which we seek to address in this chapter. Thus Creemers (1994a) observed 'until recently the state of the art of school effectiveness research was excellently described by the fact that the research reviews outnumbered the total of empirical investigations' (p. 9). Fortunately, the number of empirical studies of school effectiveness has grown rapidly during the 1990s and has focused on new and important research questions. For example, there is increasing interest in the topics of departmental effectiveness, consistency and stability as our present study (and recent work by Ainley, 1994; Luyten, 1994; Witziers, 1994; Harris, Jamieson and Russ, 1995) illustrates. A major study in Australia has also drawn increasing attention to the extent of within-school variation at the classroom level, and this by implication the importance of teacher effects (Hill and Rowe, 1996; Rowe and Hill, 1994, 1996). Nonetheless, there remains a need to focus on the integration and synthesis of the 'increasingly varied, disparate and complex bodies of knowledge which have become known collectively as school effectiveness research' (Reynolds et al., 1994, p. 1).

Some work, however, has been done on the drawing together of the field and the important contribution made by the Dutch school effectiveness tradition to the theoretical development should not be underestimated (e.g. Scheerens and Creemers, 1989; Scheerens, 1990; Creemers, 1992; Scheerens, 1992; Bosker and Scheerens, 1994; Creemers, 1994a and b; Scheerens and Bosker, 1997). Despite this, however, relatively few studies have attempted to investigate the strength of the links between the results of specific empirical studies and theories of educational effectiveness so that more can be learnt about their generalizability/context specificity (Bosker and Scheerens, 1994; Creemers and Reezigt, forthcoming, provide innovative examples of such investigations). The growth of school effectiveness research in many parts of the world is encouraging researchers to conduct collaborative international comparative studies (Creemers *et al.*, 1996) to investigate the impact of social and cultural context. Moreover, reviews of school effectiveness research (NWREL, 1995; Sammons, Hillman and Mortimore, 1995; Scheerens and Bosker, 1997) have attempted to establish the extent to which findings about the characteristics of effective schools are consistent across sectors – primary, secondary, post-school – and different contexts (socio-economic as well as national). For example, the possibilities of learning from 'high performing schools' with very different educational systems – such as in the Pacific rim – has recently been highlighted through international and national comparisons of mathematics and science performance (Reynolds and Farrell, 1996).

In this chapter we seek to examine the findings from the Differential School Effectiveness project in relation to existing theories and models of educational effectiveness and in doing so hope to increase understanding of the ways in which schools influence their students' educational outcomes. But first we address the question of why we need better theories? Some practitioners and policy makers see theoretical developments as an essentially academic exercise of little or no relevance to their concerns. Given consistent findings which can be applied, the question 'But does it work in theory?' can seem both esoteric and irrelevant. However, the alternative view can also be justified as Scheerens (1995) argues: 'there is nothing more practical than a good theory and there is nothing more relevant for school improvement than a well-designed evaluation of a programme . . . built upon the knowledge-base of school effectiveness' (p. 9). The examination of current theory in the light of research results can be especially beneficial for those concerned with school improvement because it may help to disentangle the causal chains and mechanisms which influence student achievement. This is important for those seeking to apply school effectiveness results for the purposes of improvement since it provides a guide as to the most influential factors and the way action in one area can affect other areas, and thus can be used to select specific foci for the initial phases of an improvement initiative.

Theories and models of school effectiveness

Our definition of school effectiveness is a student-achievement centred one, as we argued in Chapter 2. For us an effective school is thus one in which students progress more than might be expected on the basis of their intake characteristics (Mortimore, 1991a). We are not talking in general terms about 'good' schools, but those which are effective in promoting their students' educational outcomes (Silver, 1994, and Gray, 1995, provide a more detailed discussion of this issue). It is important, therefore, that we take a longitudinal perspective controlling for students' attainment at entry to school, and so investigate progress over subsequent years to get a measure of the *value added* by the school. We do not accept that IQ type assessments of students' ability provide the best measures of intake control, particularly if they are measured some time after students join a school. Baseline assessments of students' skills in areas relevant to the curriculum, such as reading or mathematics, provide a better basis for value added studies of school effectiveness. Given this focus on student achievement Reynolds (1995) has commented that the 'touchstone criteria to be applied to all educational matters concern whether children learn more or less because of the policy or practice. Fads, fallacies and policy and practice fantasies hopefully pass us by because we try to form our views of the educational world on a scientific basis' (p. 59). In other words, we are concerned with finding out about the school and classroom processes which help to make some schools and departments more effective than others in advancing their students' educational achievements.

In connection with the growing interest in theory development, Scheerens (1995) has argued that 'we do not just want to know what *works* in education but also *why* certain things seem to work. Not only is there an interest in the causal determinants of educational achievement but also in possible underlying explanatory mechanism' (p. 6). Similar arguments concerning the practical value of theory for practitioners have been proposed by Bush (1995) in connection with theories of educational management.

It is important to recognize that there are few generally agreed theories of educational effectiveness, although attempts have been made to borrow theories from existing disciplines such as economics, psychology and sociology to help in its interpretation. For example, organizational, contingency, catastrophe, systems and public choice theories have all been drawn on in the development of ones about educational effectiveness (Scheerens, 1992; Creemers and Scheerens, 1994; Scheerens and Bosker, 1997). School effectiveness research can be distinguished from the wider educational effectiveness field by its focus on schools and explicit attempts to specify *how* school and classroom processes influence students' educational outcomes. School effectiveness research has thus resulted in the development of causal models of educational attainment which attempt to demonstrate the nature and direction of links between particular school processes and student outcomes.

The framework of INPUT-PROCESS-OUTPUT has been commonly adopted, and in recent years the importance of CONTEXT has also been widely recognized (Teddlie, 1994a). In the Differential School Effectiveness project, we have focused on the concept of *academic effectiveness* at the secondary level, using various measures of students' public examination results at GCSE as outcome measures and controlling for prior attainment and other relevant intake characteristics.[1] Although these examination results are not the only important goals of education, there are strong arguments for emphasizing academic goals, due to the 'high stakes' nature of UK public examinations as determinants of young people's future educational and employment life chances (Mortimore and Sammons, 1997). Because we only have limited – though important – measures of students' academic outcomes at the end of compulsory schooling, we will restrict our discussions to the development of a model of 'secondary school academic effectiveness'. We use the term 'model' to indicate the partial nature of our propositions. As Creemers and Scheerens (1994) have noted, 'models and theories can be thought of as positions on a continuum. Thus theories can be seen as "improved" models, where improvement means that central propositions gain in precision and generalizability and relationships become more formalized' (p. 135). We do not think that the current 'state of the art' of school effectiveness research as yet allows more than the elementary outlines of a comprehensive educational effectiveness theory to be sketched.

The basic structure of models of school effectiveness has been outlined by Creemers and Scheerens (1994) and is shown in Figure 8.1. Such models explicitly attempt to describe the multilevel structure and linkages between levels of the CONTEXT-INPUT-PROCESS-OUTPUT chain.

The levels involved comprise the individual student, the classroom, the school and the school environment (the latter covers matters such as the national or local context which would include in the UK the influence of the NC and NA, publication of league tables of examination results, the OFSTED inspection cycle, all of which can be seen as accountability mechanisms). Creemers and Scheerens (1994) have argued that 'theories of learning and instruction, such as the Carroll model, are at the core of multilevel educational effectiveness models' (p. 137). The model they propose defines school-level factors as facilitating conditions for classroom-level factors. Due to this restriction the only school-level factors that are viewed as relevant are those 'conditional for and directly related to quality of instruction or to time allowed/opportunity to learn'. In addition, Creemers (1992) has argued that school-level factors should either promote cohesion between teachers (stimulate similar effective teacher behaviour in all classrooms) or control what is going on in classrooms. He also stresses the importance of continuity in terms of school rules and policies over several years.

In a more recent educational effectiveness model developed from theories about how students learn, Creemers (1994a) stresses the impact of three key concepts – quality, time for learning and opportunity – which are seen to be relevant to each level. Stringfield (1994b) also provides an example of a model of primary (elementary) school effects influenced by learning theories and stressing Slavin's (1987) QAIT (quality, appropriateness, incentive structures and time for instruction) research. Stringfield also emphasizes the notion of 'high reliability organizations' (HROs) in which failure is not tolerated and also draws attention to research evidence which indicates 'that the routes to becoming highly effective and highly ineffective are not mirror images of one another' (Stringfield, 1994b, p. 183).

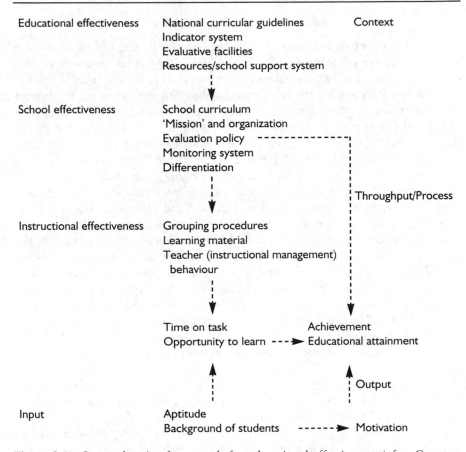

Figure 8.1 Comprehensive framework for educational effectiveness (after Creemers and Scheerens, 1994)

Scheerens (1995) has pointed out an additional complexity to model building, namely that 'combinations of effectiveness enhancing conditions may work better given specific contextual contingencies' (p. 8) i.e. some factors may have beneficial effects only in combination or may only produce positive effects in particular contexts. In commenting on the theoretical base of school effectiveness research, Mortimore (1995a) has stressed that little is known about contingency effects and unintended consequences of different improvement approaches. However, the importance of the socio-economic status (SES) context of the student body has been highlighted by work in the US (Teddlie *et al.*, 1989) and Scotland (Brown, Riddell and Duffield, 1996). Of course, interpreting this result is not easy; it may be due to lower teacher expectations for some social classes, or lower expectations amongst the peer group or students' parents. Quite probably it represents a combination of such influences. Contextual influences have important policy and practical implications which we will discuss in Chapter 9.

School versus classroom effects

Early school effectiveness research concentrated on the identification of more and less effective schools (often by means of outlier studies) and school processes related to effectiveness but paid little attention to the question of teacher effectiveness (Stringfield, 1994a). There has been an increasing recognition of the importance of classroom/teacher effects in recent years and attempts to utilize three level models to separate effects at these levels because so much of the educational process – the teaching of students – takes place in the classroom (Rowe and Hill, 1994, 1996; Luyten, 1995; Creemers and Reezigt, forthcoming). However, it is important to recognize that students commonly attend only one school at a given time, usually for a period of several years. They will experience a succession of teachers and classes during this time, especially at the secondary level, where, as in our own study, the departmental level may be particularly influential. We believe that studies which examine the effects on students of being a member of a particular secondary school over a period of years remain of considerable practical and theoretical relevance. This is because any student's educational experience involves being taught by a number of subject specialists in any year. Although students and their parents may have (usually quite heavily constrained) opportunities to choose particular schools in the UK system, this is not the case for individual classes or teachers. Moreover, students usually spend several years in one institution and therefore the question of whether over several years the particular school attended has an impact on their later educational outcomes is of prime importance. The period covered by our study from age 11 to 16 years represents nearly a third of their lifetime for secondary students.

Research which adopts a longitudinal approach, for example, using baseline measures of student achievement at entry, and which follows-up academic outcomes several years later, is more likely to identify school effects than studies (particularly in primary schools) conducted over only one year where class/teacher effects are likely to be much stronger. As Teddlie (1994b) has argued, there is a need to integrate school and teacher effectiveness research traditions 'since true change in elementary and secondary schools must occur at both the school and class levels simultaneously and since neither level (school or classroom) can be adequately studied without considering the other' (p. 113).

In our Differential School Effectiveness project, we assessed student progress from age eleven to age sixteen, the end of compulsory schooling. This approach provides an indication of the cumulative effect of attending a particular institution over five years. Also we used three successive cohorts of sixteen-year-olds so that the impact of schools could be distinguished from annual fluctuations. In this way we could establish the extent of stability in patterns of schools' academic performance at GCSE, as we described in Chapters 3 and 4. In the light of this, it is perhaps not surprising that many of the factors found to be related to academic effectiveness concerned school processes related to leadership, organization and policy (see Chapters 5 and 7).

The departmental level

On the basis of our empirical research (and other research examining the impact of the department at the secondary level such as that by Ainley, 1994; Luyten, 1994; Harris, Jamieson and Russ, 1995; Witziers, 1994) we conclude that models of secondary school effectiveness need to analyse the impact of the department explicitly. As we have argued earlier (see Chapter 4), judgements about effectiveness are complex. Effectiveness should be seen as both *outcome (i.e. subject)* and *time specific.* Our results show that, in the vast majority of cases, secondary schools cannot be readily classified as either 'effective' or 'ineffective', although the study of unusually effective outliers may be illuminating. In addition, our investigation of differential effectiveness – reported in Chapter 4 – draws attention to the need to focus on effectiveness for specific student groups, thus adding an important *equity* dimension to any model. The concept of school effectiveness needs to be qualified at the secondary level to the term school and departmental effectiveness (Sammons *et al.*, 1995a and b; Thomas *et al.*, 1997a and b).

In addition, in line with Bosker and Scheerens' (1994) conclusion, models of school effectiveness need to consider the influence of potential 'feedback loops'. Thus student intake factors may influence the nature of school and classroom experiences as well as having a direct impact on students' educational outcomes. For example, the nature of students' characteristics or achievements at intake can affect teacher expectations. There is evidence that teachers tend to rate middle class students more highly in terms of ability, even when control is made for their current attainments (Mortimore *et al.*, 1988), and this phenomenon is likely to influence their teaching approaches for such students. In addition, teachers' expectations of subsequent age groups may be influenced by the particularly good or poor results of earlier cohorts. It is in this sense that contextual or compositional effects may operate. For example, a number of studies have shown that, in addition to the impact of a student's own socio-economic status (SES) the composition of the student body in his/her school is also related to measures of academic achievement. Our current study indicates that a measure of low family income (eligibility for free school meals) is related to English GCSE performance at both the level of the individual student and at the *school level* where a contextual or compositional effect, related to the level of disadvantage in the intake as a whole, is identified. Put simply, students attending schools which serve poor areas have an additional educational disadvantage. Again this has important policy implications which we discuss in the next chapter.

Cross-level influences

If we accept that schools are best studied as organizations which are made up of nested layers – students within classrooms, departments within schools – the question of how we can conceptualize the ways in which one level influences another becomes especially important. The most pervasive view on cross-level influences in nested (i.e. multilevel) models of school effectiveness is that higher-

level conditions, aspects concerning school leadership, policy and organization, for example, in some way facilitate conditions at lower levels (the quality
of teaching and learning in classrooms). These, in turn, have a direct impact on
students' academic outcomes (see Bosker and Scheerens, 1994).

While some have argued that it is unlikely that aspects of overall school
functioning have a direct impact on students' educational outcomes, we conclude that this is not impossible. For example, a clear school policy on homework may have a direct impact on students' learning and therefore on their
educational outcomes by increasing both the time on task and opportunity to
learn, including curriculum coverage. We found qualitative evidence suggesting the value of a consistently applied school policy which stressed the importance of regularly set and marked homework in our case studies of academically
more and less effective schools. Likewise, aspects of organization and policy at
the departmental level, whilst most likely to operate indirectly by affecting the
quality of teaching and learning in the classroom, may in some circumstances
have a direct effect. For example, departmental policies on GCSE examination
entry can be viewed as having a direct impact on academic outcomes. As an
illustration, our research found clear differences between the more and less
academically effective departments in terms of the emphasis given to GCSE
entry. This can directly affect students' opportunities for academic achievement (as we described in Chapters 5 and 7).

Bosker and Scheerens (1994) examine a number of alternative interpretations of cross-level facilitation. They highlight six possibilities concerning the
nature of the impact of school-level processes:

- **Contextual effects** – in this case it is suggested that in a school with a
  majority of 'effective' teachers and feedback amongst staff, the performance
  of the *less effective minority will be improved*;
- **Mirrors** – in this case the congruence between evidence on effective schools
  and effective classrooms is highlighted. Congruence of factors (e.g. orderly
  climate, high expectations, achievement pressure etc.) *helps to create a consistent school culture* which provides a general supportive background;
- **Overt measures** – in this case specific measures are taken to create effectiveness enhancing conditions at lower levels (e.g. the classroom). Examples
  given include the positive impact of instructional leadership, increasing allocated learning time, recruiting 'effective' teachers, selecting teaching mater-
  ials, keeping records of student progress etc.; and
- **Incentives** to promote effectiveness enhancing conditions at lower levels.
  This view would cover rewards for 'effective' teachers from senior managers
  and monetary grants from their districts for schools if they achieve certain
  standards.
  The application of 'market forces' via open enrolment and publication of
  league tables can be seen as a crude focus of incentive-based approach in the
  UK context;
- **Material facilities** for conditions at lower levels. In this case the example

given is a computerized school-monitoring system implemented at the school-level which gives teachers better information on student progress; and

- **Buffers** to protect effectiveness enhancing conditions at the classroom level. This view implies minimal expectations of the direct influence of school management on what the authors call the 'education production process' and covers administrative functions such as student involvement, dealing with government regulations and external pressure etc.

Of course these different interpretations are not necessarily mutually exclusive and it seems likely that higher level conditions can operate in more than one way simultaneously. Given this, it may be hard to distinguish between them in practice.

UNDERSTANDING ACADEMIC EFFECTIVENESS

In Chapter 5, we described the results of our detailed case studies of six schools and thirty academically more and less effective departments. The conclusions we drew concerning the characteristics of more and less effective schools and departments in the results of our larger questionnaire survey of project schools are summarized in Chapter 7. The quantitative analysis of the questionnaire responses of HTs and HoDs support and extend the findings of the qualitative case studies and enhance our confidence in the conclusions. They highlighted nine factors which we think help to increase our understanding of the mechanisms of academic effectiveness at the secondary level. These are:

- high expectations;
- strong academic emphasis;
- shared vision/goals;
- clear leadership by both HTs and HoDs;
- an effective SMT;
- consistency in approach;
- quality of teaching;
- a student-centred approach; and
- parental involvement and support.

We were particularly interested to examine whether the main conclusions of the much earlier *Fifteen Thousand Hours* research on twelve inner London secondary schools remain valid, given the lapse in time and many significant changes to the educational system over the last twenty years. As we discussed in Chapter 5, the results of the two studies do not diverge greatly. In terms of school processes, Rutter *et al.* (1979) highlighted the concept of school climate in interpreting their results. Leadership was identified as important, although the impact of middle managers (the HoDs) is a feature of our results and the coherent functioning and unity of the SMT is also significant. The positive impact of shared vision and goals and consistency in approach received emphasis in both studies, but the benefits of home/school partnership are a more notable feature of our results.

Harris, Jamieson and Russ's (1995) qualitative case studies of accelerating departments in a west country city were conducted much more recently but in a different socio-economic context. This research focused explicitly on the departmental level and highlighted eleven aspects. There are a number of important similarities between our results and theirs, which we describe in Chapter 5. Our research, however, draws more attention to the importance of several school-level factors – namely high expectations, strong academic emphasis, shared vision and goals, clear leadership by the HT and an effective SMT. This is perhaps because both more and less effective departments and schools were covered in the case study phase, and for the questionnaire survey we received responses from fifty-five schools and seventy-nine departments covering a wide range of academic effectiveness. While the department level is undoubtedly very influential for students' GCSE performance in specific subjects, our results indicate that in some schools the benefits of a more supportive context (including a whole school emphasis on the central importance of student learning and achievement, high expectations and consistency in approach, particularly in relation to policy and practices concerning student behaviour) fostered the academic effectiveness of all departments. This conclusion supports Bosker and Scheerens' (1994) suggestion relating to mirrors creating a consistent culture where there is congruence of factors at the school and, in this case, the departmental level.

Interdependence of factors

In terms of empirical results, there is now a fair degree of agreement as to the factors which are important in determining the academic effectiveness of secondary schools at GCSE. However, as noted earlier, we need to explore the relationships between our empirical findings and models of academic effectiveness further to improve our understanding of the way schools and departments influence student outcomes. Creemers *et al.* (forthcoming b) have argued that educational effectiveness research has yielded a lot of classroom and school factors which are correlated with achievement to some extent. However, although there is broad agreement about the lists of factors which are relevant, they comment that such lists

> suggest that the effectiveness factors, whether they are classroom or school factors all have their own independent effects on student achievement. Moreover, the lists suggest that all factors are of equal importance and that their effects are of the same size (p. 3).

They go on to argue that:

> it is possible that not all effectiveness factors have their own independent effects. Their effectiveness may be due to their interrelatedness, at least partly. Also factors at the classroom level may influence achievement in another way than factors at the school level. Finally, factors of different levels may interact (p. 4).

Some authors have suggested that school effectiveness factors are not independent and have investigated the links between factors at different levels in order to improve understanding of the mechanisms of effectiveness (see Mortimore *et al.*,

1988). We certainly concur with Creemers' and his colleagues' comments concerning the possibility, and we suggest the strong probability, that the various factors interact, as we noted in Chapter 7. The results of our secondary school case studies, which investigate more extreme (outlier) examples of academically highly effective as well as highly ineffective schools and departments, also support this contention.

Reezigt and colleagues (forthcoming) present an interesting attempt to test empirically an educational effectiveness model of primary schools (Creemers, 1994a) by defining factors at different levels (school and classroom). This model focuses on the key concepts of quality, time and opportunity which are held to affect student learning, and also stresses the concept of consistency. Disappointingly, the results of the multilevel analysis of the model provide only a very fragmentary picture of classroom and school effects on student achievement. Factors did not always have similar effects on different subjects (language and mathematics). Reezigt et al. (forthcoming) note that, due to measurement problems in the information available about some factors, further research is needed before their school effectiveness model can be confirmed or refuted by empirical evidence.

An expanded model

In this section we seek to relate the findings from our research to the kinds of educational effectiveness models such as those developed by Creemers and Scheerens (1989) and Scheerens (1990), while incorporating an explicit departmental level into our secondary school model. Ainley (1994) has drawn attention to the importance of the subject department in secondary school effectiveness research. He observes: 'The nature of secondary schools raised additional issues because of their greater organizational complexity and because the outcomes of learning may involve a much wider range of areas of learning' (p. 14) and concludes that 'in terms of research it is important to incorporate the department as a central component of high school organization' (p. 15).

Current school effectiveness models have drawn heavily on the traditions of primary school research (e.g. Scheerens, 1990; Creemers, 1994a; Stringfield, 1994b) and seem to be particularly relevant to younger children's achievement in the basic skills. In our view such models need extension to incorporate the departmental level in order to describe adequately the educational process at the secondary level.

The model we outline (Figure 8.2) suggests that congruence between factors operating at different levels (school, department and classroom) is an important feature of academically effective schools. In particular, academic emphasis and high expectations are mirrored at the school, department and class levels, while consistency, shared vision and goals and a student-focused approach are mirrored at two levels (school and departmental). Both senior and middle management can be seen to influence academic effectiveness through the leadership of the HT and the functioning of the SMT at the school level and leadership by HoDs at the department level.

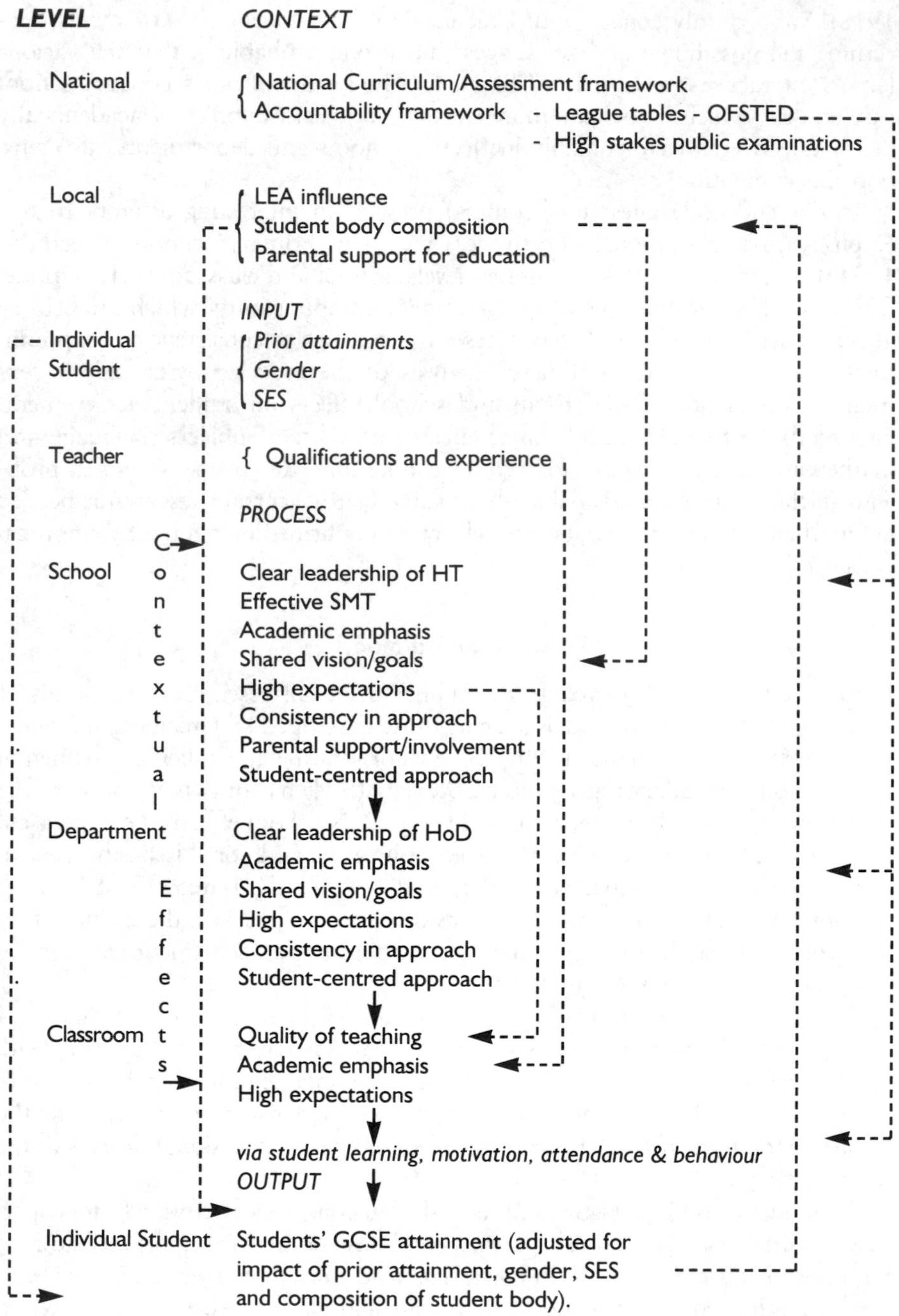

LEVEL

CONTEXT

National

{ National Curriculum/Assessment framework
{ Accountability framework   - League tables - OFSTED
                             - High stakes public examinations

Local

{ LEA influence
{ Student body composition
{ Parental support for education

INPUT

Individual
Student

{ *Prior attainments*
{ *Gender*
{ *SES*

Teacher

{ Qualifications and experience

PROCESS

School

C→
o
n
t
e
x
t
u
a
l

Clear leadership of HT
Effective SMT
Academic emphasis
Shared vision/goals
High expectations
Consistency in approach
Parental support/involvement
Student-centred approach

Department

E
f
f
e
c
t
s

Clear leadership of HoD
Academic emphasis
Shared vision/goals
High expectations
Consistency in approach
Student-centred approach

Classroom

Quality of teaching
Academic emphasis
High expectations

via student learning, motivation, attendance & behaviour
OUTPUT

Individual Student

Students' GCSE attainment (adjusted for
impact of prior attainment, gender, SES
and composition of student body).

Figure 8.2   A model of secondary school academic effectiveness

In contrast to other factors, that of parental support/involvement should be viewed as a feature only partially under the control of the school. Thus some schools are more advantaged in terms of the value placed on education and support for the school amongst the parents of students in their intakes. Nonetheless, our case studies indicate that even schools serving very socioeconomically disadvantaged intakes differed markedly in staff views of the extent of parental interest and support. Some reported much higher levels of interest, support and involvement than others and had worked hard to build better relationships and encourage such involvement.

Student attitudes/motivation, behaviour and attendance were noted as important outcomes in their own right by many practitioners in our case study schools and questionnaire survey. They can also be seen as intermediate outcomes which facilitate (or hamper) academic achievement. A safe, orderly school environment and a clear and consistently applied school policy on behaviour appeared to be necessary, though not in themselves sufficient, conditions for academic effectiveness. Classroom processes, particularly the quality of teaching, can be seen to exert a direct impact on students' learning and motivation which, in turn, affects academic outcomes. Behaviour and attendance, however, may be influenced by both school and classroom processes. Behaviour, motivation and attendance can also influence student learning directly. For example, at the student-level, studies have shown significant correlations between attendance, behaviour and attainment (Mortimore *et al.*, 1988; Sammons, 1996). Our own data also revealed significant relationships between secondary schools' impact on academic outcomes and the extent of staff satisfaction with past levels of student motivation, attendance and behaviour, as we reported in Chapter 7.

Teacher qualifications and experience can be viewed as INPUTS to the educational process which can directly influence the quality of teaching at the classroom level. We found significant correlations between English HoDs' assessment of factors such as staff knowledge of the content of subject and GCSE syllabus, their experience of teaching the subject and their qualifications and effectiveness in promoting overall GCSE performance and English performance, although associations were weaker in mathematics. Our study also pointed to the adverse impact of high levels of staff absence in the school or specific departments, and of shortages of qualified teachers. Staff shortages and high levels of absence inevitably affect the quality of teaching in individual classrooms and in departments teaching specified subjects (e.g. mathematics, science or languages in which the supply of qualified teachers has been problematic for many schools in inner city areas). However, high levels of staff absence and difficulties in recruitment/retention of good teachers may also be a symptom as well as a cause of academic ineffectiveness, being influenced by staff morale and by school and departmental leadership. Historically, staff shortages and absence levels have been higher in disadvantaged inner city contexts and this factor has important policy implications which we consider in Chapters 9 and 10.

Importance of different factors

In interpreting the results of our Differential School Effectiveness project, we integrated findings from the qualitative case studies, and from simple analyses of patterns of correlations between process variables and value added measures of school or departmental performance at GCSE. In addition, we used multilevel analyses to test the *explanatory power* of process variables in accounting directly for school level variance in academic effectiveness using three measures of student outcomes (total GCSE performance score as an overall measure of achievement, English, and mathematics GCSE scores) after control for differences in student intake (Chapter 7). In this section we revisit these multilevel analyses in an attempt to increase our understanding of the relative importance of different factors as determinants of student outcomes. Head-teachers' and English and mathematics HoDs' questionnaire responses were tested in relation to total GCSE score. In English only HTs' and HoDs' responses were analysed, and for mathematics only HTs' and mathematics' HoDs' responses, as we reported in Chapter 7. By using this approach our analyses were able to throw light on the perspectives of different players (HTs and subject leaders). In addition, because of differences in the number of respondents from the three groups in different schools and the need to exclude non-respondents to specific questions, our analyses were based on sub-samples of the ninety-four project schools. Given this, the extent of correspondence in results based on different categories of respondent and rather different sub-samples enhances our confidence in the main findings. However, where results were different it is not possible to say whether this is due to a slightly different sample of schools included in the analysis or to 'real' differences in the impact of particular process factors for different GCSE outcome measures.

School culture

Our findings point to the importance of *school and departmental ethos or culture* in determining the academic effectiveness of secondary schools. Most of the items found to be significant in accounting for variations in academic effectiveness in our multilevel analysis fall into three broad categories (see Appendix 3). The three aspects or dimensions of culture concern are: order (behaviour policy and practice); task achievement (academic emphasis); and relationships (a student-focused approach). In academically more effective schools the school and departmental cultures mirror and reinforce one another.

Order – behaviour, policy and practice
The empirical results reveal the positive impact of behaviour policy and practice. The benefits of a clear and consistently applied whole-school approach to student behaviour and discipline and high staff expectations for student behaviour were evident in the explanation of better than predicted total GCSE and English performance. In contrast, significant behaviour problems and an inconsistent approach were related to poorer than predicted mathematics results.

In order to achieve positive student behaviour, it is evident that staff at all levels need to share a common vision/goals and accept the need for consistency in approach. The outcome is a safe, orderly working environment both in the classrooms and around the schools, maximizing time and energy for teaching and learning.

It should be noted that efforts to create this environment may be a particular requirement for academic effectiveness at the secondary level for schools which serve socio-economically disadvantaged communities in inner city contexts, where social fragmentation and disorder may be a greater feature of students' lives outside school. Such an environment can be viewed as a necessary pre-condition for effective teaching and learning. Its importance is likely to be most evident in studies which analyse student progress over several years where cumulative effects may be anticipated. The positive effects on student learning are likely to operate through patterns of better attendance, behaviour and motivation providing greater learning time and opportunities.

Academic emphasis

While a safe and orderly working environment can be viewed as a necessary – but not in itself sufficient – condition for effectiveness, an academic emphasis must be seen as absolutely essential. Such an emphasis involves agreement amongst all staff, teachers, middle and senior managers on the importance of teaching and learning in the school and acceptance that examination uptake and results are important in judging both school and departmental effective-ness. A weak academic emphasis in the school and in the English department were found to be significant in accounting for poorer than predicted English and total GCSE scores in particular. Our value added analyses demonstrated a somewhat closer relationship between schools' overall academic effectiveness in terms of total GCSE performance score and English than mathematics scores. Nonetheless, for mathematics, the emphasis placed on a high level of achievement in examinations as a factor for judging school effectiveness and staff and students' shared belief that the school is primarily a place for teaching and learning were important. From a 'common sense' view, it is not very surprising that academic emphasis is important for academic effectiveness! Yet the importance ascribed to public examination results, as reported by HTs and HoDs, did vary markedly amongst our sample of schools, especially in the past. For example, where the English HoDs thought that the creation of con-fident, articulate people was a key factor in judging school effectiveness rather than academic outcomes, English results were significantly poorer than pre-dicted. However, where uptake at GCSE/A-level was regarded by the HoD as a key factor which ought to be taken into account in judging departmental performance, the opposite occurred. Too little emphasis on homework – identified as a key factor holding the department back from greater effective-ness by the English HoD – was also found to be significant in the explanation of poorer than predicted English results.

As with behaviour and the creation of safe, orderly working environment, achieving a strong academic emphasis also implies the existence of shared vision/goals, high expectations and consistency in approach, and supportive conditions at different levels. In other words, the school's academic emphasis is mirrored at the departmental and classroom level.

Student-focused approach

This third strand of school culture or ethos also exerts a powerful impact on academic effectiveness. Items related to this aspect focus on the student's experience of schooling. 'Students feel valued as people' (identified as a key factor contributing to their school's effectiveness) was significant in accounting for better than predicted total GCSE performance. 'A caring pastoral environment' and 'student satisfaction' identified as key factors which ought to be taken into account in judging school effectiveness were relevant for English. In addition, 'creating a positive climate for learning', 'promoting student responsibility' and 'promoting students' ability to learn independently', all found to be significant for English GCSE results, can be seen to contribute to a student-focused approach.

A student-focused approach is indicative of a positive affective environment, an emphasis on the quality of staff-student relationships and enjoyment in the process of learning. It is related to higher levels of student motivation. Our results demonstrate that a student-focused approach is important for academic outcomes. Task achievement (enabled by an academic emphasis and an orderly environment) needs to be supplemented by an acknowledgement of the importance of individuality, the quality of the learning experience and positive patterns of attendance and behaviour.

Teaching

At first sight it is rather surprising that none of the items specifically related to the quality of teaching was found to be significant in explaining differences in academic effectiveness at GCSE when tested in combination with other items in the multilevel analysis. It should be remembered that, when tested individually, these showed strong relationships with schools' value added results and all correlations were in the directions expected from the existing school effective knowledge base (Sammons, Hillman and Mortimore, 1995). However, our multilevel analyses did provide clear evidence of the adverse impact of shortages of teaching staff and high levels of staff absence in relation to students' subsequent GCSE performance. There may be a number of explanations for our findings. The first is related to our focus on students' academic progress over five years from secondary transfer at age 11 to GCSE performance at 16, using three consecutive age cohorts in the study. It is likely that school level factors may be more influential than classroom factors in accounting for overall measures of academic achievement. This is because students would have been taught by many teachers in a variety of subjects and classes during their five years at secondary school. In addition, items related to quality of teaching were themselves negatively associated with staff shortages, high levels of staff absence and a weak academic emphasis, as might be expected.

Of course, our results are not meant to imply that quality of teaching is unimportant – we identified it as one of nine key factors because clear differences were evident in both the case studies and questionnaire findings. Also two general items – 'insufficient high quality teaching in some classes' and 'dissatisfaction with the performance of the teaching staff' – as assessed by HoDs were relevant for the explanation of poorer value added results in mathematics and overall GCSE scores. Specific aspects of quality of teaching, however, are likely to be more variable over time and between classes than measures of the items found to contribute to the culture or ethos of the school. The research message from our attempts to explain statistically variations in academic effectiveness at GCSE and the importance of different aspects of school processes is that, although quality of teaching is highly relevant, the three aspects of school culture we highlight appear, in combination, to be more powerful. Where these are positive at each level – school, department *and* classroom – it is likely that the quality of teaching will also be favourable.

Leadership

Our multilevel analyses drew attention to the impact of leadership at different levels within the school. For example, items related to the 'quality of the HT's leadership', 'a strong cohesive SMT' were related to greater value added in total GCSE scores when tested with other process items. In contrast, 'considerable teacher involvement in decision making' was not. Items concerning the leadership of subject leaders were also significant in the analyses of subject (English and mathematics) performance. Leadership, of course, has an important part to play in the creation and maintenance of positive school and departmental cultures.

External influences

Two other items found to be relevant in the explanation of academic effectiveness relate to possible external influences and to the impact of national or local context. One was the negative impact of a falling student roll. Of course, this may be viewed as a symptom as much as a cause of ineffectiveness. Parents may choose not to send their children to a secondary school perceived to have 'problems' in terms of academic results or student behaviour. Thus there is likely to be a negative feedback loop between low examination results in absolute terms and the composition of student intakes. Indeed, the last government's explicit intention in *Choice and Diversity* (DFE, 1992) was stated as the 'withering away' of poor schools via the application of market forces. However, no reference was made to the consequences of this policy for students currently attending such schools. Our results suggest that, controlling for intake and school processes, a falling roll tends to have a detrimental impact on the education of existing students. This may be due to the financial consequences affecting the school's ability to retain teachers (especially older, experienced and therefore more expensive staff) or to recruit good teachers, which, in turn, can lower staff morale.

The second item concerns the apparently positive impact of 'pressure of external changes' (NC, LMS, etc.). This item was included as a possible barrier to greater effectiveness but in the questionnaire survey was found to be important in accounting for better value added results in overall GCSE performance. Again, the interpretation of this is not straightforward. As we noted in our case studies, the respondents in less effective schools generally stressed internal problems as barriers to effectiveness whereas in the more effective schools internal problems were fairly minor with external pressures identified as problem areas. Nonetheless, given that intake and process items were included in our analyses, the result may indicate that schools highlighting external changes as a barrier have reacted more strongly to the perceived need to enhance their academic emphasis. This interpretation remains very tentative but would suggest that the national context has an impact on standards and is in line with Gray *et al*.'s (1996) report on the jump in raw GCSE results which occurred over and above a broadly rising trend associated with the first annual publication of secondary school league tables (1992). This can be interpreted as indicating that as a direct consequence of the use of league tables for accountability purposes, schools entered more students and gave greater attention to GCSE performance.

DISCUSSION

In an extensive American research review on the topic of effective secondary schools, Lee, Bryk and Smith (1993) have pointed out that the faculty is an important feature of school organization. Nonetheless, these authors found evidence that schools with a common sense of purpose and a strong communal organization (involving collegial relationships among staff and positive adult-student relationships) are effective in promoting a range of student academic and social outcomes, reflecting student engagement and commitment. They stress the importance of student and staff's experience of the school as a social organization and the quality of human relationships experienced within it. Lee, Bryk and Smith (1993) also concluded, however, that attention to social relations reflecting a common aim and perspective is not sufficient: 'it is clear to us that 'good' or 'effective' schools must couple concern for social relations with an appreciation for the structural and functional aspects that instrumentally affect instruction and academic learning' (p. 228). In the very different context of Hong Kong, Ming and Cheong's (1995) primary research has also drawn attention to the benefits of a caring and supportive climate and a cohesive student-centred philosophy of teaching for the entire school.

A somewhat similar thesis to that of Lee, Bryk and Smith (1993) is argued by Hargreaves (1995a). He also draws attention to the relevance of the concept of school culture to both school effectiveness and school improvement research. He argues that the school as a social institution has two domains which are potentially in tension. The *instrumental* is concerned with task achievement and social control, and requires teachers and students to work together in orderly ways; whereas the *expressive* – social cohesion – involves the maintenance of good relations both amongst staff and between staff and students. Hargreaves suggests that there is an optimal level of both domains which avoids four extremes which he typifies as A 'traditional', B 'welfarist', C 'hothouse' and D 'anomic'.

In reality Hargreaves acknowledges that few actual school cultures fall into these extremes. However, although Weberian 'ideal types' do not exist, he suggests that they are helpful in interpreting real institutional cultures. Over time, he argues, a real school moves its position and, because schools are 'loosely coupled' institutions, different parts of the school could be located in a different segment from the rest of the school. In his model the effective school's culture

> is around the centre (E), striving to hold its optimal position in the social control and social cohesion domains. Expectations of work and conduct are high – the principal's expectations of staff and teachers' of students. Yet these standards are not perceived to be unreasonable: everyone is supported in striving for them and rewarded for reaching them. For both teachers and students, such a school is a demanding but enjoyable place to be. (p. 28)

The Hargreaves typology avoids the common implication that there is a linear continuum from the least to the most effective school. Moreover, it recognizes the potential of internal variation in school effectiveness (different departments or classes may vary in their positions across the two dimensions), and suggests that there may be 'different ways of being ineffective excessive formalism, welfarisms and survivalist' (p. 29). It also implies the notion of change, because over time a school (or sub-units within the school) may vary in its position. The evidence from our study gives some support for these arguments. Certainly our case studies of academically ineffective schools and departments provided evidence of ineffectiveness related to both the 'welfarist' and the 'anomic' school cultures. Given the inner city and, by national standards, socio-economically disadvantaged nature of our sample it is perhaps not surprising that we found no evidence suggestive of the 'traditional' and 'hot house' school cultures. If our sample had included selective schools, this might not have been the case.

Our research, particularly the case studies of mixed schools in which highly academically effective and ineffective departments coexist (Chapter 5), also supports the view that many schools are 'loosely coupled' institutions and that some departments may successfully create a positive culture which enhances students' academic results, whereas others for a variety of reasons do not. Our case studies indicate the importance of individual department and school histories and draw attention to the need to treat effectiveness as a time as well as an outcome specific concept (Sammons, 1996).

In contrast to Hargreave's arguments, however, we found less evidence for the view that there may be many ways to be effective, although our results are likely to be most applicable to schools in inner city contexts. Whilst effective schools and departments were not identical, consistent results both from our qualitative case studies and the empirical testing of questionnaire data concerning the correlates of effectiveness were found. Moreover, we were able to go beyond interpreting patterns of correlations and through our multilevel analysis demonstrate that it is possible to account for much of the variation in academic effectiveness (Reynolds, 1996). Such analyses help to provide firmer evidence of causal connections, as we demonstrated in Chapter 7.

In the context of schooling, there seems to be a variety of paths to ineffectiveness. As Reynolds and Packer (1992), Gray and Wilcox (1995) and Stoll and Myers (1997) have argued, we need to know more about the functioning of ineffective institutions, although we believe that our research provides some important pointers about aspects which hinder secondary school academic effectiveness. Nonetheless, there appears to be greater consensus about the requirements for academic effectiveness. Our findings are in accord with Reynolds' (1995) argument that 'the ineffective school may also have inside itself 'multiple schools' formed around cliques and friendship groups . . . there will be none of the organization, social, cultural and symbolic "tightness" of the effective school' (p. 61). Such tightness appears to be a particular requirement for academic effectiveness in the context of the inner city.

CONCLUSIONS

In this chapter, we have attempted to tease out the most important factors in the explanation of academic effectiveness, linking our empirical results with models of school effectiveness. Our findings strongly suggest that effective secondary schools are *not* simply schools with effective teachers. Although the quality of teaching is undoubtedly very important, it is not by itself seen to be sufficient for general academic effectiveness at the secondary level. Our proposed model of secondary school academic effectiveness highlights the importance of the school and additional departmental levels. This is likely to be, at least in part, due to the longitudinal approach we have adopted looking from entry to performance five years later. Students may experience in excess of thirty different subject teachers during their secondary school careers. Our analyses also cover three consecutive age groups. This repeated measures design inevitably provides a much better indication of the impact of the school than studies which look at student progress over one or two years. Again the greater stability of overall measures of academic effectiveness (like total GCSE performance score) over time also supports the contention that the school attended can have a consistent impact on students' overall academic performance, for good or ill. We also think that current models of school effectiveness are most applicable to the primary sector where the importance of the classroom level is likely to be much greater.

In interpreting our model it is important to stress its multilevel nature. Our results suggest that cross-level relationships are fundamental (school to department, department to classroom). Teaching and learning takes place in the classroom and most of the school and department's influence is thus likely to be indirect, operating through the culture or ethos. Where culture and ethos at different levels – school, department and classroom – are mirrored, their impact becomes more powerful, due to consistency in students' educational experiences over several years. Nonetheless, overt measures may both contribute to the culture and also have a direct impact on student learning – for example, school-wide policies consistently applied in areas such as behaviour, marking/assessment or homework.

The three aspects of culture or ethos we find to be most significant in determining academic effectiveness at GCSE demonstrate how an effective school manages to achieve an optimal balance between the social control task achievement and the expressive social cohesion domains identified by Hargreaves (1995a). Both behaviour policy and practice, leading to a safe orderly working environment and an academic emphasis, are necessary for task achievement (effective teaching and learning and thus students' academic progress), while the student-focused environment concerns social cohesion and creates a positive climate for learning. The school experience thus becomes both demanding and enjoyable for teachers and students alike. Thus, while it is not possible to claim that school culture necessarily has a direct impact on student learning and achievement, its indirect effects may be profound.

The importance of school culture or ethos has implications for management at both the school and the department level. Effective leadership by both the HT, the SMT and the HoDs will be necessary to foster or maintain a positive and consistent culture. Reynolds (1995) has drawn attention to the 'increased value heterogeneity within societies, and the lack of consistency between socializing agencies of the family, the society and the community, [which] may combine to potentially elevate the consistency of the school's socialization process to an importance it would not formerly have had' (p. 65). In an inner city context this *socialization* process may be of especial relevance. The achievement of a positive and consistent school culture thus appears to be crucial for academic effectiveness at the secondary level.

SUMMARY

In seeking to examine the relationship between the results of our Differential School Effectiveness project and theoretical accounts of educational effectiveness, we have outlined existing models of school effectiveness and explored how our findings relate to these, stressing the need to incorporate the departmental level into current models of school effectiveness. We argue that such models help to improve our understanding of the ways schools influence their students' academic outcomes. In particular we focus on the concept of school culture or ethos and identify three strands which, in combination, are highly significant in accounting for variations in academic effectiveness. These findings have important messages for schools involved in the processes of self-evaluation and review and concerned with school improvement (see also Reynolds *et al.*, 1996). In the next chapter we move on to discuss in more detail the implications of our results for policy makers, practitioners and other players in the educational process, linking school effectiveness with the concerns of school improvement.

NOTES

1 West and Hopkins (1996) have argued for a broader definition of effectiveness encompassing a range of student and teacher outcomes. We accept the value of such a broad perspective but suggest that this relates to more general concepts such as what constitutes a 'good' or 'successful' school.

9

Implications for School Improvement

INTRODUCTION

We have already alluded to the growing concern amongst politicians and the wider public about 'educational standards', particularly levels of literacy and numeracy, over the last twenty years. Regular reports that school leavers lack the skills needed by employers still appear in the contemporary press. This concern is not unique to the UK system, although to practitioners it sometimes seems as though 'teacher bashing' is a peculiarly English phenomenon! (The term 'English' is used deliberately, for studies suggest that public satisfaction may be higher north of the border.) Visitors to countries such as the US, Canada, New Zealand or Australia, however, will also hear debates about 'failing schools' and falling educational standards that have a very familiar ring.

In fact there is little hard evidence about whether educational standards have actually fallen – reliable information enabling comparisons over decades simply is not available. The tendency to look back to a mythical 'golden age' ignores the trend for many more young people to stay on at school and enter further and higher education, and there can be no doubt that access to educational qualifications has widened considerably, particularly for girls. The introduction of the GCSE, removing the two-tier GCE/CSE divide, is generally regarded as having had a beneficial impact, and a gently rising trend in GCSE performance has been evident over the last decade.

These improvements in educational opportunities should be welcomed and are a cause for celebration – but there is no room for complacency (see the Labour Literacy Taskforce, 1997, for example). Although we do not think there is convincing evidence that standards have fallen in the UK, international comparisons strongly suggest that our educational system is not working to maintain competitiveness with other nations as well as it should. Too few young people obtain vocationally relevant qualifications and, although substantially more enter higher education than previously, the proportion remains lower than in most post-industrial societies. It must, however, be recognized that international comparisons are fraught with difficulties (Goldstein, 1996). In areas such as mathematics, recent reviews suggest that our education system continues to serve more able students well, but that it has a much longer 'trailing edge' than is evident in many other countries, particularly the 'tiger' economies of the Pacific rim

(Reynolds and Farrell, 1996). While the reasons which underlie these differences are likely to be complex and probably reflect cultural traditions and resourcing as much as variations in the processes of schooling, such international comparisons suggest that we should pay much more attention to ways of raising standards for average and below average students.

There is, therefore, a growing awareness that our current education system continues to serve the bottom 30 per cent of our young people relatively poorly. This has important equal opportunities as well as economic implications. Such students are over-represented in inner city areas and there is considerable concern about the long-term social consequences of their educational under-achievement. Additionally, poor and ethnic minority students are geographically concentrated in such areas and thus are disproportionately affected. There are also growing gender differences in achievement at GCSE, which can be seen as the gateway or, for those failing to gain A-C grades, the stumbling block to continuing in education after age sixteen. Gender, ethnic and socio-economic factors do not operate in isolation, however, and in recent years the poor achievement of white working class and Afro-Caribbean boys has attracted much media attention (e.g. Sammons, 1995; Gillborn and Gipps, 1996). Allied to problems of academic under-performance, there is growing concern about increasing behaviour and attendance problems in schools, both amongst their staff as well as the wider public (Barber and Dann, 1996). Recent tragedies such as the shooting of primary pupils at Dunblane (March 1996, the murder of a London headteacher (Philip Lawrence), and the well-publicized disruption at the Ridings School in Yorkshire, appear to have induced a sense of moral panic in the public at large. Moreover, there is growing evidence that the number of exclusions has risen from 1991 onwards (TES, 9.11.96., p. 1; Gillborn and Gipps, 1996).

There are, of course, strong links between students' academic achievement, motivation, behaviour, attendance and self-esteem. These links are often reciprocal, poor attainment increasing the risk of subsequent poor behaviour and attendance and vice versa (Mortimore *et al.*, 1988). As we have argued elsewhere, there are strong arguments for focusing on these links since programmes which address only one aspect in isolation, be it academic achievement, attendance, behaviour or self-esteem, are liable to have less impact in the long term. A failure to address the needs of the 'trailing edge' has serious consequences for democracy and social cohesion, as is demonstrated by the rise of an increasingly alienated underclass of mainly male, young, unemployed people concentrated in decaying, inner city environments with rising crime rates.

School effectiveness research has indicated that there are greater variations between schools in their effectiveness in the UK than in many other education systems where school differences are far smaller (Reynolds, 1995). The results of our study of departmental differences in secondary school effectiveness are highly relevant to all those concerned with raising educational standards and school improvement. We have identified the existence of both statistically, and – much more importantly – educationally significant differences in academic effectiveness between schools. We also highlight the need to look at within-school differences in effectiveness, and our case studies show links with behaviour and attendance patterns. Our sample covered eight inner city LEAs and ninety-four schools: because of this and the nature of the student population we studied, it is of particular relevance to those concerned with raising educational standards for average and below average groups, and to those committed to improving the quality of schooling in socio-economically disadvantaged and ethnically diverse urban areas.

School improvement has been defined as 'a strategy for educational change that enhances student outcomes as well as strengthening the school's capacity for managing change' (Hopkins, 1994, p. 3). In this chapter, therefore, we will examine the implications of our research for the various partners involved in educational policy making and the delivery of education in schools, as well as for the consumers of the service – the students and their parents.

IMPLICATIONS FOR POLICY MAKERS – GOVERNMENT AND LEAS

The last two decades have seen many important and controversial changes to the education system. For secondary schools the most significant have probably been those arising from the implementation of the Education Reform Act (1988) leading to greater autonomy and accountability via the introduction of LMS and open enrolment, the National Curriculum and associated National Assessment (NC and NA) at KS 3, and national publication of examination results from 1992 – the so-called 'league table' policy. Changes in teacher pay and conditions (e.g. the introduction of directed time) and the creation of the Office for Standards in Education (OFSTED) and the development of a national framework for regular inspection on a four-year cycle have also been highly influential with the identification of 'failing' schools and of those with serious weaknesses requiring 'special measures'.

Detailed discussion of these changes is beyond the scope of this chapter – see Barber, 1996(a) and (b), for recent analyses of these developments. In brief, however, they have involved attempts to apply market forces to education as outlined in *Choice and Diversity* (DFE, 1992). It was claimed that the combination of open enrolment (with student numbers driving funding formulae) and publication of league tables of NA and public examination results would lead to the 'withering away' of 'poor' schools if they fail to improve, because parents would choose to send their children to schools with better results. Significantly, nothing was said about the impact of this policy for the quality of education available to students attending these schools during this process of withering! In the early 1990s government policy substantially reduced the powers of LEAs, including the abolition of the former Inner London Education Authority in the capital (and the future and role of LEAs remained in some doubt). It also reduced the support available to schools, through both local management of schools (LMS) and the encouragement of schools to opt out of local control by becoming Grant Maintained (GM). The existence of greater diversity in schools (including plans to increase schools' abilities to select students and more recently the last Prime Minister's advocacy of a 'grammar' school in every town) was ostensibly designed to make schools more responsive to local needs and allow greater consumer choice.

Although many of the changes outlined here were intended to make schools more autonomous and to encourage diversity, they also involved a great increase in the powers and responsibilities of the secretary of state and greater centralization and standardization (for example, of the curriculum, of funding arrangements, and a much higher profile for inspection). As a result, the trend towards greater autonomy of individual schools is in tension with that towards centralization, standardization and control. Likewise, the move towards increasing accountability at the individual school level conflicts with the reduction in powers of the LEA, which erodes accountability to the local electorate. Furthermore, there is also a tension between the policy of enhancing parental choice and encouraging diversity amongst schools to widen such choice, and that of promoting selection which inevitably enhances schools' abilities to choose students and, therefore, reduces options for the majority.

Our research contains a number of important messages for policy makers concerned with raising educational standards. These include implications for: the judgement of performance and mechanisms for ensuring accountability; the inspection process and teacher training; and the intake and resourcing of schools.

Judging school performance

It is evident from the findings of our secondary school research that schools do indeed differ in their effectiveness. Even within the relatively socio-economically disadvantaged and ethnically diverse context of inner London, some schools were much better than others at promoting their students' academic outcomes over several years. As we illustrated in Chapter 3, the differences for individual students in terms of GCSE results could be striking (e.g. differences for the average student between six Grade Ds and six Grade Bs at the most extreme). Some students' future educational and employment prospects were significantly enhanced by their positive educational experiences, while others were much less fortunate. As in an earlier primary school study (Mortimore *et al.*, 1988), we can conclude that secondary schools also matter. Even in the face of very difficult circumstances schools can have a beneficial impact on their students' lives. It is vitally important that schools receive feedback about their effectiveness because such information can help them evaluate their performance, set targets, assist in school development planning and stimulate improvement initiatives.

League tables and value added
Our study also makes it quite clear that the current publication of raw 'league tables' of schools' public examination results is not justified as a mechanism for accountability. As we have shown, schools vary markedly in the nature of

their student intakes and valid comparisons cannot be made without reference to this. There is a long tradition of sociological and educational research (for a review of this see Sammons *et al.*, 1994) which demonstrates the strength of relationships between students' background characteristics, particularly socio-economic factors such as parents' education, occupation and income, and their educational outcomes. It is unrealistic to expect schools to compensate for all the ills of society. Raw league tables make invalid comparisons because they are not conducted on a 'like with like' basis. Schools in affluent suburban areas are compared with those receiving students from very different backgrounds in inner city areas. Such comparisons are likely to lead to complacency on the part of more advantaged schools and demoralization on the part of staff in schools serving disadvantaged areas, which face very different challenges. We must stress that this is not to condone low expectations of students by staff in such schools. Rather we argue that judgements about performance should take account of differences in intake so that comparisons are only made between schools receiving similar kinds of students.

One of the purposes of research shows how value added approaches can be used to study school effectiveness. These focus on student progress over time, for example, from secondary transfer at age eleven to the end of compulsory schooling, and separate the schools' contribution from that which relates to intake by controlling for prior attainment and other background factors. Such information shows whether students in a given school made more or less progress than similar students in other schools. We argue that such value added information is much more useful to practitioners in schools than raw league tables, and also is more relevant to inspectors and those concerned with accountability and promoting school improvement. We believe strongly that the proper criterion for measuring school effectiveness is their impact on students' educational outcomes, and that measures of academic progress are important indicators. Schools are thus held accountable for what they are designed to influence – students' progress – which can be seen as the fundamental purpose of education. They should not be held responsible for all the pre-existing inequalities in society (Mortimore, Sammons and Thomas, 1994).

OFSTED has shown some interest in the development of contextualized measures of secondary school performance (Sammons *et al.*, 1994) and, after some initial reluctance, the DFE (1995) and SCAA (1995) have accepted the need for value added measures. However, there has been considerable reluctance to take on board the message from school effectiveness research that, in addition to prior attainment, other factors to do with students' backgrounds (most notably socio-economic disadvantage as measured by eligibility for free school meals, but also gender) also exert an influence. Our research shows that such factors continue to influence students' GCSE results. Ignoring such differences inevitably penalizes inner city schools (Willms, 1992; Sammons *et al.*, 1994) and does nothing to remove the link between socio-economic disadvantage and school achievement. In order to be accepted by practitioners it is vital that school comparisons are seen to be fair.

Arguments against value added approaches have stressed the need for 'simplicity' although, strangely, complexity appears to be quite acceptable in other areas such as economic modelling or police pay formulae! There is, however, an important distinction between simplicity and the adoption of simplistic but inappropriate solutions. Value added approaches have been used to give feedback about school performance for over a decade and, in our experience, both practitioners and parents accept the message that student progress is at the heart of an effective school. Examples of LEAs which have developed value added indicators of performance include pioneering work by the former ILEA (later extended by the Association of Metropolitan Authorities), Lancashire, Shropshire, Suffolk, and Surrey. The ALIS system has also operated in many parts of the country to give schools valued added feedback on A-level performance, and more recently has extended to GCSE. In our experience the development of such measures has been welcomed by schools which are keen to obtain comparative feedback about their performance (Fitz-Gibbon, 1991, 1992; Thomas and Mortimore, 1996).

It is important to stress, however, that ranking schools on the basis of their value added GCSE results (as is the practice in raw league tables) is not justified (Goldstein et al., 1993; Sammons et al., 1993; Goldstein and Thomas, 1996). As we have shown in the research reported in this book, it is possible to identify schools in which students' GCSE results were significantly better or worse than predicted on the basis of intake, but for many schools GCSE results were in line with those predicted, and thus could not be differentiated. Fine distinctions, such as rank ordering, are simply not statistically valid.

In addition, our analyses of GCSE performance demonstrate that comparisons of schools based on only one measure (e.g. the percentage gaining five A-C GCSE grades) are inadequate. Even using value added approaches reliance on only one measure will obscure the existence of internal variations in effectiveness. As our results illustrate, there can be marked variations in effectiveness in different GCSE subjects, pointing to the importance of the departmental level. Although a few outliers can be identified (broadly effective or broadly ineffective across a range of subjects) for most schools, the situation is much more complex and indeed in some institutions we found highly effective and highly ineffective departments coexisting. The use of only one overall measure can obscure such internal variations. For most schools simplistic distinctions such as 'good' or 'bad' are therefore inappropriate. We conclude that the concept of school effectiveness should be amended to that of *school and departmental effectiveness*.

Trends over time

Our research also highlights the need to look at school performance across several years, three being the minimum required to identify trends and five years giving a even better picture (Gray et al., 1996). We argue that value added information about trends is much more useful to practitioners as well as to parents whose children usually spend five years in one secondary school before entering for GCSEs. It is also more relevant to inspectors concerned with judging the quality of education provided and identifying areas for improvement.

The question of differential effectiveness is also relevant for all concerned with social justice and democracy. Is a school equally effective for different student groups or for boys or girls? How do those of different ethnic or socioeconomic backgrounds and those who enter secondary schooling with below or with above average prior attainment fare?

We recommend that either nationally or at LEA level, as is already done very successfully in some areas, appropriate value added frameworks be developed which will provide schools with good quality comparative information about their performance on a year-by-year basis. Such information should use both an overall indicator, such as total GCSE performance score, and performance in core subjects (e.g. English, mathematics and science). In this context we note the work of the SCAA value added working group (SCAA, 1995). However, we believe that the attempt to use national assessment data for these purposes is problematic. Such measures were not designed with the requirements of establishing a value added framework in mind and therefore may not provide sufficiently detailed information about student attainment *at entry* to secondary school. The use of standardized assessments in reading and mathematics, which are good predictors of later GCSE results, are greatly preferable. IQ-type measures, particularly if not taken at entry, are also considered inappropriate because they do not relate to the curriculum. Our study has demonstrated the continuing strength of socio-economic and other background influences, value added frameworks should be established which explicitly model such effects. Only in this way can we be confident that like is properly being compared with like, as we showed in Chapter 3.

In addition, we believe that such a system should attempt to provide measures of effectiveness for different sub-groups of students. The three questions that should guide the development of such a system are:

- Differential effectiveness – Effective for whom (which student groups)?
- Consistency – Effective for what kinds of outcomes? (different subjects etc.)?
- Improvement – Effective over what time period (what are the trends in performance)?

Intake and resourcing of schools

School effectiveness research has revealed the importance of taking account of the differences between schools in their intakes. In our study we were able to demonstrate the existence of substantial differences between schools in the prior attainments of their students at age eleven, as well as in measures of socio-economic and ethnic diversity. Although resources were not identified as a key factor influencing school effectiveness, some schools had experienced great difficulties in attracting and retaining experienced and qualified staff.

This has obvious implications for the quality and consistency of students' learning experiences. Of course, as we note in Chapter 7, such difficulties may be as much a symptom as a cause of ineffectiveness in some schools. Nonetheless, they remain powerful barriers to improvement. Sadly, in a case study drawn from the highly ineffective group, finally having in-post 'the full complement of staff' was cited as perhaps the major achievement of the new head's time in their school!

The challenges faced by schools in socio-economically disadvantaged areas require serious recognition. Ways of improving such schools' attractiveness to teachers need to be developed. Current policies – such as the publication of raw league tables – are likely to add to staff demoralization in such areas. This tends to discourage teachers from applying for jobs in these schools because of the risk of association with institutions which are more likely to be identified as 'failing' or requiring special measures. The rewards for headteachers in such schools also need to be improved, given evidence of growing difficulties in attracting good candidates reported in recent years. Although resources are certainly not the answer to all educational problems, ways of ensuring that inner city schools can attract and retain good staff at all levels need to be identified and given a high priority.

Experience of the educational priority policies of the 1970s suggests that it is important that additional resources do not reward schools with poor results (Sammons, Kysel and Mortimore, 1983). Under LMS, however, there are restrictions which limit LEAs' abilities to direct additional resources to schools with serving students with additional educational needs. Some LEAs make no provision, many use crude measures of the percentage of students eligible for free school meals. The way such funding formulae are applied, however, means that students with the same characteristics in different areas will attract different resources to their schools (Sammons, 1993). Even more difficult, there is no mechanism for ensuring that any resources allocated to schools on the basis of their students' special needs are actually used to benefit those students – except in the case of statemented children.

Given the strong links, illustrated by this study but also to be found in many others, between low levels of attainment at age eleven and students' GCSE results, and also the impact of other factors like low family income, we think there is a very strong case for the development of a national funding formula for schools. This should take into account the *risk* of low achievement and direct extra resources to schools which serve higher numbers of such students. This would remove the geographical 'lottery' which currently characterizes the operation of LMS. If such a formula were based on student intakes to school, e.g. at secondary transfer at eleven, probably using low KS2 results as a basis, the danger of rewarding past poor performance would be eliminated. There would be an additional advantage to such a system, since it would help to counteract the 'market forces' pressure on schools to recruit as many high attaining non-disadvantaged students who are likely to do well at GCSE and therefore boost a school's raw league table position. To put it crudely, under the present system schools which can recruit more than average numbers of middle class girls will tend to shine, whereas schools which have the most disadvantaged cannot.

Of course extra resources by themselves will be no guarantee of effectiveness (a point we discuss in more depth later). It is *vital* that such resources are specifically targeted at students in most need. This was a crucial weakness of earlier educational priority policies of the 1970s and 1980s (Sammons, Kysel and Mortimore, 1983; Sammons, 1993), and remains a weakness in the way resources are allocated for special educational needs under LMS. Students falling below a certain level of performance could be identified as at risk of low attainment or viewed as entitled to extra provision, probably in literacy and numeracy, designed to bring low attaining 7 and 8 year students up to a specified level which would enable them to benefit more fully from the rest of the secondary curriculum. The design of special programmes for such groups, if used positively, could help to raise rather than depress teachers' expectations.

The ways in which resources could be so targeted have been clearly demonstrated by the success of the Reading Recovery programme with younger age groups (Sylva and Hurry, 1995). Given the strong link between poor attainment, especially in reading and for boys, and low self-esteem, plus behaviour and attendance problems, intervention in the early years of secondary schooling and careful monitoring of student progress should have beneficial effects on a range of student outcomes, not only academic performance. The deliberate targeting of resources on the basis of education need to benefit those students who are the 'trailing' edge in our system and who are at most risk of becoming the so called 'disaffected (and disappeared)' (Barber, 1996a) would help to ensure that schools in the most difficult circumstances had better odds in the struggle to raise standards.

In this book we focus on the implications of our research for secondary schools in particular. Nonetheless, our other studies have pointed to the importance of primary education and the variations in effectiveness of such schools (Mortimore et al., 1988). We have also drawn attention to the long term impact of primary schools (Sammons et al., 1995) on later GCSE results. Early identification of children with low levels of reading attainment in particular (for example via schemes such as Reading Recovery) will prove most cost-effective in the long term, and enable students to progress into secondary schooling more readily (Sylva and Hurry, 1995). Again, the arguments we have made about the need to provide and target resources for secondary schools also apply to the primary sector.

Selection
Our research, as noted earlier, demonstrates the strong links between individual student intake characteristics and academic results. In addition, we found some indications of *contextual* effects related to the proportion of disadvantaged students, i.e. those eligible for free school meals in a school, in spite of the fact that our sample came from an inner city area well known for encour-

aging a balanced intake (see Chapter 3). The implication of our findings is that in schools with a higher concentration of disadvantaged students the performance of all students, regardless of their own background, tends to be depressed. This tendency was most evident for performance in English at GCSE, reflecting the stronger links between performance in this subject and background. We would argue that this tendency would be more pronounced in areas where there are greater variations between schools in their intakes, especially where there are selective schools.

The early *Fifteen Thousand Hours* study in inner London (Rutter *et al.*, 1979) and also work in Scotland (e.g. Willms, 1986) have also drawn attention to the impact of socio-economic and academic balance in schools. Of course, schools' intakes vary greatly according to the socio-economic characteristics of their local catchment areas, but the influence of other factors, such as the availability of an alternative school, also has an important effect. Schools in middle-class suburbs usually have a more favourable academic balance. Even without selection, in some areas true 'comprehensives' may be hard to find. However, where selection operates, local comprehensives are creamed. The last government's plans to increase schools' abilities to select their students, at the extreme proposals for a grammar school in every town, would, inevitably, mean that the majority of other (non-selective) schools will have less balanced intakes.

As Mortimore (1995c) has argued, the beneficial influence of a balance of academically able students in a school gives a powerful boost to the ethos of the school and thus to its ability to be effective and promote progress. Teachers also commonly value the opportunity for a genuine balance of teaching assignments and in this research we found that academic balance was an important issue for many respondents. Unfortunately, although research as well as practitioners' experience suggests that academic balance is desirable, recent policy with its emphasis on diversity has promoted the opposite trend. Proposals to increase selection via the re-introduction of grammar schools would, we believe, have increased the wide gap in performance, already wider in the UK than in many other countries, between the highest and lowest performing students rather than reduce it. This would exacerbate the problem of the 'trailing edge' of the bottom 30 per cent of students. Also, as we have noted before the variation between schools in the UK is also substantially larger than in many other systems. Increasing selection could thus also serve to widen the 'trailing edge' of schools as well as of students.

There is, unfortunately, no easy solution to this problem. How can the maximum academic balance of students be encouraged for the maximum number of schools, thus benefiting the academic achievement of the majority of students, while, at the same time, allowing the flexibility of parental choice? Can a balance between diversity and equity be encouraged as Barber (1996a), has suggested, which will avoid the recreation of a two-tier system of schools with the inevitable sense of failure for the majority of children at eleven-plus, and the consequent reduction in their choice of schools which a fully selective system inevitably creates?

LEAs no longer have the power to intervene in admission arrangements in the way they once did. In these circumstances, how can a satisfactory overall pattern of schools be created? One possible solution may be to allow only partial selection of academically high attaining students (perhaps the maximum of 15 per cent currently allowed for GM schools), while at the same time allocating significant extra resources for those with additional educational needs. If resources were targeted at the student level as we discussed above, this would act as a powerful incentive to schools to maintain a wide balance in their intakes. It would also benefit students in schools serving areas in which there were, as a consequence of the social geography of the locality, inevitably higher numbers of disadvantaged and low attaining students.

Although it might not prove feasible to have a quota of low attaining students (as was tried with limited success in the former ILEA), by linking resources *directly* to the admission of low attaining students at secondary transfer, and ensuring they were specifically used to benefit these students, the current powerful incentives to schools to recruit as many able students as possible would at least be reduced, if not eliminated. Also the status of such students could be enhanced by specific recognition of their needs, if properly designed programmes were instituted. If the lowest scoring 20–25 per cent of students in terms of national primary school Key Stage 2 assessments were identified before secondary transfer, their choices of secondary schools might be enhanced. Clearly, in socio-economically disadvantaged areas more students would be identified than would be the case in say suburban ones. Yet this would help to recognize and, hopefully, address the additional challenges currently faced by such schools. If the results of primary school assessments were used, there would be no danger of rewarding low performing secondary schools, a very important consideration if the aim is to raise national educational standards. Also, analysing the value added scores for the low attaining group after a period of time in secondary school (e.g. from age eleven to KS3) would provide one method of evaluating whether the additional funds had helped improve performance for these students.

As noted earlier, additional resources cannot by themselves raise standards. Our research was conducted amongst ninety-four inner London schools with broadly similar funding levels (a legacy of the former ILEA) and favourable resource levels in comparison with secondary schools elsewhere in the country. Resourcing levels were not found to differentiate the most and the least effective schools in our case studies, even though all respondents felt more resources would be beneficial. In terms of policy implications we are not suggesting a dramatic increase in resourcing to finance the targeting of specific funds for the lowest attaining groups at secondary transfer. A modest increase in educational funding, however, would surely have a considerable psychological impact especially if guaranteed to continue over several successive years. However, if a national pupil-based funding formula was developed with an explicit and fairly substantial needs-based element as we have proposed, this would have a *redistributive* effect. We argue that it is this redistributive aspect which would create a tension between the current pressure on schools to maximize the number of high ability socio-economically advantaged students who will perform well in league tables and pose fewer behaviour and attendance problems, by a direct financial incentive to recruit more low attaining, disadvantaged students. This tension, we think, would act as a powerful mechanism for encouraging schools to maintain a balanced intake which would, nationally, benefit the attainment of the majority of students.

The amount of the educational budget which should be allocated to enable such redistribution is a matter which would require consultation, but a figure of 15–20 per cent of the total allocated on the basis of pupil numbers might be sufficient.

Inspection

The creation of OFSTED in 1993 was a significant and ambitious policy initiative designed to serve two main functions – to promote accountability and to stimulate improvement. Matthews and Smith (1995) provide a clear account of the underlying rationale. Before OFSTED's inception, 'the inspection manual was a fairly closely guarded secret' (Wilcox and Gray, 1996, p. 139). OFSTED, to its credit, has sought to be open via publication of its handbook and consultations prior to its revision in 1995. The OFSTED Handbook can be seen to embody not only a model of inspection, but also an implicit model of the school (Wilcox and Gray, 1996).

The inspection system prior to 1993 could be criticized for its infrequency and therefore the remote possibility of identifying schools which were failing to provide a satisfactory education for their students. The opposite extreme has been reached with a four-year inspection cycle and whether spending the large sums entailed is the best way to achieve school improvement remains to be proved (see Hargreaves, 1995b; Mortimore, 1996; Earley, Fidler and Ouston, 1996). The current move to a six-year inspection cycle, with more frequent inspection of schools for which there is concern, is likely to prove more acceptable and manageable, and should release additional resources which could be used to provide a higher level of support post-inspection than is currently the case. There are very good arguments for ensuring that inspections provide both 'support as well as pressure' (Fullan, 1993; Stoll and Thomson, 1996). In our view, the separation of advisory and inspection functions is unfortunate and does not provide the best basis for post-inspection action planning.

Our study of secondary school effectiveness has, we think, important implications for the operation of the inspection process. The discussion of league tables and accountability is clearly relevant to the judgement of educational standards and quality of education in secondary schools. It is essential that comparisons are made on a 'like with like' basis, given the consequences of being categorized as a 'failing' or requiring special measures. The inspection process should use information about student intakes (as provided in the Pre-

Inspection Context Indicators reports) to assist in the contextualization of inspectors' judgements of performance (Sammons *et al.*, 1994). Where available, value added data or information about the attainments of students at secondary transfer should be obtained to assist in this process and schools should be encouraged to engage in internal monitoring of pupil progress using such methods. Targeting and benchmarking, if contextualized, may prove a valuable stimulus for school-based monitoring and focusing on improving educational standards.

The results of our analysis of the mechanisms underlying secondary and departmental effectiveness support the emphasis given by OFSTED to the crucial role of the management of schools. We identified the leadership of the headteacher and senior management team as important factors which contribute to the academic success of the school. Their influence operates through the creation of shared vision and goals, high expectations, and a climate which is conducive to teaching and learning in the classroom. Concern with administrative and financial matters was not allowed to obscure the prime focus of the school on students' outcomes. The development and consistent implementation of whole school policies (e.g. marking, assessment, behaviour, homework) had a high priority. Likewise, the institution of effective mechanisms for the regular monitoring and review of student progress and outcomes was regarded as important. Such leadership sought to involve as well as influence staff behaviour. Communication and consultation with staff was given a high priority and, in the more effective schools, a sense of whole school ownership of policies was engendered as a result.

Our research also draws attention to the significant role of middle managers. Heads of department played an important part in promoting GCSE subject results. In some schools both highly effective and highly ineffective departments co-existed. The identification of lead departments may be one way to raise the performance of others. Studies of school improvement suggest that it is important to build on and celebrate existing strengths while targeting weaknesses. This can be a positive outcome of inspection and help to empower staff managers and the governing body through recognition of the need to act to raise standards in specific subjects.

The inspection process can be used to help clarify the role and responsibilities of heads of department and to identify training needs. Key features include policy and consistent current examination entry, assessment and record keeping, homework, marking and feedback to students, and the department's methods for monitoring, reviewing and rewarding student progress. As with the school as a whole, the individual department's history, especially staff changes and shortages, will be highly relevant.

Getting the right blend of advice and inspection inevitably demands local knowledge at the level of the school and the LEA, as well as appropriate experience and skills. Good subject specialist advice will be particularly important for schools with difficulties in particular departments. The provision of post-inspection support by OFSTED is likely to make its commitment to promoting improvement more of a reality. It is also likely to improve schools' abilities to accept and act on the judgements made by inspectors.

The findings of our questionnaire survey indicated that the majority of those already inspected had found the process helpful rather than unhelpful. We suggest the process of significant self-evaluation and review stimulated by the knowledge in advance when the school would be 'OFSTEDed' is likely to have been at least as important as the inspection process itself. Ironically, in some schools the prospect of inspection appeared to have engendered a sense of whole staff unity and encouraged a level of collaboration which was previously lacking. Whether this is sustained post-inspection of course may be another matter. For long lasting improvement a change of culture from within the school is a necessary pre-condition (Stoll and Fink, 1996). Such a change in culture cannot be externally mandated, though appropriate advice and support may be highly beneficial.

The most workable and cost-effective system may prove to be a more flexible inspection system with specific criteria to trigger earlier inspection where deemed necessary, for example, related to a declining trend of examination or NA results, attendance or increase indicators of behaviour problems, such as exclusions, but a longer inspection cycle for other schools and lighter reporting. For schools with severe difficulties there may be a need for long term – two to three years – external support to promote school improvement. Such support, however, should have a definite time scale and be evaluated carefully by means of clear targets and criteria. Although it is recognized that improvement may take several years for most schools, in extreme cases the power to close schools should be retained where problems continue unchecked for a specified period. Turning around 'failing' schools may prove too time consuming or difficult in some instances and time is very costly to the students involved.

OFSTED has had a highly controversial first four years in operation. We consider it important that achievements in providing an external framework for evaluating schools should be built on. However, whether the considerable resources involved are the best way to promote school improvement remains open to question. A more flexible, somewhat less frequent inspection cycle which combined support/advice as well as judgement would, we think, prove more efficacious. In our view, the highly political role adopted by its current chief inspector (in contrast to his predecessor) threatens to bring the system into disrepute and alienate teachers and senior managers. Without their support and goodwill, raising educational standards will be impossible. This controversial and adversarial approach is preventing the useful contribution which a more flexible inspection system could make to promoting good practice and improving opportunities for students.

IMPLICATIONS FOR PRACTITIONERS IN SCHOOLS

Staff in schools are chiefly responsible for the quality of students' educational experiences. Our study shows that even in difficult circumstances they can and do make a difference. Where learning is valued and academic matters are seen to be relevant for all students, staff recognize that they can make an important contribution. School effectiveness research has consistently demonstrated that schools cannot lay all the blame for failure at the doors of parents and society, powerful though such influences can be (Reynolds, 1994b; Mortimore, 1995a).

Stoll and Fink (1996) have provided a definition of an effective school which links well with schools' interests in improvement. This covers four aspects:

- promoting progress for *all* students beyond what would be expected given consideration of initial attainment and background factors;
- ensuring that each pupil achieves the highest standards possible;
- enhancing all aspects of pupil achievement and development; and
- continuing to improve from year to year (p. 28).

The Senior Management Team

Unsurprisingly our research drew attention to the importance of the Senior Management Team (SMT) in promoting secondary schools' academic effectiveness. As Wallace and Hall (1994) have shown in their detailed study of different SMTs, it is essential that the SMT do in fact work together effectively as a team. They stated that lack of teamwork is the 'Achilles heel' of SMT: 'together, team members make the team, individually they can break it. The culture of teamwork is no stronger than individuals' commitment . . . the onus is on every member to accept equal responsibility for making the SMT work' (p. 198). Our research supports this emphasis on the need for teamwork and individual as well as collective responsibility for ensuring this.

In this sub-section we highlight some of the most important practical messages from our research for the SMT.

Monitoring

There are a number of simple but informative ways in which individual schools can analyse their own data to enhance their monitoring capacity and this section provides some suggestions concerning this.

By linking information about students' prior attainment and later performance we can investigate the value added by the school. Where a school has access to information about its own results set in the context of other schools and convering three or more years, changes in performance can be studied over time. In Figure 9.1 we show for a sample of our schools, the trends in average prior attainment over three years (the mean LRT score) at secondary transfer. From such a plot a school can see whether its intake is changing from year to year and also how it compares with other schools. In Figure 9.2 the trend in overall examination performance, i.e. mean total GCSE score, is shown for the same three student cohorts at age sixteen. This illustrates an overall upward trend in GCSE results across most schools. Differences between schools in both

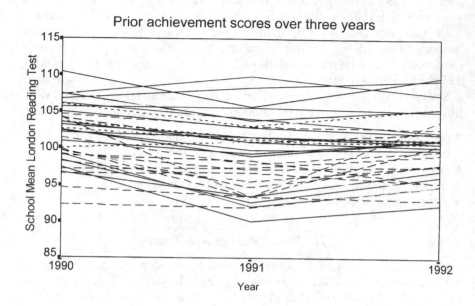

Figure 9.1   Differences between secondary schools in students' average prior attainment levels at secondary transfer for three GCSE cohorts (1990–92)

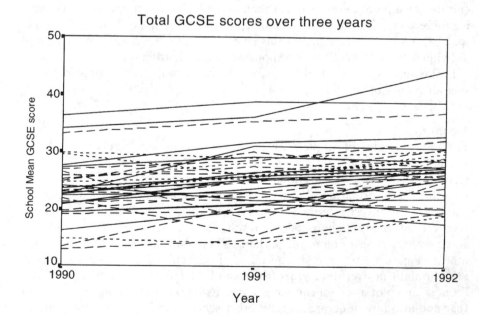

Figure 9.2   Differences between secondary schools in students' average Total GCSE performance score for three GCSE cohorts (1990–92)

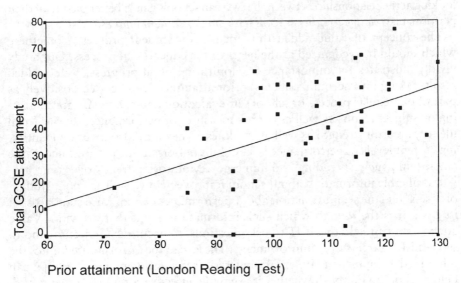

Correlation = 0.47

Figure 9.3   Scatterplot of the relationship between students' Prior attainment and later Total GCSE performance score for a **more academically effective** school

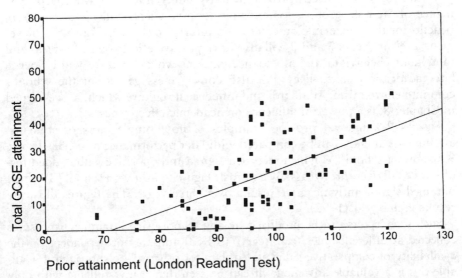

Correlation = 0.64

Figure 9.4   Scatterplot of the relationship between students' Prior attainment and later Total GCSE performance score for a **less academically effective** school

prior attainment and GCSE outcomes are quite marked in both these plots. Only by looking at the relationship between the two can schools gain a better picture of their performance *relative to other schools with similar student intakes.*

The concept of value added thus focuses on student progress, something which should be recognized as the heart of the educational process. Our study vividly illustrates the importance of monitoring pupil progress. Value added results taking into account students' prior attainment can be used positively as part of the regular process of school self-evaluation and review. By concentrating on subject results as well as overall measures of performance, the SMT can identify areas of strength as well as weakness. They may also focus on identifying current levels of performance in key skills important for progress across the curriculum, such as reading and numeracy. Monitoring trends over time provides valuable information about school improvement as well as about student progress. Of course, information about performance cannot raise standards on its own. It is the *uses* to which such information is put that are vital. Value added data can help the SMT to ask questions, to encourage reflection and to set realistic targets for improvement. These can be incorporated into the school's development plan. Analysing results for different pupil groups can help a school to establish whether it is equally effective for all its students and, if not, help to set priorities for the future. They can thus contribute to the school's equal opportunities policy.

Collecting detailed information about students' achievement at entry in key skills such as reading and numeracy is essential to help the school decide priorities for special needs provision. Early intervention to raise the performance of 'at risk' groups, for example, poor readers, will have long term benefits for their academic outcomes and future life chances. Raising achievement levels in Years 7 and 8 will also have positive effects on self-esteem and motivation, behaviour and attendance patterns which, in turn, will influence later academic results. They will also convey messages about the school's commitment to raising standards and influence its culture which, as we argued in Chapter 8, is a powerful influence on academic effectiveness.

Figures 9.3 and 9.4 provide examples of how simple plots of students' attainments at entry can be compared with later performance at GCSE. Figure 9.3 shows a school (A) which recorded significantly positive value added results at GCSE over three years. By contrast, Figure 9.4 shows a school (B) which obtained significantly negative results over three years. The figures illustrate results in one year (1992).

Such scatterplots can be produced by any school using attainment measures collected at different times (e.g. Year 7 to KS3) and are not dependent on the availability of comparative value added data for other schools, though if available this is a valuable advantage. It can be seen that many students with only average levels of prior reading attainment (100 in this illustration) did well at GCSE in school A, whereas in school B quite a number of initial good readers went on to obtain poor GCSE results. Overall, school A had added considerably more value to its students' GCSE performance. Schools can also explore gender differences in achievement patterns using separate plots for males and females. As we discuss in the next section individual departments can use similar methods to investigate their own subject results. Where the SMT review departmental performance we believe such simple plots can be a valuable tool.

Schools should remember, however, that the data is retrospective and that it is quite possible that the results of future cohorts may reveal a changing pattern. For example, note the increasing trend overall in GCSE attainment. Crucially, this means that the widespread practice of predicting the GCSE grades of individual Year 7 students on the basis of attainment at entry should be treated with some caution, as it is important that predictions do not depress teacher or student expectations.

In addition to monitoring academic results, analysing information about behaviour/attendance and listening to the students' views (Ruddock *et al.*, 1996) should be key activities for the SMT. As we noted in Chapter 8, there are three important aspects of school ethos and culture which are important for the academic effectiveness of secondary schools: order (behaviour policy and practice), task achievement (academic emphasis) and relationships (a student-focused approach). Ensuring a safe and orderly working environment in school is a necessary prerequisite for effective learning. Although all staff, both teaching and support, must contribute to this, the SMT are best placed to take a whole school view. Our case studies showed that improvement in 'interim outcomes', that is to say behaviour, motivation and attendance, may be evident before any changes in academic results occur. Collecting and using information about such social outcomes and about students' views also provide important feedback on the quality of students' educational experiences. Evidence of improvements in 'interim outcomes' can boost staff morale, raise expectations and help to maintain staff commitment to promoting academic outcomes in the long term.

Leadership
One clear message, from both our research and other school effectiveness studies, is the need for leadership. The HT has a particularly important role to play in exercising this, and his/her leadership helps to establish a clear and consistent vision (agreed goals) for the school, which emphasizes the prime purposes of the school as teaching and learning and is highly visible to both staff and students. Staff collaboration and involvement is emphasized and the headteacher takes a keen interest in monitoring pupil progress and in the quality of teaching.

Although the headteacher is a key figure, as we have shown, our research also highlights the need for an effective SMT which promotes staff morale and exemplifies teamwork. The academically least effective schools in our case studies suffered from marked division between individuals and personality conflicts which prevented teamwork and cohesion of approach. The SMT should play an important part in promoting the shared vision and goals of the school, an academic emphasis and high expectations. The effective SMT recognizes the need for consistency in approach in terms of agreed policies and practice in the key areas of behaviour, rules and management, assessment and marking, homework, and parental involvement. It ensures high levels of staff consultation and involvement in the development of such policies and it is also deeply involved in the process of self-evaluation and review, monitoring the performance of different departments on a regular basis and encouraging them to give regular feedback to their students. The effective SMT thus seeks to promote a culture of continuous improvement in the school.

There is increasing recognition of the need for schools to become learning organizations in which all participants – SMT, HoDs and teachers as well as students – are actively involved in learning. Southworth (1994) has drawn attention to some of the key features of a learning organization. He notes, 'what really holds members of staff together is a sense of shared values . . . the development of shared beliefs takes time and requires more than formal structures that invite staff to plan and evaluate together' (p. 71). Our research draws attention to the impact of school culture in creating academic effectiveness. Bush (1995) has noted the value of cultural models in his discussion of theories of educational management. He notes that cultural models provide a focus for organizational action, and that there is a strong connection between the way we think and the way we act. 'Leaders may focus on influencing values so that they become closer to, if not identical with, their own beliefs. In this way they hope to achieve widespread support for, or "ownership" of, new policies. . . . An appreciation of the salience of values and beliefs, and the ritual that underpins them, is an important element in the management of schools and colleges'. (p. 140). Other authors have also highlighted the concept of culture. In their discussion of school development planning, Hargreaves and Hopkins (1993) argue that ' when research-based knowledge is put to the test of practice, the result will be more schools which educate *all* of their pupils' (p.239). However, they also emphasize that a profound change in school culture is required for many schools to take on board the messages of school effectiveness research, that it is possible to raise the achievement of all children. Stoll and Fink (1996) likewise draw attention to the need to change school culture, although writing more recently in connection with schools in difficulties they note that change takes time and there are 'no quick fixes'.

Inspection evidence has also drawn attention to the creation of a reflective, consultative, self-critical approach which has become 'enshrined in the school's culture'. Based on HMI visits to over thirty schools identified as good or improving and committed to quality management, Coleman and Matthews (1996) identified four common features: a marked capacity for self-assessment; concern for the views of pupils and parents; effective strategies for improving teaching; and inspiring leadership and effective management.

Practical strategies for improvement

Discussion of the results of our study of secondary school and departmental effectiveness with practitioners suggest a number of practical strategies which

SMT can adopt to improve their school's effectiveness.

(1) *Explore staff views about the school's current goals and effectiveness*
   A number of questions can be used to initiate discussion and reflection
   amongst the SMT and staff as a whole. They can enable the SMT to
   examine the extent of shared vision/goals and to identify common perceptions of areas of strength and weakness. The questions we developed and
   piloted in our research may prove useful for the SMT in identifying important differences in focus between different groups (the SMT itself,
   HoDs, classroom teachers).

   - What would you say are the principal educational goals that this school tries
     to achieve for its students? Have these changed over the last five years?
   - Which factors do you think ought to be taken into account in judging the
     effectiveness of any secondary school?
   - Which factors contribute most to the current effectiveness of this school?
   - What (if anything) holds this school back from being more effective?

   It is important to encourage all staff to focus on areas of success and
   achievement as well as challenges or problems. Collecting and discussing
   staff views of major successes/achievements over a given time period (such
   as the last five years) and examining major problems/challenges which the
   school has faced can prove a useful exercise. Open discussion of the results
   of such a survey will help to identify areas of agreement as well as difference. Feeding the results into school development planning/identifying
   agreed specific foci for action (including staff involved, resources and time
   scale) are important components in an on-going process or cycle of self-
   evaluation/review – action – reflection – evaluation/review. Such a strategy
   can help to address feelings of powerlessness amongst staff and managers
   which are often present in schools experiencing serious difficulties. Of
   course, very deep divisions may exist in some schools – open discussion
   may appear to exacerbate some of these at first but nonetheless some,
   perhaps unanticipated, areas of agreement may be found which can be
   built on and the deeper difficulties may be resolved as a result of the
   process of discussion.

(2) *Encourage the regular collection and use of information about students'
   educational outcomes at all levels – classroom, department and whole
   school*
   As well as the statistical analysis of results suggested earlier, regular reviews of samples of students' work can contribute to the monitoring of
   different departments and year groups. They can also help to establish
   whether assessment/marking and homework policies are being followed
   consistently and whether students do get regular and constructive feedback
   on their performance and on how to improve their work.
   Information about behaviour and attendance can be used to identify 'at
   risk' students who require greater particular pastoral care. Early interven-

tion and ensuring that behaviour standards are agreed amongst staff and consistently applied are likely to be most effective where students themselves are involved in developing the school's code of conduct. A 'firm but fair' approach focusing on positive reinforcement strategies is most productive. No magic solutions are on offer but helpful approaches to attendance problems and behaviour difficulties have been described and applied (e.g. MacBeath, 1994; Watkins, 1995). Specific anti-bullying programmes may be appropriate for some schools.

Utilizing questionnaire surveys of particular year groups is a strategy that is proving beneficial in an increasing number of schools. This can help to identify whether significant numbers of students experience bullying and the context in which it occurs. Such surveys can also prove revealing in relation to students' views of academic matters such as homework, feedback on work and teacher-student relationships and teaching quality.

As Ruddock et al. (1996) have argued, in many schools too little attention is commonly given to listening to and learning from the students' voices in many schools. Seeking to find out about, and valuing, students' views can be an important first step in creating a sense of whole school identity and common purpose. An example of the way student attitudes can be measured by questionnaires and used as an important indicator of educational outcomes has been provided in an ongoing school improvement study in Scotland (see Thomas, Smees and McCall, 1997).

Focusing attention on early identification of at risk students (in terms of behaviour and attendance), especially for those in Years 7 and 8 before a pattern becomes firmly embedded, is also likely to be most fruitful and will have a beneficial impact on these students' later achievement. Given the known links between attendance and behaviour problems and poor academic achievement, efforts to identify and improve the basic skills of at risk students is likely to benefit social outcomes including self-esteem. This, in turn, can have a positive impact on learning.

(3) *Focus on staff morale*
Poor staff morale is probably as much a symptom as a cause of ineffectiveness. There is no doubt from our research that this was an important issue for schools in our sample, and perhaps nationally, during the first half of the 1990s. Schools in the inner city serve the most disadvantaged communities and, whilst not unique in this respect, serve above-average numbers of students with attendance, behaviour and learning difficulties. In raw league table terms these schools fare badly and annual press publication can prove demoralizing for teaching staff. Inner London schools, in particular, have experienced a range of major changes compressed into a relatively short period. In addition to all the major national educational changes related to the introduction of the National Curriculum, national assessment, LMS, directed time and national OFSTED inspections, these schools simultaneously had to cope with the abolition of the ILEA. Not

surprisingly, levels of stress related to the pace and pressure of external change were reported to be high and staff morale was felt to have been adversely affected.

Nonetheless, some schools coped with change far better than others and, in line with national trends, overall GCSE standards were rising. In particular, the number of students achieving no qualifications at all has fallen across the sample. Some schools also reported improving attendance, motivation and behaviour amongst their students.

Linked with staff morale, poor staff attendance was identified as a significant problem in a minority of schools. Unsurprisingly, high staff absence levels in the previous five years had a negative impact on students' progress, as measured by our value added analyses.

Poor staff attendance was associated with a tendency to blame external factors (especially students/parents/community) for the school's problems as well as low expectations. Remedying unacceptably high levels of staff absence must have a high priority for the SMT, linked with development of a shared vision and goals and raising expectations.

Encouraging departments to cover for absent colleagues wherever possible, and ensuring that classwork and homework is set and marked, can help to maintain some continuity for students. Poor attendance may not only be evident amongst classroom teachers, of course, and where HoDs or members of the SMT itself have a poor attendance record over an extended period, action by the headteacher and other SMT members, perhaps involving the governing body, will be needed. High levels of staff as well as of student absence have a powerful impact on the culture of any secondary school and demonstrate that teaching and learning are not regarded as the highest priority of the school. As well as conveying an adverse message to students about the value of education, high staff absence rates directly affect the quality and continuity of students' educational experiences.

(4) *Working with middle managers*

One method of enhancing academic success at GCSE was evident from our case studies, concerning a strong SMT commitment to working closely with HoDs, particularly new ones and those whose departments were not felt to be achieving as well as others in the school. Learning from good practice developed in particularly effective departments was another strategy. For example, adopting a particularly effective department's marking or homework policy for the whole school could be considered. It is notable that, in interviews, HoDs stressed the benefits of clear *whole-school policies* on behaviour, assessment and marking and homework which were followed in *all* departments.

In the sample of schools as a whole we found that many HoDs wanted a clearer definition of their role and greater involvement with the SMT in decision making. Regular department review (one per term) may prove to be a useful mechanism for encouraging such involvement and providing HoDs with both recognition for current achievements, pressure for improvement where necessary and support. Pairing departments may also prove beneficial if conducted sensitively.

In connection with the need for a clearer definition of their role, the Teacher Training Agencies' (TTAs') work on the development of a National Professional Qualification for Subject Leaders (NPQSL) is highly relevant. This is intended to provide a framework for the training, development, assessment and accreditation of such post holders. The stated objective of the qualification is to help to identify and describe national standards. One of the key principles outlined in the TTA consultation document was that it should be rooted in school improvement and build on current best practice in effective schools and outside education. We return to this topic in more detail in the next section when we focus on implications of our research for HoDs. For school management and leadership we suggest that the SMT may find that the development of national standards and a national professional qualification will help to provide the greater clarity about roles and responsibilities needed by HoDs as well as improving their status. It may prove to be a valuable mechanism for encouraging HoDs to focus on establishing and ensuring high standards of teaching and learning in their subject, for contributing to policy development in the school and by evaluating its impact.

We welcome the fact that the proposed NPQSL lays great stress on monitoring and promoting standards of student achievement and believe this should help to foster the academic emphasis and high expectations, which our research shows are essential components of the institutional culture of academically effective schools.

Heads of Department

Our study explicitly sought to investigate the nature and extent of internal variations in school effectiveness. Its findings demonstrate that, although a small number of schools were found to be consistent outliers (either academically very effective or ineffective), for *most* schools the picture was far more complicated with significant differences at the subject level over three consecutive years. We analysed information about performance in terms of the three core areas of the national curriculum – English and English literature; mathematics and science (highest grade in any science subject). We also obtained details for French and history because these subjects were taken by larger numbers of students in our sample than any others. In some schools results were highly mixed, with ineffective and effective departments co-existing in the same institution. This clearly demonstrates the importance of the subject department in any discussion of secondary school academic effectiveness. Going beyond earlier work (Smith and Tomlinson, 1989; Witziers, 1994; Luyten, 1995) we related information about school and departmental processes to students' GCSE results.

Our case studies of six schools and thirty different subject departments provide rich qualitative insights into what enabled some departments to be more effective in promoting their students' achievement than others. By studying both consistently more effective and less effective departments, and by focusing on change over a five-year period, better understanding of factors which contribute to, or are barriers to, greater effectiveness, was possible. We also obtained important insights into the processes and factors which influence change and foster improvement. Our questionnaire survey of HoDs enabled us to test out the qualitative findings using a larger sample.

HoD leadership

The leadership role of the HoD was found to be important but all too often ill-defined. HoDs have the primary responsibility to monitor pupil progress and raise achievement levels for all students of their subject. To achieve this it is important that they create or maintain a shared vision of their subject and foster high expectations for all students (boys and girls, different ethnic groups, those of high or low initial attainment levels) amongst their department's teachers.

Good record keeping and a clear assessment and marking policy which facilitates the monitoring of individual students' progress and those of different student groups both within and across years is a characteristic of more effective departments. As well as oral comments, marking, tests and records of achievement all provide opportunities to give students constructive feedback on their performance and, more importantly, how to improve the quality of their work. HoDs who monitored the setting and marking of homework and quality of classwork – by looking at lesson plans and via observation – were better able to ensure consistency in the implementation of departmental and school policy. Regularly examining samples of students' work books and GCSE coursework and discussion with students provide valuable sources of information for the HoD to help evaluate the performance of their department.

Monitoring pupil progress over several years helps HoDs to identify areas of success or of under-achievement. Investigating trends over time is essential to establish evidence of improvement. Obtaining information about student attainment at entry gives a baseline for plotting later results (annually or at Key Stage 3) as well as linking to final GCSE performance. It is important that such information is recorded at the level of the individual student. In addition to examining their own school's data, it is valuable for HoDs to compare the department's performance with that of other departments elsewhere using value added measures (these may be available at the LEA or via consultancy projects such as the NFER). If value added data are not available, it may prove possible to compare the department's results with those of other schools known to serve a similar catchment area, e.g. white working class council estate, ethnically diverse inner city with a high proportion of E2L students; or mainly middle class suburban with few students eligible for free school meals. Better still, different intakes with a similar profile, in terms of percentage of free school meals, ethnic and language composition, could be compared. This can help to give HoDs an indication of relative performance on a contextualized or 'like with like' basis. Such comparisons can enable challenging but realistic targets to be set for improvement based on past performance and performance of similar schools. The DfEE, OFSTED and SCAA are currently showing much interest in the way benchmarking and target-setting can be used to help schools identify realistic goals for their improvement. In particular, SCAA is exploring ways of providing schools with information about the performance of schools from similar groups (e.g. by their profile in terms of indicators such as the percentage of students eligible for free meals, the percentage of E2L). In the absence of value added measures, this may well prove helpful for more rigorous school self-evaluation and more accurate target-setting.

The HoDs of more effective departments attached considerable importance both to team building and to actual teamwork in their departments. In contrast, the absence of teamwork was frequently cited as a source of much difficulty in the less effective departments. Low morale and high staff absence, as might be expected, were more common in departments which lacked a clear direction and a team spirit. Analysing performance data, however, is only one important activity for HoDs.

In our study, we found that effective HoDs often sought to lead by example in a variety of ways, including teaching and raising expectations of both staff and students. They also sought to ensure that departmental policies were developed through a process of discussion which helped promote a sense of common ownership. Regular departmental meetings to discuss policies and practice and to evaluate student progress were seen to be important in fostering teamwork, identifying areas for improvement and setting targets as well as discussing departmental policies. The ability to listen to staff and to maintain constructive relationships was seen by many HoDs to be an essential part of their work. Equally important was providing a clear direction and having high expectations of staff. Personality conflicts and 'dead wood' (uncommitted members of staff who were not felt to pull their weight) were a feature of the less effective case studies. Shortages of staff and high levels of absence were also seen as major barriers to greater effectiveness by this group.

Quality of teaching
There was strong evidence, as would be expected, that the quality of teaching is a crucial component of departmental effectiveness. Important factors which our research suggest can form a helpful basis for departmental reviews include the following:

- work focus of lessons (are most students on-task most of the time?);
- strong academic emphasis;
- clarity of goals for student learning;
- student responsibility (independent learning is encouraged);

- lessons generally challenge students of *all* ability levels;
- teacher enthusiasm;
- effective classroom control;
- high teacher expectations for student performance and behaviour;
- promptness starting and finishing lessons;
- regular monitoring of student progress;
- consistently applied marking policy;
- homework given a high priority and homework policy consistently applied by all teachers;
- teachers' knowledge of the content of the subject and the GCSE syllabus.

These are all aspects of teaching which might form a useful basis for the observation of lessons both by the HoD and by other subject teachers. Conducted with sensitivity and honesty, observations could provide a valuable opportunity to discuss teaching approaches, to identify training needs and to give constructive feedback for all subject teachers, including the HoD. Further consideration of teaching approaches is given in the section on implications for classroom practitioners.

Questions which may prove helpful in stimulating discussion at the departmental level include the following:

- which factors do you think ought to be taken into account in judging the effectiveness of any department;
- which factors contribute most to the current effectiveness of this department, and
- what, if anything, holds the department back from being more effective?

Examining Boards

Our research provided little support for the view that the particular examining board chosen was a significant factor in determining departmental effectiveness. Indeed amongst our case studies examples of the most and least effective departments used the same boards and syllabus. Factors which were more important related to covering the syllabus, ensuring students had completed the required course work, and a strong emphasis on entering students for examinations whenever possible, as well as the quality of teaching and staff expectations.

Ability grouping

Likewise, the use of ability grouping did *not* emerge as a key feature in relation to academic effectiveness. None of our sample of schools used rigid streaming, preferring the more flexible approach of setting for specific subjects and specific year groups. Most schools set into student ability groups for Years 10 and 11 (the GCSE period). We found that some of the less effective case studies, which had used mixed-ability approaches, planned to introduce more setting in the hope of raising standards, but, in other schools, good value added results had been achieved in a mixed ability context – although some staff there also thought the use of setting from Year 9 onwards might lead to further improvements. From the questionnaire survey we found setting from a younger age (e.g. Years 7 or 8) for all subjects was associated with greater effectiveness in overall GCSE results, but this was not identified as a key factor in the multilevel analysis. Also in mathematics, the subject in which setting by ability was most common, a greater use of setting from a younger age was weakly negatively associated with effectiveness.

We can conclude therefore that prescriptive, and we suggest simplistic, organizational solutions concerning the merits of streaming or ability grouping versus mixed ability approaches are unlikely to be the key to raising performance. The quality of teaching, high expectations, good student-teacher relationships and classroom control, and an academic emphasis are much more important. Whatever approach to student grouping is adopted, it is important that departmental staff are involved in the decision-making process, that they share common goals, and that a department's policies are agreed and consistently applied by all its teaching staff.

Classroom teachers

As we have noted elsewhere, our research has a vitally important and positive message for classroom practitioners. It demonstrates clearly that individual schools and departments can and do make a different to secondary students' progress between the ages eleven and sixteen years. Even in some of the most disadvantaged LEAs in the country, individual schools and departments were much more effective than others. Although students' background characteristics exert a powerful influence, which needs to be recognized, the quality of teaching and educational experiences at secondary school can significantly raise achievement levels and affect the subsequent life chances of students. We conclude that teachers do make a difference.

Due to the retrospective nature of our research we did not observe teaching in individual classes in any of our sample of schools, thus we cannot evaluate or make detailed comments about specific teaching practices. Nonetheless, the evidence from both the case studies and questionnaire surveys confirms the importance of high quality teaching as vital determinants of academic effectiveness to both SMTs and HoDs.

Purposeful teaching, creating a learning environment and high expectations are seen as indicators of high quality teaching. Naturally, it is vital to recognize that teachers do not operate in isolation. Other aspects we have already referred to concerning the implications of the study for the SMT and middle managers facilitate (in effective schools) the teaching and learning process in individual classrooms. Leadership and management, organization and policy, goals and expectations in combination influence the school and individual departments' cultures. We can conclude that a more supportive environment for classroom practitioners and for teaching and learning is provided by:

- effective leadership
- shared vision/goals (fostering consistency of practice, and collegiality)
- a clear focus on monitoring student progress, and departmental reviews
- a student-focused approach (with positive staff-student relationships and emphasis on students' rights and responsibilities.

Teaching styles
In the light of the recent resurrection of the teaching styles debate following publication of international reviews which highlighted the UK's poor performance in mathematics in particular (Reynolds and Farrell, 1996), it is important to note that, on the basis of available evidence, no one 'style' can be seen to be more effective than others. Indeed, our experience in the field indicates that teachers' practice is far more complex than simplistic notions of teaching style, such as formal versus informal allow (Mortimore, 1993; Sammons, forthcoming). Elsewhere, on the basis of an extensive review of school and teacher effectiveness literature, we observed 'in our view debates about the virtues of one particular style over another are too simplistic and have become sterile. Efficient organization, fitness for purpose, flexibility of approach and intellectual challenge are of greater relevance' (Sammons, Hillman and Mortimore, 1995, p. 25).

Factors which the present research indicates are relevant for effective classroom practice point to the importance of teachers' curriculum, pedagogical and school and classroom process knowledge as well as their skills in organization, analysis, synthesis, presentation management, assessment and evaluation. There are no easy recipes or blue-prints for 'good teaching'. Teachers need to blend together skills and knowledge for particular purposes, taking into account the context of the age, prior attainments and interests of a particular class of students. Imagination, creativity and sensitivity are also needed to communicate with and to inspire students (Mortimore, 1993).

While there is no prescription for good teaching, the benefits of a fairly structured approach, of teacher enthusiasm, positive student-teacher relationships, clear planning and good order and control in the classroom for promoting students' academic achievement were evident from comments by headteachers, deputies and HoDs in our research, and are in accord with the results of reviews of the school and teacher effectiveness literature (Sammons, Hillman and Mortimore, 1995). From our case studies it was apparent that five years previously in many departments there had been concern about variability of teaching quality between individual teachers. Especially in the less effective departments concerns about lack of interest and relevance to students, over-reliance on a passive role for students in lessons, too much emphasis on students working individually in isolation were perhaps best characterized by comments like 'death by a thousand worksheets'. Lack of preparation, little academic emphasis, low expectations and unclear goals were also criticized and in some instances poor behaviour management by some teachers was a serious handicap.

Reflecting on personal practice

Particular features which were found to be associated with academic effectiveness were noted earlier under implications for middle managers. These were suggested as a helpful basis for departmental reviews. They can also, we think, provide useful pointers for teacher reflection on their own practice, and for observations and constructive critique of colleagues in terms of three activities: planning, management and feedback.

(1) Planning
- teachers' knowledge of the content of the subject;
- teachers' knowledge of the content of the GCSE syllabus in use;
- clarity of goals for student learning;
- homework given a high priority and homework policy consistently applied;
- strong academic emphasis; and
- lessons to generally challenge students of *all* ability levels.

(2) Management
- work focus of lessons (most students on-task most of the time);
- high teacher expectations for student performance and behaviour;
- student responsibility (independent learning is encouraged);
- effective classroom control;
- promptness starting and finishing lessons;
- teacher enthusiasm (for subject and teaching); and
- quality of teacher-student relationships.

(3) Feedback
- assessment information used for regular monitoring of student progress;
- emphasis given to providing students with constructive feedback (verbal and written); and
- consistently applied marking policy.

IMPLICATIONS FOR STUDENTS AND PARENTS

In terms of fundamental underlying values a concern for equity, promoting the educational achievements of *all* students regardless of their gender, ethnic or socio-economic status, has been – and continues to be – a driving force in school effectiveness research. As Reynolds (1995) has argued, the impact on students is the 'touchstone' for school effectiveness research. In earlier chapters, we highlighted the ways some schools and individual departments were able to promote students' progress during their time at secondary school from transfer at age eleven to sixteen.

Our research has focused on secondary schools' academic effectiveness at GCSE, although we have also noted the important interdependencies between attainment, behaviour, attendance, motivation and self-esteem. We have not attempted to address the concept of a 'good' school – interesting discussions of this have been made by writers such as Silver (1994) and Gray and Wilcox

(1995). We doubt whether agreement on what constitutes a 'good' school could be achieved or would be desirable. Quite rightly parents and students will have their own views on this reflecting their particular interests and values. However, while we would acknowledge that a good school will be much more than an academically effective one, we remain convinced that it is a *necessary*, if not sufficient, condition (Sammons and Reynolds, 1997).

The prime purpose of schooling, we argue, is the promotion of student progress. The concept of value added – the school's particular contribution to the progress a student makes while attending his or her secondary school, commonly over five years – is thus essential to allow informed judgements about a school's performance to be made.

In our experience, parents are keenly aware of the importance of measuring progress and are anxious to receive regular and comprehensible information about this from their child's school. Parents recognize the significance of the 'high stakes' assessment by public examination at GCSE and the implications of success or failure for their children's later education and employment prospects. Many realize that current raw league tables may not provide a good guide to school effectiveness, but the absence of other comparative published material means that such tables are still consumed avidly. Given this, we believe our study of departmental differences in secondary school effectiveness has very important implications and messages for both parents and students which we will attempt to summarize here.

Choosing schools

Our research has examined internal variations in secondary schools' performance over three years. When we focus on the value added by schools (taking into account differences between schools in their intakes of students at eleven years), it is quite clear that crude distinctions such as 'good' or 'bad' school are inappropriate for the vast majority. Over three years only a very small number of schools were found to be highly effective across the board, and very few to be consistently ineffective. In some schools 'average' overall GCSE results may mask the existence of significant subject variations. Highly effective and ineffective departments can co-exist in the same institution.

Raw league tables, which only show the percentage of the fifteen-plus age cohort attaining five A-C grades, cannot tell parents and prospective students how a school performs, nor particular subjects which may be of interest, for example, those in which a child has shown an aptitude or interest at primary school. They also cannot demonstrate whether a school is differentially effective for some student groups, such as boys or girls or different ethnic groups. Yet this sort of detailed information is of interest to prospective parents and students.

Our research shows that, in the real world, judgements about school performance are fairly complex (Sammons, 1996). We believe that steps to provide non-statistical information about the value added by schools to students' progress would be more useful than crude league tables. Developments in school

Table 9.1   Example of presenting value added information about school effectiveness over two years

	Total GCSE scores	English	Mathematics
School A	+ [+]	+ [E]	−[−]
School B	E [E]	− [E]	+ [+]
School C	E [E]	E [+]	− [E]
School D	E [+]	E [+]	E [+]
School E	+ [E]	+ [E]	E [−]

[ ] Previous year's results shown in brackets for comparison
Where: E means results as expected (in line with predictions based on intake)
   + means results are significantly better than predicted (p<0.05)
   − means results are significantly below those predicted (p<0.05)

effectiveness research will hopefully provide more accurate information about school effectiveness. For example, in Table 9.1 we show how value added measures could be shown comparing results over two years. It is suggested that parents need information which shows whether a school's performance is significantly above that expected on the basis of its intake, broadly as expected for its intake or significantly below that expected on the basis of its intake. This example illustrates how results for five fictitious schools could be shown in terms of overall GCSE performance and two subjects, mathematics and English. It can be seen that School A performed well (significantly above expected) in overall GCSE results and in English but results for mathematics are poor (significantly below expected). School E is doing well in overall results and English, and in all three years performance is better than the previous year.

Parents would not need any particular statistical expertise to interpret value added results presented in this way. Using such a form of presentation would avoid all the misleading properties of raw ranked league tables which appear to show differences amongst individual schools which are statistically invalid. By presenting results for key core subjects (such as English and mathematics) and by including total GCSE performance score as an overall indicator, a broader picture of schools' academic effectiveness could be given. We further propose that value added results be presented for at least two years and preferably three consecutive years, so that trends can be seen.

Of course, it must be stressed that schools are subject to change and over time a school may improve its performance or decline may ensue. When students and parents choose a secondary school even the best value added indicators of examination results can only give a *retrospective* indication of performance. There is no guarantee that the school which is performing above expectation now will still be in this position in six years' time when prospective students take their GCSE results. In our view, value added information is probably most useful for schools to encourage rigorous self-evaluation and review, to guide target-setting and to help evaluate success of improvement initiatives. Nonetheless, in an open and democratic society it is only right that value added information is made available in addition to raw results (Tomlinson, Mortimore and Sammons, 1988).

In addition to information about examination results we believe that, as many parents do now, discussion with the parents of students already at schools which their child might attend should be encouraged. Details about attendance and behaviour will be relevant as well as visits to the school, informal observations in and around the school and talking to current students. Published inspection results can also be a useful source of information.

Parents of students in Year 6 of primary school also need to consider the pupil's views about secondary schools, and issues about the benefits of proximity, maintaining primary school friendships and so on. We believe that the factors which our research highlights as important for promoting academic effectiveness (described in earlier chapters) also provide an excellent basis for parents in evaluating what they see in their school visits, and provide points to questions which may be helpful, for example, concerning homework policy and practice, subject setting, assessment, the code of practice on student behaviour, etc.

It must be remembered that, in many ways, the concept of parental choice can be rather misleading in itself. Parents have a right to express a preference for a particular school but cannot be guaranteed a place if the school is popular. Where a school is over-subscribed, schools will make choices according to specific criteria. For some schools (e.g. church schools or GM schools) criteria can differ. Also it should be remembered that, in many areas of the country, there may in practice be very little choice because of the practicalities of transport to and from the school. Where selection exists, choice will be restricted with schools selecting students rather than parents choosing schools. Parents with a better knowledge of the education system and with access to a car will usually have access to greater choice than others.

In addition, whilst parents have some (usually restricted) choice, in practice choosing a school is a difficult decision, and it is important to remember that parents have no say about individual teachers. In a typical secondary school career a student may be taught by perhaps thirty or more different ones. Inevitably, some students will respond better when taught by particular teachers. From our research the school's culture or ethos is perhaps the key factor parents and students should get a feel for when visiting potential schools. The three features of school culture which we found were important in determining academic effectiveness were:

- order (behaviour, policy and practice);
- task achievement (academic emphasis); and
- relationships (a student-focused approach).

Parental involvement

Much research has pointed to the value of parental involvement in their children's education both at home (especially in the early years) and at school (Coleman, 1994). However, such research has tended to focus very much on pre-school and primary school children. Our study demonstrates that parental involvement is also important at the secondary level. Some schools in our research were better able to involve parents and had a more positive attitude towards their potential contribution. Parents have an important role in encouraging and supporting their children's efforts right through secondary school. Many, however, would welcome clear advice from, and encouragement by, the school concerning practical strategies for helping their children. The more effective schools in our case studies tended to harness parents, encouraging them to monitor students' homework, such as by signing a diary on a regular basis, sent home regular newsletters, and provided regular feedback about students' progress and achievements. They were also likely to be proactive about enlisting parental support concerning any behaviour or attendance problems at an early date. Celebrating student achievements (by letter or certificate) is just as important as involving parents when things go wrong. More effective schools tend to be better, as MacBeath (1994) has argued, in making demands on parents as well as providing them with opportunities for involvement and ensuring a welcoming atmosphere in the school.

Parental contracts are achieving much publicity in the UK given the new Labour Government's commitment to them. We doubt whether such contracts are legally enforceable but, in principle, we feel that stressing both the rights and responsibilities of parents as well as students may be one way in which schools could help to maximize parental support and involvement to the benefit of young people's secondary education.

SUMMARY

In this chapter we have sought to examine some of the implications of our research for different players in the educational process: politicians and policy makers; inspectors; the senior management team, middle managers, classroom teachers and finally for parents and students.

The key message from our research concerns the positive impact secondary schools can have, even in disadvantaged areas such as inner London, on students' academic performance. What schools and teachers do really can make a difference (Mortimore, 1995b). We believe that our findings are relevant to all those interested in school improvement, and hope they will stimulate reflection by both policy makers and practitioners. It is important to recognize that there are no solutions or magic recipes for school effectiveness (Myers, 1995; Stoll and Fink, 1996). Like Hopkins (1994), who argued in connection with school improvement, 'the knowledge is there not to control, but to inform and discipline practice' (p. 89), we believe that our findings may be best used as tools to assist the development of schools as learning institutions. It is clear, however, that our research does not support the 'back to the 1950s' lobby which argues that traditional approaches (streaming, selection, whole class teaching, caning, uniforms) are the solution to all our educational ills.

Various authors including Ainscow and Hopkins (1992), Hargreaves

(1995a and b) and Stoll and Fink (1996) have drawn attention to the need to focus on obtaining a better understanding of the social organization of schools and how they create their particular cultures. Although it is important to recognize that schools are in many ways non-rational organizations that are resistant to external pressure for change, we believe that by focusing on the different components of the school's culture and by monitoring student progress, departmental and whole-school performance, educational standards can be raised. Involving students and parents, seeking their views and addressing their concerns is equally important. Where expectations are high and all participants share the view that their school is primarily a place for teaching and learning, where student progress is encouraged, celebrated and seen as the 'touchstone' for evaluating school, departmental and teaching practices, our research suggests that improvement will follow.

10

Last words

Like most books, this one has several purposes. We wanted the opportunity to consider in depth the results and the implications emanating from our empirical study of secondary schools: a full length book allows the space for this. We also hoped that a book would draw the attention of policy makers and practitioners to our work. Traditionally, in this country, research papers published in academic journals have been read mainly by fellow researchers, although we have been encouraged by the number of teachers who, in recent years, have begun to do likewise. By publishing our work in a book designed for a general readership, we have sought to extend its messages to a wider audience.

THE EDUCATIONAL CONTEXT AT THE START OF THE STUDY

We wrote the proposal for this study in the year after the last Conservative government had enacted the most ambitious educational reforms for forty years in the UK. Ministers had propelled a highly controversial bill (ERA 1988) through long parliamentary sessions with the argument that radical change was essential. The strength of the opposition to the proposals was revealed only when an interested individual – Julian Haviland – published the results of weeks of collating the individual submissions in the House of Commons Library. With a large majority, however, the government could overcome all opposition, whether from opposing members of parliament, the church, LEAs, the Teacher Associations or from individuals.

The atmosphere within secondary schools at the start of the study, therefore, was strained. The introduction of the national curriculum and of the local management of schools (LMS) was generally welcomed but, while many teachers accepted that greater accountability was due and that established systems required *re-tuning* from time to time, few welcomed the last government's wholehearted embrace of market forces. In particular, teachers were suspicious of the new status of grant maintained schools and were resentful of the extra funding available for such schools. Practitioners generally condemned the publicity given to the publication of examination results league tables and were wary of the same treatment being given to the National Curriculum Assessments which were to be developed as part of the reforms. This was the context in which we embarked upon our study of academic effectiveness in

GCSE, a summative measure of student performance taken at the end of compulsory schooling.

The judgement of school performance

We believe that our study has pioneered a new phase in school effectiveness work by starting to unpack the concept of effectiveness by looking at both internal variations and trends over time. We have been greatly assisted in this task by the availability of multilevel modelling through which we have been able to gain some estimates of the value added to student effort by the secondary school attended. We have considered the issue of consistency across different subject outcomes as well as in relation to stability and differential effectiveness for particular student groups. We have argued that attempts to describe schools uniformly as '*good*' or '*bad*' are genuinely unhelpful. In contrast, we believe that effectiveness should only be judged on the basis of, at least, three years' performance and should best be seen as outcome-specific. As we have noted, these findings weaken the arguments for the use of league tables. We consider the last government's encouragement of the press to produce spurious school-by-school rankings without taking account of confidence intervals of the data to be irresponsible. In contrast, we believe the use of appropriate statistical tests which use both statistical and educational significance to identify differences is helpful to parents, schools and those responsible for national monitoring. Importantly this approach also emphasizes the precision that is possible in measuring effectiveness. We hope that, under a new administration, a greater use of value added approaches focusing on student progress and encouraging schools to engage in a continuous process of self-evaluation and review will be encouraged by bodies such as OFSTED and the DfEE's new Standards and Effectiveness Unit.

Understanding academic effectiveness

Our results also provide support for the findings of previous research. In particular the data from our school case studies add flesh to the bones of early studies such as *Fifteen Thousand Hours*. The robustness of the findings on school processes is encouraging. The original choice of factors in *Fifteen Thousand Hours* was made on the basis of a set of correlations. These indicated that there was a statistical association between two specific factors – an outcome measure based on student performance and a process measure which described the conditions or some other characteristic of the school. Correlations are useful in alerting researchers to relationships which might otherwise remain hidden. Their weakness is that they can work in either direction. In other words, the outcome may be influenced by the particular conditions in the school, but it is also possible that the outcome has influenced the process characteristic. Only a clear theory, able to point to one direction, can aid interpretation of the data. Without this, the value of statistical tools is limited.

We believe this study has made some contribution to the development of such a theory. In contrast to much of the work on primary schools which has come out of the Netherlands – where there is a flourishing group of school effectiveness researchers – our work covers the secondary age range.[1] We collected data relating to three years of student outcomes and to five years of school processes at school and at subject department level. The major difference between primary and secondary schools is that the latter employ specialist teachers and that each student is taught by approximately eight teachers each school year. For this reason it is perhaps not surprising that 'culture' emerges as an important unifying feature of schools and departments. Our analyses suggest that culture provides an important key to the understanding of secondary school academic effectiveness. A grander theory, attempting to explain the effectiveness of all schools – primary, secondary and special – and taking into account such differences, has yet to be formulated and may prove unobtainable.

A focus on the individual school

The focus on the individual school is also relevant because, whilst students and parents may have had some choice of school, they will seldom have been in a position to choose a particular set of teachers. We do not believe that effective schools are so because, by chance, they have accumulated the best teachers; we consider that the way those teachers are socialized and grow into the job within the particular school culture is important. Support for this conclusion is provided by a case study of another secondary school which was not part of this project. Here we found that both teachers and students shared a positive view of academic work and achievement and that each party was able to reinforce this view in the other (Mortimore et al., 1995). The research reported here suggests that the impact of such culture on students' achievement over five years – almost a third of their lifetime – is strong. This has important implications, for both practitioners and all concerned with school improvement.

Our findings also indicate that, while effective schools share many common features, the same is not true for ineffective schools, where there appear to be a multiplicity of routes. Our results suggest that a different form of school culture is operating in such schools and that one of its strongest characteristics is a lack of common purpose and a widespread inconsistency – but firm conclusions must await further empirical work.

THE EDUCATIONAL CONTEXT AT THE END OF THE STUDY

Eight years on from the beginning of our fieldwork, the context of education is different. The reforms have had time to 'bed down': practitioners have accepted some but remain unhappy about others. Thus, the National Curriculum and LMS, after teething difficulties, began to have a positive impact. Yet the increased use of league tables, in order to 'shame and blame' schools into improvement, and the continuing unpopularity of the OFSTED system of school inspection are contributing to a negative view of schooling and have led to an unprecedented number of teachers and HTs seeking early retirement.

One major weakness of the reforms is that too many have been imposed on the profession. This may have been necessary initially but the 'macho' style of innovation has become counterproductive. One clear lesson is that for reforms to succeed those introducing them must work *with* – rather than against – teachers, since it is on them that any such reforms ultimately depend. This provides a considerable challenge to a new government: how to develop ways of working with – rather than against – teachers.

Implications of the study for policy makers and practitioners

We have spelled out the main implications of our work in Chapter 9. The key message is that schools can have positive effects even in the most disadvantaged areas. What teachers and school managers do makes a vital difference. The catch is that in order to make the crucial difference, HTs and teachers, in areas of disadvantage, have to make *more* effort, give *more* commitment and be *more* resourceful and energetic. They are working against the grain and, as a result, have to exceed the efforts of their peers in schools with more advantaged students. The question is whether it is possible to maintain these levels of commitment indefinitely.

Other implications to which we have drawn attention concern the impact of the market driven reforms. Our work suggests that many of these are likely to exacerbate the problems of what is sometimes known as the 'trailing edge': schools which serve students who are 'hard to teach'. Many of these students are barely tolerated in schools and yet – without some positive school experience – they are likely to drop out and join an underclass of school failures. For these schools, the reforms have had negative effects. If more schools become selective, such schools will be further creamed of any balance in intake. It is difficult to see how, in such circumstances, a downward spiral can be averted.

We have proposed, therefore, that 'hard to teach' students are identified on entry to school and that they receive extra resources to be used in special programmes designed to raise their academic level and their self-efficacy. This would be contrary to policies over the last decade which have favoured schools which recruit the more advantaged students. Unlike earlier positive discrimination schemes, an important feature of our proposal is to target individual students. Clearly, considerable care would need to be taken so as to avoid public labelling and shaming of such students. Just as many schools found ways to conceal which students receive free meals, ways would have to be found to provide the extra support in a sensitive manner. The aim must be both to raise the expectations – of teachers, students and parents – and to provide support and widen opportunities.

Our research also points to the vital importance of school self-evaluation and review activities. The collection and analysis of school data on student performance is the first step on such a programme. Our colleagues MacGilchrist, Myers and Reed (1997) argue that modern schools have to become 'intelligent' in order to manage themselves. This intelligence includes learning how to use the schools' data to set targets, monitor and evaluate progress. Our findings are that a school culture which fosters a strongly student-focused approach, an academic focus, and an orderly school climate and where students' academic outcomes are seen as the highest priority in their classes, their subject departments and at the whole school level, has the best chance of promoting progress and thus giving a high value added component to their students.

International comparisons

Throughout the world, governments and educationalists are reviewing their systems of schooling. Two pressures are motivating them: one – stimulated by a concern that we are moving into a period when the most valued commodity will be knowledge rather than any goods or minerals – focuses on quality; the other is driven by rising costs and a fear that public education will stretch the public purse to unacceptable levels.

The availability of information also means that comparative data are more readily available than at any time in our history. The *Education at a Glance* series produced by the Organization for Economic Co-operation and Development (OECD), for instance, produces comparisons of educational provision and achievement between the world's most developed nations. These data are reliable but there are also dangers associated with their use (Alexander, 1996; Goldstein, 1995). In particular, governments suffer from the temptation to 'cherry pick' particular findings and to use these to berate their own school systems, regardless of the different cultural contexts in which they have been identified. Nevertheless, the availability of information has served to make us more internationally aware.

At a time when we accept the possibility that those currently attending school may, in the course of their working lives, be employed in different countries, inculcating a broader view is important. Understanding the cultural contexts of different countries is aided by collaboration with local researchers. In the Institute of Education colleagues are conducting a project on successful schools with disadvantaged intakes of students. This involves case studies of schools in Hong Kong, Singapore and Shanghai, as well as London. We wish to see if any of the features of the London schools can be identified in schools with Chinese cultures or if the contexts are so different that no lessons can be drawn.

Costs of education are also difficult to compare, as different countries operate different systems and have different priorities. Most countries, however, define their gross domestic product in a broadly similar way and it is usually possible to express the education budget as a proportion of this figure in order to obtain a comparable figure. In 1975, for instance, the UK spent 6.8 per cent of our gross domestic product on education (1 per cent above the average) and were ranked fifth out of eighteen countries. The latest figures show that our spending has dropped to 5.1 per cent (0.7 per cent below the average) and we are now ranked fourteenth. The contrast with the trend in a country such as Norway is telling. Norway spent only 6.4 per cent on education in 1975 (ranked eighth) but by 1993 had increased this figure to 9 per cent (ranked first).

Considerable injustice in our system is also caused by the very *uneven* distribution of resources to schools. This has been exacerbated by differential funding between grant maintained and LEA managed schools. Where you live and which type of school your child attends – rather than any needs they might have – can make a significant difference to the amount of public money being spent on their schooling. It may be difficult for a government to put right long standing differences between schools but, as we argued in Chapter 9, an equitable funding formula should be introduced across all schools as a matter of the utmost priority. This should place an emphasis on increasing resources for those students forming the 'trailing edge' in our current system.

Change in the education system

Our Differential School Effectiveness project has drawn attention to the difficulties that some schools have experienced as a result of government-inspired reforms during the 1990s. We have condemned the use of a 'shame and blame' strategy to achieve change. We believe this can encourage complacency and an unwillingness to change in those schools which – for geographical or historical reasons – tend to receive a favoured intake of students and, similarly, induce feelings of hopelessness amongst schools where high proportions of students come from disadvantaged backgrounds. The question, therefore, of how best to introduce change is not easily answered but at least we should know some of the barriers to it. By studying what has gone wrong in the past, it should be possible to avoid some pitfalls, encourage successful innovation and frame some principles for future governments.

Principle 1. Consult genuinely and amend appropriately
We have learned how shortsighted it is for government to consult on policies but then ignore the outcome and even, on occasions, to conceal its nature. But for the persistence of Julian Haviland, the weight of objections to aspects of the Education Reform Bill of 1987/88 would have remained secret. It seems an obvious lesson, therefore, that consultation must be a genuine search for reactions to a proposal and must incorporate a willingness to modify the proposal in the light of a negative response.

One helpful strategy could be to adopt the 'middle-top-down' consultation model advocated by Hirotaka Takeuchi, a Japanese management expert. Government would consult initially with HTs and teachers on educational changes before turning to local authorities and others concerned with the management of schools. It would then consult with those whose lives would be directly influenced by the changes – parents and students. General agreement would give government a mandate for change. A unanimous negative reaction would be a clear indication that the policy was flawed. Differences in views would mean that government would have to decide which should predominate or find ways of accommodating those differences.

Principle 2. Pilot as fully as possible

We now know that trying to introduce a major change across the system as a whole, without adequate piloting, is usually a grave mistake. The system of assessment introduced after the Education Reform Act consumed a vast amount of energy in every school yet proved unworkable. Sir Ron Dearing had to revise it drastically before it became acceptable. The lesson is that no matter how much politicians *want* something to happen, if the policy is not technically deliverable, they will be disappointed.

Adequate piloting is, therefore, essential but – even so – it cannot guarantee success. Volunteers in pilot projects are usually more tolerant than the pressed folk who ultimately have to deal with the policy. Furthermore, pilot studies usually provide extra resources to attract volunteers and make the extra effort worthwhile. When change is fully implemented – but without the extra resources – problems are more likely to emerge. The only viable solution is to seek a compromise: making sure all the technical processes work and then taking the risk. Had the last government been able to demonstrate that tests were manageable, valid and reliable when it introduced a new assessment regime, the tests would have been more readily accepted.

Principle 3. Fund change equitably

It has also become clear that it is impossible to introduce policies or practices that benefit a minority of schools without generating resentment among the others. The introduction of generously funded City Technology Colleges (CTCs), for instance, offended the British sense of fair play which dictates that equity in funding is crucial.

So does this mean that all institutions should receive roughly the same level of resources? In general terms, we believe it does, although there must always be scope for special funding in particular circumstances. Schools that cope with a high proportion of 'hard to teach' students deserve, and should receive, proportionately more resources than those which do not. But giving extra resources to schools that are already advantaged creates resentment. In times of scarcity it is even more important to fund equitably. Governors and teachers will be more likely to accept change if they are convinced that such a principle is being followed.

Of course there is no guarantee that adherence to these three principles will always result in governors and teachers accepting a new policy or practice but it *will* guarantee that three of the most powerful barriers to change will have been removed.

RESTORING CONFIDENCE IN THE SYSTEM

The teaching profession has increasingly been subject to attacks by politicians, officials and the media during the period of our research. Teachers have been presented as being unambitious on behalf of their students. There is little recognition that teaching is actually a very difficult job, often embraced by those with a sense of vocation. Even in comparison with others with challenging occupations, teaching is hard: striving to motivate a class of young people who do not want to be in school is not for the faint-hearted. Unlike many other professions, teaching is both public and isolated, and teachers, accordingly, have vulnerable roles. Of course, the work is often highly rewarding and many teachers today – despite the problems – refuse to be cast as victims but celebrate the opportunity they have to influence the next generation by changing the lives of individual students.

How can the government maintain and enhance this positive spirit, whilst rewarding more appropriately those who are feeling unappreciated? Creating a General Teaching Council (GTC) and strengthening the commitment to an all graduate profession would help. A GTC, with responsibility for entry qualifications and the discipline of members, working with universities to provide a route from beginner teacher to highly skilled 'practitioner', would, we believe, do wonders to lift the standing and morale of the profession.

Level of resources devoted to education

No one visiting schools can fail to notice that many buildings are in poor shape. Similarly, there are shortages of books and computers. School governors will know that some schools are having to make teachers redundant. As we have already noted, the resources devoted to education in Britain are relatively low in comparison with other OECD countries. Even though modern governments appear to have rejected policies involving high levels of taxation, money to support education will have to be found if a slide into a two-tier system with a growing gap between public and private provision is to be avoided.

The 'pecking order' of schools

The range of independent schools, selective grammar schools and church schools has in recent years been increased to include city technology colleges and grant maintained and technology schools. The result is a sophisticated 'pecking order', starting with Eton and ending with the currently most unpopular school receiving media attention.

Changing public perceptions of schools is not easy and some will take years to recover from the damaging effects of league tables. But, as the good work on failing schools undertaken by OFSTED demonstrates, with hard work and extra resources, it is possible to improve the school's image and, more importantly, its impact on students (DfEE, 1997). Creating an equitable funding formula will help convince teachers that the government is trying to improve *all* schools rather than consciously trying to create and sustain a hierarchy of school status. Such a strategy is also more likely – ultimately – to satisfy a greater proportion of parents.

CONCLUSIONS

We believe that our empirical research, carried out in collaboration with practitioners, over a number of years and incorporating a mixture of quantitative and qualitative analyses, provides us with scope to comment on the organization and performance of the secondary school system. We are conscious that we have gone beyond the data in our last chapter in order to express views on contemporary educational issues, writing in the wake of a general election campaign in which education was at the forefront of political debate. We believe, however, that this is justified and that our recommendations spring from our data and its interpretation. As with all research, it will be for others to challenge our findings and the inferences we have drawn from them.

We have enjoyed working on this project. The study of schools is fascinating and education will undoubtedly be one of the major themes of public life as we enter the new millennium and as more nations realize the crucial importance of knowledge creation. We look forward to a more genuine appreciation of education by the newly elected (at the time of writing) Labour government in the UK. Part of this appreciation must include a more positive view of teachers. No nation will prosper in its educational endeavours if it fails to value its teachers. They need to be valued – not because they are particularly sensitive or weaker than other groups in society – but because they are symbols of our corporate need to learn. Treating them shabbily – as we believe has happened – sends negative messages to children about the value of learning.

Our work has been carried out in secondary schools. The next century may well see radical changes in the way these are organized. The greater availability, at lower prices, of information technology may herald a revolution as great as the industrial revolution of the last century. It is too early to tell how much such a revolution would change learning. Our view is that it will not make teachers redundant though it may alter the way they work. They will no longer be the sole authority on any topic – the Internet will be able to link any learner to an expert system. They will not be the only keeper of progress measures – the computer is much more effective in such tasks. They will not be the source of authority in the classroom – the use of IT requires a very active role for learners. But none of these changes removes the necessity for them. Teachers will still be needed to inspire, to instruct, to counsel and advise and, where appropriate, to assess and evaluate standards of work.

Schools, too, may look very different in the future. The factory approach that we have inherited from the last century is likely to disappear. The control and conformity that has to be a part of such an approach will be less obvious. There will be more individuality, as recognition grows that learners learn in different ways. There may also be more mixing of the ages, although it is likely that for a variety of reasons, including socialization, child care and protection, younger students will continue to be grouped together. In these circumstances, we believe the principles that underpin our view of an effective school culture – appropriate order, academic emphasis and student focus – will continue to serve an important purpose.

NOTE

1 An excellent international overview of the foundations of the educational effectiveness field has been provided by Scheerens and Bosker (1997).

Appendices

APPENDIX 1

Model II Multilevel analysis of total examination score (1990–92)

Fixed Part	Estimate	Standard Error
	TSCORE	
Intercept	24.9	0.8647
Girls-Boys	4.153	0.2953
Age-Mth	0.2664	0.03085
Year 91-Year 90	2.13	0.4403
Year 92-Year 90	4.401	0.474
PCTFSM	−0.07999	0.02286
FSM-NO FSM	−6.296	0.2583
African-White	3.692	0.6039
Caribbean-White	−2.785	0.3544
Indian-White	6.61	0.6031
Pakistani-White	8.606	0.8067
Bangladeshi-White	5.897	0.793
Other-White	3.606	0.3613

Random Part		Estimate	Standard Error
Between Schools	(σ^2)	14.85	2.562
Between Cohorts	(σ^2)	2.124	0.6007
Between Students	(σ^2)	207.6	2.21

Notes: Students = 17,850   Cohorts = 213   Schools = 94

Where: FSM   = Entitlement to free school meals
PCTFSM= Percentage of pupils in school entitled to FSM
ns   = Not significant (at 0.05 level)

APPENDIX 2

Table 1   Example of multilevel analysis of total GCSE performance score: testing HT variables

Fixed Part		Estimate	Standard Error
Intercept		14.43	1.116
LSLRT		0.4429	0.01277
LSLRT^2		0.002861	0.0005165
VR1-VR3		13.80	0.4988
VR2-VR3		5.896	0.3441
Age in months		0.05101	0.03258
Year 91–90		2.811	0.4314
Year 92–90		4.303	0.4570
PCTFSM		−0.01159	0.01992
FSM-no FSM		−3.609	0.2719
African-White		5.959	0.6952
Caribbean-White		0.7894	0.3456
Indian-White		7.819	0.6409
Pakistani-White		10.450	0.9067
Bangladeshi-White		9.746	0.3815
Other-White		6.210	0.4416
Girls		2.552	0.2875
Process variables			
C124		2.327	0.6475
C125		1.398	0.5938
* C126		0.7593 ns	0.5323
* C130		0.9738 ns	0.5877
C131		−2.573	0.8342
C146		−0.6209	0.2624

Random Part			Estimate	Standard Error
School level				
Intercept	σ^2		1.656	0.6242
Year				
Intercept	σ^2		1.111	0.4515
Student				
Intercept	σ^2		89.22	5.496
LSLRT/intercept			0.5887	0.09993
LSLRT^2/intercept			−0.005068	0.003628
VR1/intercept			17.64	3.763
VR2/intercept			16.91	2.326
Girls/intercept			−3.711	1.672
Year91/intercept			7.634	2.005
Year92/intercept			8.127	2.121
FSM/intercept			6.637	1.910
Caribbean/intercept			−10.54	2.043

* Items retained in model because exclusion affected estimate for C125, and removal of both had a significant impact on the model's explanation of variance at level 3 (the school).

C124 *Strong support from parents/community*   [n=46 schools / 9047 students]
      (identified by HT as a key factor contributing to the school's effectiveness)
C125 *Students feel valued as people*
      (identified by HT as a key factor contributing to the school's effectiveness)
C126 *Clear and consistently applied whole school approach to pupil behaviour and discipline*
      (identified by HT as a key factor contributing to the school's effectiveness)
C130 *Pressure of external change*
      (identified by HT as a key factor holding the school back from being more effective)
C131 *Falling pupil roll*
      (identified by HT as a key factor holding the school back from being more effective)
C146 *Academic emphasis of English department in the past (5 years ago)*
      (rated by HT from 1 – very strong emphasis to 5 – weak emphasis)

Where: LSLRT   = London Standardized London Reading Test Score
       VR1   = Verbal Reasoning Band 1 (approximately top 25 per cent)
       VR2   = Verbal Reasoning Band 2 (approximately middle 50 per cent)
       VR3   = Verbal Reasoning Band 3 (approximately bottom 25 per cent)
       FSM   = Entitlement to free school meals
       PCTFSM   = Percentage of pupils in school entitled to FSM
       ns   = Not significant (at 0.05 level)

Table 2   Examples of multilevel analysis of English score (1990–92): testing HoD English questionnaire items

Fixed Part	Estimate	Standard Error
Intercept	2.072	0.1877
LSLRT	0.05352	0.001556
LSLRT^2	−0.0002183	6.341e−05
VR1-VR3	1.327	0.06413
VR2-VR3	0.5631	0.04888
Girls-boys	0.4908	0.03668
Age in months	0.006393	0.004162
Year 91–90	0.1548	0.05167
Year 92–90	0.2413	0.05579
PCTFSM	0.0009005	0.002277
FSM-no FSM	−0.3432	0.03648
African-White	0.7033	0.09637
Caribbean-White	0.2716	0.04711
Indian-White	0.7223	0.07952
Pakistani-White	0.8070	0.1068
Bangladeshi-White	0.9660	0.1093
Other-White	0.4359	0.05725
Process variables		
C101	0.1919	0.0586
C104	0.2327	0.0586
C105	−0.1396	0.05901
C108	0.1659	0.0659
C124	0.1512	0.04822
C128	0.3116	0.0585
C129	−0.2235	0.06885
C142	0.3562	0.06704
C151	−0.2422	0.09299

Random Part		Estimate	Standard Error
Between schools			
Intercept	σ^2	0.00551	0.004823
Between years			
Intercept	σ^2	0.01093	0.005787
Between students			
Intercept	σ^2	2.089	0.06317
LSLRT/intercept		0.003369	0.001154
LSLRT^2/intercept		−0.0002491	4.788e−05
VR1/intercept		−0.1079	0.03762
Girls/intercept		−0.1486	0.02913
Year92/intercept		−0.1474	0.0264
FSM/intercept		0.181	0.03378
Caribbean/intercept		−0.1265	0.03774

[n=38 schools / 8006 students]

C101 *Promoting students' ability to learn independently*
(identified by HoD as a principal goal of school 5 years before)

C104 *A caring pastoral environment*
(identified by HoD as a key factor which ought to be taken into account in judging school effectiveness)

C105 *The creation of confident, articulate people*
(identified by HoD as a key factor which ought to be taken into account judging school effectiveness)

C108 *A strong, cohesive SMT*
(identified by HoD as a key factor contributing to school's current effectiveness)

C124 *Level of staff shortage in school five years before*
(rated by HoD from 1 – high to 3 – shortages rare)

C128 *Shortages of teaching staff*
(identified by HoD as a major challenge faced by department over last 5 years)

C129 *Difficulties getting parent/community support*
(identified by HoD as a major challenge faced by department over last 5 years)

C142 *Uptake at GCSE and A-level*
(identified by HoD as a key factor which ought to be taken into account in judging department effectiveness)

C151 *Too little emphasis on homework by staff*
(identified by HoD as a key factor holding the department back from greater effectiveness)

Table 3   Example of multilevel analysis of Mathematics score (1990–92): testing HoD Mathematics questionnaire items

Fixed Part	Estimate	Standard Error
Intercept	2.169	0.3243
LSLRT	0.04857	0.002023
LSLRT^2	0.0002978	8.114e–05
VR1-VR3	2.037	0.07949
VR2-VR3	0.8637	0.05579
Girls-boys	−0.2033	0.04816
Age in months	0.004826	0.005231
Year91–90	0.1357	0.08341
Year92–90	0.1092	0.08808
PCTFSM	0.00644	0.003145
FSM-no FSM	−0.3248	0.04464
African-White	0.3417	0.1220
Caribbean-White	−0.2236	0.05983
Indian-White	0.7758	0.1016
Pakistani-White	0.9543	0.1402
Bangladeshi-White	0.9540	0.1386
Other-White	0.4696	0.06023
Process variables		
C105	0.3611	0.1164
C114	0.2709	0.09262
C123	−0.2713	0.0543
C128	−0.1186	0.04916
C131	−0.1778	0.07145
C136	0.3373	0.1036
C137	−0.4188	0.18925
C155	−0.2895	0.07609
C166	0.2800	0.07341

Random Part		Estimate	Standard Error
Between schools			
Intercept	σ^2	0.00	0.00
Between years			
Intercept	σ^2	0.04697	0.012
Between students			
Intercept	σ^2	1.716	0.1117
LSLRT/intercept		0.007559	0.002162
LSLRT^2/intercept		−0.0001757	7.69e–05
VR1/intercept		0.4476	0.08278
VR2/intercept		0.4674	0.05276
Girls/intercept		−0.1289	0.03761
Year92/intercept		0.1662	0.03881
FSM/intercept		0.1491	0.04401
Caribbean/intercept		−0.1419	0.05018

[n=34 schools / 7150 students]

C105 *A high level of academic achievement in examinations*
      (identified by HoD as a factor which ought to be taken into account in judging
      school effectiveness)
C114 *Staff and students' shared belief that the school is primarily a place for
      teaching and learning*
      (identified by HoD as a key factor contributing to the school's current
      effectiveness)
C123 *Student motivation*
      (HoD's overall satisfaction with student motivation in the school 5 years ago –
      rated from – 1 very satisfied to 5 very dissatisfied)
C128 *Level of teacher absence in the school five years before*
      (rated by HoD from 1 – fairly high to 5 – very low)
C131 *Persuasion rather than coercion*
      (HoD identified as a key feature of their leadership style)
C136 *Student motivation*
      (identified by HoD as a major challenge faced by department over last 5 years)
C137 *Significant student behaviour problems*
      (identified by HoD as a major challenge faced by department over last 5 years)
C155 *Insufficient high quality teaching in some classes*
      (identified by HoD as a key factor holding department back from greater
      effectiveness)
C166 *Staff shortages in department were rare five years before*

APPENDIX 3

Three components of school culture

Items Identified as Statistically Significant in the Multilevel Analysis of Process Data in Relation to Measures of Academic Effective[1]

Order – Behaviour Policy and Practice
- A clear and consistently applied whole-school approach to student behaviour and discipline (identified by the HT as a key factor contributing to their school's effectiveness)
[+] TSCORE ENGLISH
- Inconsistent approach to student behaviour and discipline matters in school (identified by the HT as a major problem faced by their school over the last five years)   [–] MATHEMATICS
- Teaching staff expectations for student behaviour poor (HoD of English's assessment of English staff expectations five years ago)   [–] TSCORE
- Significant student behaviour problems (identified by HoD mathematics as a major challenge faced by their department in the past five years)
[–] MATHEMATICS

Task Achievement – Academic Emphasis
- Ensuring each student obtains the highest qualification possible (identified by HoD mathematics as a principal educational goal of the school five years before)   [+] TSCORE
- Examination results (identified by HoD mathematics as a factor which ought to be taken into account in judging departmental effectiveness)
[+] TSCORE
- Weak academic emphasis of English department five years' before (HT's rating)   [–] TSCORE
- Insufficient academic emphasis in the school (identified by the HT as a key factor holding their school back from being more effective)   [–] ENGLISH
- A high level of achievement in examinations (identified by HoD mathematics as a key factor which ought to be taken into account in judging school effectiveness   [+] MATHEMATICS
- The creation of confident, articulate people (identified by HoD English as a factor which ought to be taken into account in judging school effectiveness)   [–] ENGLISH
- Uptake at GCSE and A-level (identified by HoD English as a factor which ought to be taken into account in judging departmental effectiveness)
[+] ENGLISH
- Too little emphasis on homework by English staff (identified by HoD English as a key factor holding back their department from being more effective)   [–] ENGLISH

- Promoting students' ability to learn independently (identified by HoD English as a principal educational goal five years ago)   [+] ENGLISH
- Insufficient high quality teaching in some classes (identified by HoD Mathematics as a key factor holding their department back from greater effectiveness)   [–] MATHEMATICS

Quality Relationships and Learning Experience – A Student-Focused Approach
- Student feel valued as people (identified by HT as a key factor contributing to the effectiveness of their school)   [+] TSCORE
- Promoting student responsibility (identified by HT as a principal educational goal for the school five years ago)   [+] MATHEMATICS
- The creation of a positive climate for learning (identified by the HT as a key factor which ought to be taken into account in judging school effectiveness)   [+] MATHEMATICS
- Staff and students' shared belief that the school is primarily a place for teaching and learning (identified by HoD Mathematics as a key factor contributing to their school's effectiveness)   [+] MATHEMATICS
- Low student motivation (HoD Mathematics level of satisfaction with student motivation five years before)   [–] MATHEMATICS
- A caring pastoral environment (identified by HT as a key factor which ought to be taken into account in judging school effectiveness)
                                                            [+] ENGLISH
- A caring pastoral environment (identified by HoD English as a factor which ought to be taken into account in judging school effectiveness)
                                                            [+] ENGLISH
- Student satisfaction (identified by the HT as a key factor which ought to be taken into account in judging school effectiveness)   [+] ENGLISH

1. For full details see Sammons, Thomas and Mortimore, 1995.

Glossary

AMA	Association of Metropolitan Authorities
APU	Assessment Performance Unit
DfEE	Department for Education and Employment
DHT	Deputy Headteacher
ERA	Education Reform Act 1988
ESRC	Economic and Social Research Council
FSM	Free School Meal
GCSE	General Certificate of Secondary Education
HMI	Her Majesty's Inspectorate
HoD	Head of Department
HRO	High Reliability Organization
HT	Headteacher
ILEA	Inner London Education Authority (abolished 1990)
LEA	Local Education Authority
LMS	Local Management of Schools
LRT	London Reading Test
NA	National Assessment
NC	National Curriculum
NCER	National Consortium for Examination Results
NPQSL	National Professional Qualification for Subject Leaders
OECD	Organization for Economic Co-operation and Development
OFSTED	Office for Standards in Education
SCAA	School Curriculum and Assessment Authority
SDP	School Development Plan
SEN	Special Education Needs
SES	Socio-Economic Status
TScore	Total Examination Score
TTA	Teachers' Training Agency

References

Ainley, J. (1994) *Curriculum Areas in Secondary Schools: Differences in Student Response*. Paper presented at the International Congress of School Effectiveness and Improvement, Melbourne: January.

Ainscow, M. and Hopkins, D. (1992) Aboard the moving school, *Educational Leadership*. Vol. 50, no. 3, pp. 79–81.

Alexander, R. (1996) *Other Primary Schools and Ours: Hazards of International Comparison*. CREPE Occasional Paper, Warwick.

Ball, S. J. (1994) *Comprehensive Schooling Effectiveness and Control: An Analysis of Educational Discourses*. Centre for Educational Studies, King's College, London.

Barber, M. (1996a) *The Learning Game: Arguments for an Education Revolution*. Victor Gollanz, London.

Barber, M. (1996b) *The Curricula, the Minister, His Boss and Her Hairdresser*. Curriculum Association, London.

Barber, M. and Dann, R. (eds.) (1996) *Raising Educational Standards in the Inner City: Practical Initiatives in Action*. Cassell, London.

Bassey, M. (1996) Democracy needs research: editorial, *Research Intelligence*, Vol 55, p. 20.

Bolam, R., McMahon, A., Pocklington, K. and Wendling, D. (1993) *Effective Management in Schools*. HMSO, London.

Borger, J. B. (1984) Effective Schools: A quantitative synthesis of constructs, *Journal of Classroom Interaction*, Vol. 20, pp. 12–17.

Bosker, R. J. and Scheerens, J. (1989) Issues in the interpretation of the results of school effectiveness research, *International Journal of Educational Research*. Vol. 13, no. 7, pp. 741–751.

Bosker, R. J. and Scheerens, J. (1994) Alternative models of school effectiveness put to the test, in R. J. Bosker, B. P. M. Creemers and J. Scheerens (eds.) *Conceptual and Methodological Advances in Educational Effective Research: special issue of the International Journal of Educational Research*. Vol. 21, no. 2, pp. 159–180.

Brown, M. and Rutherford, D. (1995) *Successful Leadership for School Improvement in Areas of Urban Deprivation: A Framework for Development and Research*. Schools of Education, Universities of Manchester and Birmingham.

Brown, S., Riddell, S. and Duffield, J. (1996) Possibilities and problems of small-scale studies to unpack the findings of large scale studies of school effectiveness, in J. Gray, D. Reynolds, C. Fitz-Gibbon and D. Jesson (eds.) *Merging Traditions: The Future of Research on School Effectiveness and School Improvement*. Cassell, London.

Bush, T. (1995) *Theories of Educational Management* (2nd edition), Paul Chapman, London.

Coleman, M., and Matthews, P. (1996) *Initiative or Strategy: The Chicken and the Egg of School Improvement*. Paper presented at the British Educational Research Association Conference, University of Lancaster, September.

Coleman, P. (1994) *Learning About Schools: What Parents Need to Know and How They Can Find Out*, Institute for Research on Public Policy, Montreal, Canada.

Coleman, P., Collinge, J. and Tabin, Y. (1994) *Improving School from the Inside Out: A Progress Report on the Coproduction of Learning Project in British Columbia*, *Canada*. Faculty of Education, Simon Fraser University, Burnaby, BC, Canada.

Creemers, B. P. M. (1992) School effectiveness, effective instruction and school improvement in the Netherlands, in D. Reynolds and P. Cuttance (eds.) *School Effectiveness Research, Policy and Practice*. Cassell, London.

Creemers, B. P. M. (1994a) The history, value and purpose of school effectiveness studies, in D. Reynolds, B. P. M. Creemers, P. S. Nesselrodt, E. C. Schaffer, S. Stringfield and C. Teddlie (eds.) *Advances in School Effectiveness Research and Practice*. Pergamon, Oxford.

Creemers, B. P. M. (1994b) *The Effective Classroom*. Cassell, London.

Creemers, B. P. M. (1994c) Effective instruction: an empirical basis for a theory of educational effectiveness, in D. Reynolds, B. P. M. Creemers, P. S. Nesselrodt, E. C. Schaffer, S. Stringfield and C. Teddlie (eds.) *Advances in School Effectiveness Research and Practice*. Pergamon, Oxford.

Creemers, B. P. M. (1995) Process indicators on school functioning and the generalisability of school factor models across countries, in *Measuring the Quality of Schools*, pp. 105–119. OECD, Paris.

Creemers, B. and Reezigt, G. (forthcoming) School level conditions affecting the effectiveness of instruction, *School Effectiveness and School Improvement*.

Creemers, B., Reynolds, D., Stringfield, S. and Teddlie, C. (1996) *World Class Schools: Some Further Findings*. Paper presented at the AERA Conference, New York: April.

Creemers, B. and Scheerens, J. (1989) Conceptualizing school effectiveness: developments in school effectiveness research, *International Journal of Educational Research*, Vol. 13, no. 7, pp. 691–706.

Creemers, B. and Scheerens, J. (1994) Developments in the educational effectiveness research programme, *International Journal of Educational Research*. Vol. 21, no. 2, pp. 125–139.

Cuttance, P. (1987) *Modelling Variation in the Effectiveness of Schooling*. Centre for Educational Sociology, Edinburgh.

DFE (1992) *Choice and Diversity: A New Framework for Schools*. DFE, London.

DFE (1995) *Value Added in Education: A Briefing Paper*. DFE, London.

DfEE (1997) *The Road to Success: Four Case Studies of Schools Which No Longer Require Special Measures*. DfEE/University of London, Institute of Education, London.

Dearing, Sir R. (1993) *The National Curriculum: Final Report*. School Curriculum and Assessment Authority, London.

Earley, P., Fidler, B. and Ouston, J. (1996) *Improvement Through Inspection?* David Fulton, London.

Edmonds, R. R. (1979) Effective schools for the urban poor, *Educational Leadership*. Vol. 37, no. 1, pp. 15–27.

Elliott, J. (1996) School effectiveness research and its critics: alternative visions of schooling, *Cambridge Journal of Education*. Vol. 26, no. 2, pp. 199–223.

Fitz-Gibbon, C. (1991) Multilevel modelling in an indicator system, in S. W. Raudenbush and J. D. Willms (eds.) *Schools, Classrooms and Pupils International Studies of Schooling from a Multilevel Perspective*. Academic Press, San Diego.

Fitz-Gibbon, C. (1992) School effects at A-level: genesis of an information system, in D. Reynolds and P. Cuttance (eds.) *School Effectiveness Research, Policy and Practice*. Cassell, London.

Fitz-Gibbon, C. (1995) *The Value Added National Project: Issues to be Considered in the Design of a National Value Added System*. School Curriculum and Assessment Authority, London.

Fullan, M. (1993) *Change Forces: Probing the Depths of Educational Reform*. Falmer Press, London.

Gillborn, D. and Gipps, C. (1996) *Recent Research on the Achievements of Ethnic Minority Pupils*. OFSTED Reviews of Research, London.

Goldstein, H. (1987) *Multilevel Models in Educational and Social Research*. Charles Griffin and Co., London and Oxford University Press, New York.

Goldstein, H. (1995) *Multilevel Statistical Models* (2nd edn). Edward Arnold, London and Halsted Press, New York.

Goldstein, H. (1996) Relegate the leagues, *New Economy*. The Dryden Press, London.

Goldstein, H., Rasbash, J., Yang, M., Woodhouse, G., Pan, H., Nuttall, D. and Thomas, S. (1993) A multilevel analysis of school examination results, *Oxford Review of Education*. Vol. 19, no. 4, pp. 425–33.

Goldstein, H. and Spiegelhalter, D. (1996) League tables and their limitations: statistical issues in comparisons of institutional performance, *Journal of the Royal Statistical Society A*. Vol. 159, no. 3, pp. 385–443.

Goldstein, H. and Thomas, S. (1996) Using examination results as indicators of school and college performance, *Journal of the Royal Statistical Society A*. Vol. 159, no. 1, pp. 149–163.

Gray, J. (1990) The quality of schooling: frameworks for judgement, *British Journal of Educational*.

Gray, J. (1993) *Value Added Approaches in School Evaluation: The Experiences of Three LEAs*. Audit Unit, HM Inspector of Schools, The Scottish Office, Edinburgh.

Gray, J. (1995) The quality of schooling frameworks for judgement, in J. Gray and B. Wilcox (eds.) *Good School, Bad School*. Open University Press, Buckingham.

Gray, J., Goldstein, H. and Jesson, D. (1996) Changes and improvements in schools' effectiveness: trends over five years, *Research Papers in Education*. Vol. 11, no. 1, pp. 35–51.

Gray, J., Jesson, D., Goldstein, H., Hedger, K. and Rasbash, J. (1993) *A Multi-Level Analysis of School Improvement: Changes in Schools' Performance Over Time*. Paper presented at the 5th European Conference of the European Association for Research on Learning and Instruction, Aix-en-Provence, France: 3 September.

Gray, J., Jesson, D., Goldstein, H., Hedger, K. and Rasbash, J. (1995) A multilevel analysis of school improvement: changes in schools' performance over time, *School Effectiveness and School Improvement*. Vol. 6, no. 2, pp. 97–114.

Gray, J., Jesson, D. and Sime, N. (1990) Estimating differences in the examination performance of secondary schools in six LEAs: a multilevel approach to school effectiveness, *Oxford Review of Education*. Vol. 16, no. 2, pp. 137–158.

Gray, J. and Wilcox, B. (eds.) (1995) *Good School, Bad School: Evaluating Performance and Encouraging Improvement*. Open University Press, Buckingham.

Hamilton, D. (1996) Peddling feel-good fictions: reflections on key characteristics of effective schools, *Forum*. Vol. 38, no. 2, pp. 54–56.

Hargreaves, D. (1995a) School effectiveness, school change and school improvement: the relevance of the concept of culture. *School Effectiveness and School Improvement*, Vol. 6, no. 1, pp. 23–46.

Hargreaves, D. (1995b) Inspection and school improvement, *Cambridge Journal of Education*. Vol. 25, no. 1, pp. 117–125.

Hargreaves, D. and Hopkins, D. (1993) School effectiveness, school improvement and development planning, Chapter 19 in M. Preedy (ed.) *Managing The Effective School*, OUP/Paul Chapman, London.

Harris, A., Jamieson, I. and Russ, J. (1995) A study of 'effective' departments in secondary schools, *School Organisation*. Vol. 15, no. 3, pp. 283–299.

Hill, N. (1994) *Value Added Analysis: Current Practice in Local Educational Authorities*. National Foundation for Educational Research in England and Wales, Education Management Information Exchange, Slough.

Hill, P., and Rowe, K. (1996) Multilevel modelling in school effectiveness research, *School Effectiveness and School Improvement*, Vol. 7, no. 1, pp. 1–34.

Hopkins, D. (1994) School improvement in an era of change, in P. Ribbins and E. Burridge (eds.) *Improving Education: Promoting Quality in Schools*. Cassell, London.

Jesson, D. and Gray, J. (1991) Slants on slopes: using multi-level models to investigate differential school effectiveness and its impact on pupils' examination results, *School Effectiveness and School Improvement*. Vol. 2, no. 3, pp. 230–271.

Lawton, D. (1994) Defining quality, in P. Ribbins and E. Burridge (eds.) *Improving Education: Promoting Quality in Schools*. Cassell, London.

Lee, V., Bryk, S. and Smith, J. (1993) The organization of effective secondary schools, in L. Darling-Hammond (ed.) *Review of Research in Education*. Vol. 19, pp. 171–226, AERA, Washington, DC.

Levine, D. (1992) An interpretive review of US research and practice dealing with unusually effective schools, in D. Reynolds and P. Cuttance (eds.) *School Effectiveness: Research, Policy and Practice*. Cassell, London.

Literary Taskforce (1997) *A Reading Revolution: Preliminary Report of the Literary Taskforce,* chaired by Professor Michael Barber. Institute of Education, University of London, London.

Luyten, H. (1994) Stability of school effects in Dutch secondary education: the impact of variance across subjects and years, *International Journal of Educational Research*. Vol. 21, no. 2, pp. 197–216.

Luyten, H. (1995) Teacher change and instability across grades, *School Effectiveness and School Improvement*. Vol. 1, no. 1, pp. 67–89.

MacBeath, J. (1994) A role for parents, students and teachers in school self-evaluation and development planning, in K. A. Riley and D. L. Nuttall (eds.) *Measuring Quality: Education Indicators – United Kingdom and International Perspective*. Falmer Press, London.

MacBeath, J., and Mortimore, P., (1993) *Improving School Effectiveness*, Proposal for a Research Project for the Scottish Office Education Department, Quality in Education Centre, University of Strathclyde, Glasgow.

McGaw, B. *et al.* (1992) *Making Schools More Effective*. Australian Council for Educational Research, Victoria, Australia.

MacGilchrist,B., Myers, K., and Reed, J. (1997) *The Intelligent School*, Paul Chapman, London.

Matthews, P. and Smith, G. (1995) OFSTED: inspecting schools and improvement through inspection, *Cambridge Journal of Education*. Vol. 25, no. 1, pp. 23–34.

Ming, T. W. and Cheong, C. Y. (1995) *School Environment and Student Performance: A Multilevel Analysis*. Paper presented at the International Congress of School Effectiveness and Improvement, Leeuwarden, The Netherlands: January.

Mortimore, P. (1991a) The nature and findings of research on school effectiveness in the primary sector, in S. Riddell and S. Brown (eds.) *School Effectiveness Research: Its Messages for School Improvement*. HMSO, London.

Mortimore, P. (1991b) School effectiveness research: which way at the crossroads? *School Effectiveness and School Improvement*. Vol. 2, no. 3, pp. 213–229.

Mortimore, P. (1993) Managing teaching and learning: the search for a match, in M. Busher and M. Smith (eds.) *Managing Educational Institutions: Sheffield Papers in Educational Management*. University of Sheffield.

Mortimore, P. (1995a) *Effective Schools: Current Impact and Future Possibilities*. The Director's Inaugural Lecture, 7 February, Institute of Education, University of London.

Mortimore, P. (1995b) The positive effects of schooling, in M. Rutter (ed.) *Psycho-Social Disturbances in Young People: Challenges for Prevention*. Cambridge University Press, Cambridge.

Mortimore, P. (1995c) The Balancing Act, *Education Guardian*, 28 February.

Mortimore, P. (1996) We should inspect our obsession with failure, *The Independent Section 2*, 25 July, p. 17.

Mortimore, P., Davies, H. and Portway, S. (1996) Burntwood Secondary Girls' School, Chapter 6 in *Success Against the Odds*. National Commission on Education. Routledge, London.

Mortimore, P., Sammons, S. and Ecob, R. (1988) Expressing the magnitude of school effects – a reply to Peter Preece, *Research Papers in Education*. Vol. 3, no. 2, pp. 99–101.

Mortimore, P., Sammons, P. and Thomas, S. (1994) School effectiveness and value added measures, *Assessment in Education: Principles, Policy and Practice.* Vol. 1, no. 3, pp. 315–332.

Mortimore, P. and Stone, C. (1991) Measuring educational quality, *British Journal of Educational Studies.* Vol. 39, no. 1, pp. 69–82.

Mortimore, P., Sammons, P., Stoll, L., Lewis, D. and Ecob, R. (1988) *School Matters: The Junior Years.* Paul Chapman, London.

Mortimore, P. and Sammons, P. (1997) Endpiece: a welcome and a riposte to critics etc . . . Chapter 10 in J. White and M. Barber (eds.) *Perspectives on School Effectiveness and Improvement.* Bedford Way Paper, Institute of Education, London.

Myers, K. (1995) *School Improvement in Practice: Accounts from the Schools Make a Difference Project.* Falmer Press, London.

North West Regional Educational Laboratory (1995) *Effective Schooling Practices: A Research Synthesis – 1995 update.* NWREL School Improvement Research Series, Portland, Oregon.

Nuttall, D. (1990) *Differences in Examination Performance.* RS 1277/90, Research and Statistics Branch, ILEA, London.

Nuttall, D., Goldstein, H., Prosser, R. and Rasbash, J. (1989) Differential school effectiveness, in *International Journal of Educational Research, special issue Developments in School Effectiveness Research.* Vol. 13, no. 7, pp. 769–776.

Nuttall, D., Thomas, S. and Goldstein, H. (1992) *Report on Analysis of 1990 Examination Results, January 1992.* Association of Metropolitan Authorities, London.

OECD (1989) *Schools and Quality. An International Report.* OECD, Paris.

Paterson, L. and Goldstein H. (1991) New statistical methods of analysing social structures: an introduction to multilevel models, *British Educational Research Journal.* Vol. 17, no. 4, pp. 387–393.

Phillips, M. (1996) *All Must Have Prizes.* Little, London.

Preece, P. (1989) Pitfalls in research on school and teacher effectiveness, *Research Papers in Education.* Vol. 4, no. 3, pp. 47–69.

Pring, R. (1995) Educating persons: putting education back into educational research (the 1995 SERA lecture), *Scottish Educational Research Journal,* Vol. 27, pp. 101–12.

Reezigt, G., Guldemond, H. and Creemers, B. (forthcoming) Empirical validity for a comprehensive model on educational effectiveness, *School Effectiveness and School Improvement.*

Reynolds, D. (1976) The Delinquent School, in P. Woods (ed.) *The Process of Schooling,* Routledge and Kegan Paul, London.

Reynolds, D. (1982) The search for effective schools, *School Organisation.* Vol. 2, no. 3, pp. 215–37.

Reynolds, D. (1992) School effectiveness and school improvement: an updated review of the British literature, in D. Reynolds and P. Cuttance (eds.) *School Effectiveness Research, Policy and Practice.* Cassell, London.

Reynolds, D. (1994a) School effectiveness research: a review of the international literature, in D. Reynolds, B. P. M. Creemers, P. S. Nesselradt, E. C. Schaffer, S. Stringfield and C. Teddlie (eds.) *Advances in School Effectiveness Research and Practice.* Pergamon, Oxford.

Reynolds, D. (1994b) Inaugural Lecture, 19 October, University of Newcastle-Upon-Tyne.

Reynolds, D. (1995) The effective school: An inaugural lecture, *Evaluation and Research in Education.* Vol. 9, no. 2, pp. 57–73.

Reynolds, D. (1996) Turning around ineffective schools: some evidence and some speculations, in J. Gray, D. Reynolds, C. Fitz-Gibbon and D. Jesson (eds.) *Merging Traditions: The Future of Research on School Effectiveness and School Improvement.* Cassell, London.

Reynolds, D. and Farrell, S. (1996) *Worlds Apart? A Review of International Surveys of Educational Achievement involving England.* OFSTED Reviews of Research, HMSO, London.

Reynolds, D. and Packer, A. (1992) School effectiveness and school improvement in the 1990s, in D. Reynolds and P. Cuttance (eds.) *School Effectiveness Research, Policy and Practice.* Cassell, London.

Reynolds, D., Creemers, B., Nesselrodt, P. S., Schaffer, E. C., Stringfield, S. and Teddlie, C. (1994) *Advances in School Effectiveness Research and Practice.* Pergamon, Oxford.

Reynolds, P., Bollen, R., Creemers, B., Hopkins, D., Stoll, L. and Lagerweij, N. (eds.) (1996a) *Making Good Schools: Linking School Effectiveness and School Improvement.* Routledge, London.

Reynolds, D., Sammons, P., Stoll, L., Barber, M. and Hillman, J. (1996b) School effectiveness and school improvement in the United Kingdom, *School Effectiveness and School Improvement (special issue of country reports).* Vol. 7, no. 2, pp. 133–58.

Robertson, P. and Sammons, P. (1997) *Improving School Effectiveness: A Project in Progress.* Paper presented at the Tenth International Congress for School Effectiveness and Improvement. Memphis, Tennessee, 5–8 January.

Rowe, K. J. and Hill, P. W. (1994) *Multilevel Modelling in School Effectiveness Research: How many levels?.* Paper presented at the International Congress for School Effectiveness and Improvement, Melbourne: 3–6 January.

Rowe, K., and Hill, P. (1996) Assessing, recording and reporting students' educational progress, *Assessment in Education,* Vol. 3, pp. 309–352.

Ruddock, J., Chaplain, R. and Wallace, G. (1996) *School Improvement: What Can Pupils Tell Us?* David Fulton, London.

Rutter, M., Maugham, B., Mortimore, P. and Ouston, J. (1979) *Fifteen Thousand Hours: Secondary Schools and Their Effects on Children.* Paul Chapman, London.

SCAA (1995) *The Value Added National Project: General and Technical Reports.* SCAA, London.

Sammons, P. (1993) *Measuring and Resourcing Educational Needs: Variations in LEAs' LMS Policies in inner London.* Clare Market Paper No 6, Centre for Educational Research, LSE, London.

Sammons, P. (1994) Findings from school effectiveness research: some implications for improving the quality of schools, in P. Ribbins and E. Burridge (eds.) *Improving Education: Promoting Quality in Schools.* Cassell, London.

Sammons, P. (1995) Gender, ethnic and socio-economic differences in attainment and progress: a longitudinal analysis of student achievement over nine years, *British Educational Research Journal.* Vol. 21, no. 4, pp. 465–485.

Sammons, P. (1996) Complexities in the judgement of school effectiveness, *Educational Research and Evaluation.* Vol. 2, no. 2, pp. 113–149.

Sammons, P. (forthcoming) Diversity in classrooms: effects on educational outcomes, in D. Shorrocks-Taylor and D. Childs (eds.) *Directions in Educational Psychology.* Whurr.

Sammons, P., Hillman, J. and Mortimore, P. (1995) *Key Characteristics of Effective Schools: A Review of School Effectiveness Research.* OFSTED and University of London, Institute of Education, London.

Sammons, P., Kysel, F. and Mortimore, P. (1983) Educational priority indices: a new perspective, *British Educational Research Journal.* Vol. 9, no. 1, pp. 27–40.

Sammons, P., Mortimore, P. and Hillman, J. (1996) A response to David Hamilton's reflections, *Forum.* Vol. 38, no. 3, pp. 88–90.

Sammons, P., Mortimore, P. and Thomas, S. (1996) Do schools perform consistently across outcomes and areas? in J. Gray, D. Reynolds, C. Fitz-Gibbon and D. Jesson (eds.) *Merging Traditions: The Future of Research on School Effectiveness and School Improvement.* Cassell, London.

Sammons, P., Nuttall, D. and Cuttance, P. (1993) Differential school effectiveness: results from a reanalysis of the Inner London Education Authority's junior school project data, *British Educational Research Journal*. Vol. 19, no. 4, pp. 381–405.

Sammons, P. and Reynolds, D. (1997) A partisan evaluation: John Elliott on school effectiveness, *Cambridge Journal of Education*. Vol. 27, no. 1, pp. 123–126.

Sammons, P., Thomas, S. and Mortimore, P. (1995a) *Accounting for Variations in Academic Effectiveness Between Schools and Departments: Results from the 'Differential Secondary School Effectiveness Project' – a three-year study of GCSE performance*. Paper presented at the European Conference on Educational Research/ BERA Annual Conference, Bath: 14–17 September. University of London, Institute of Education, London.

Sammons, P., Thomas, S. and Mortimore, P. (1995) *Differential School Effectiveness: Departmental variations in GCSE Attainment*. ESRC End of Award Report, Project R000 234130. University of London, Institute of Education, London.

Sammons, P., Thomas, S. and Mortimore, P. (1996) Promoting school and departmental effectiveness, *Management in Education*. Vol. 10, no. 1, pp. 22–24.

Sammons, P., Thomas, S., Mortimore, P., Owen, C. and Pennell, H. (1994) *Assessing School Effectiveness: Developing Measures to put School Performance in Context*. Office for Standards in Education [OFSTED], London.

Sammons, P., Nuttall, D., Cuttance, P. and Thomas, S. (1995) Continuity of school effects: a longitudinal analysis of primary and secondary school effects on GCSE performance, *School Effectiveness and School Improvement*. Vol. 6, no. 4, pp. 285–307.

Sammons, P., Thomas, S., Mortimore, P., Cairns, R., Bausor, J. and Walker, A. (forthcoming) Understanding School and Departmental Differences in Academic Effectiveness: Findings from case studies of selected outlier secondary schools in inner London. *School Effectiveness and School Improvement* (forthcoming).

Scheerens, J. (1990) School effectiveness research and the development of process indicators of school functioning, *School Effectiveness and School Improvement*, Vol. 1, no. 1, pp. 61–80.

Scheerens, J. (1992) *Effective Schooling: Research, Theory and Practice*. Cassell, London.

Scheerens, J. (1995) *School Effectiveness as a Research Discipline*, paper presented at the International Congress of School Effectiveness and School Improvement, Leeuwarden, The Netherlands: 3–6 January.

Scheerens, J. and Creemers, B. P. M. (1989) Conceptualizing school effectiveness, *International Journal of Educational Research*. Vol. 13, no. 7, pp. 691–706.

Scheerens, J. and Bosker, R. (1997) *The Foundations of Educational Effectiveness*. Pergamon, Oxford.

Silver, H. (1994) *Good Schools, Effective Schools and Judgements and Their Histories*. Cassell, London.

Sirotnik, K. A. (1985) School effectiveness: a bandwagon in search of a tune, *Education Administration Quarterly*. Vol. 21, no. 2, pp. 135–140.

Slavin, R. E. (1987) A theory of school and classroom organisation, *Educational Psychologist*. Vol. 22, no. 2, pp. 89–108.

Smith, D. J. and Tomlinson, S. (1989) *The School Effect: A Study of Multi-Racial Comprehensives*. Policy Studies Institute, London.

Southworth, G. (1994) The learning school, in P. Ribbens and E. Burridge (eds.) *Improving Education: Promoting Quality in Schools*. Cassell, London.

Stoll, L. (1996) Linking school effectiveness and school improvement: issues and possibilities, in J. Gray, D. Reynolds, C. Fitz-Gibbon and D. Jesson (eds.), *Merging Traditions: The Future of School Effectiveness and School Improvement*. Cassell, London.

Stoll, L. and Fink, D. (1996) *Changing Our Schools: Linking School Effectiveness and School Improvement*. Open University Press, Buckingham.

Stoll, L. and Thomson, M. (1996) Moving together: a partnership approach to improvement, in P. Earley, B. Fidler and J. Ouston (eds.), *Improvement Through Inspection?* David Fulton, Cambridge.

Stoll, L., and Myers, K. (1997) *No Quick Fixes Perspectives on School In Difficulty.* Falmer Press, London.

Stringfield, S. (1994a) Outlier studies of School Effectiveness, in D. Reynolds *et al.* (eds.) *Advances in School Effectiveness Research and Practice.* Pergamon, Oxford.

Stringfield, S (1994b) A model of elementary school effects, in D. Reynolds *et al.* (eds.) *Advances in School Effectiveness Research and Practice.* Pergamon, Oxford.

Sylva, K. and Hurry, J. (1995) *The Effectiveness of Reading Recovery and Phonological Training for Children with Reading Problems.* Full Report Prepared for the School Curriculum and Assessment Authority, Thomas Coram Research Unit, University of London, Institute of Education.

Teddlie, C. (1994a) The study of context in school effects research: history, methods, results and theoretical implications, in D. Reynolds *et al.* (eds.) *Advances in School Effectiveness Research and Practice.* Pergamon, Oxford.

Teddlie, C. (1994b) The integration of classroom and school process data in school effectiveness research, in D. Reynolds *et al.* (eds.) *Advances in School Effectiveness Research and Practice.* Pergamon, Oxford.

Teddlie, C. and Stringfield, S. (1993) *Schools Make a Difference: Lessons Learned from a 10-year Study of School Effects.* Teachers College Press, New York.

Teddlie, C., Stringfield, S., Wimpelberg, R. and Kirby, P. (1989) Contextual differences in model for effective schooling in the USA, in B. Creemers, T. Peters and D. Reynolds (eds.) *School Effectiveness and School Improvement.* Swets and Zeitlinger, Lisse.

Thomas, S (1995a) Considering primary school effectiveness: an analysis of 1992 Key Stage 1 results, *The Curriculum Journal.* Vol. 6, no. 3, pp. 279–295.

Thomas, S. (1995b) *Optimal Multilevel Models of School Effectiveness: Comparative Analyses Across Regions.* ESRC proposal, Institute of Education, University of London.

Thomas, S. and Goldstein, H. (1995) Questionable value, *Education.* Vol. 185, no.11, pp. 17.

Thomas, S. and Mortimore, P. (1996) Comparison of value added models for secondary school effectiveness, *Research Papers in Education.* Vol. 11, no. 1, pp. 5–33.

Thomas, S., Nuttall, D. and Goldstein, H. (1992) *The Guardian Survey (of A-level examination results) October 1992.* The *Guardian*: 20 October.

Thomas, S., Nuttall, D. and Goldstein, H. (1993a) *The Guardian Survey (of A-level examination results) November 1993.* The *Guardian*: 30 November.

Thomas, S., Nuttall, D. and Goldstein, H. (1993b) *Report on Analysis of 1991 Examination Results.* Association of Metropolitan Authorities, London.

Thomas, S., Pan, H. and Goldstein, H. (1994a) *Report on Analysis of 1992 Examination Results.* Association of Metropolitan Authorities, London.

Thomas, S., Sammons, P. and Mortimore, P. (1994b) *Stability and Consistency in Secondary Schools' Effects on Students' GCSE Outcomes: Initial Results.* Paper presented at the annual conference of the British Educational Research Association, St Anne's College, University of Oxford: 9 September.

Thomas, S., Sammons, P. and Mortimore, P. (1995) Determining what 'adds value' to student achievement, *Educational Leadership International.* Vol. 52, no. 6, pp. 19–22.

Thomas, S., Sammons, P., Mortimore, P. and Smees, R. (1997a) Stability and Consistency in Secondary Schools' Effects on Students' GCSE Outcomes over 3 years. *School Effectiveness and School Improvement*, Vol. 8, pp. 169–197.

Thomas, S., Sammons, P., Mortimore, P. and Smees, R. (1997b) Differential secondary school effectiveness: Examining the size, extent and consistency of school and departmental effects on GCSE outcomes for different groups of students over three years. *British Educational Research Journal*, Vol. 23, pp. 451–469.

Thomas, S., Sammons, P. and Street, H. (1997) Value added approaches: fairer ways of comparing schools, *Research Matters*. No 7, School Improvement Network, Institute of Education, University of London.

Thomas, S., Smees, R. and McCall, J. (1997) *Room for Improvement: Analysis of ISEP primary baseline measures,* paper presented at a symposium Critical Issues in School Effectiveness Research at 10th International Congress for School Effectiveness and Improvement, Memphis, Tennessee, January 1997.

Times Educational Supplement, 9 November 1996, p. 1.

Tizard, B., Blatchford, P., Burke, J., Farquhar, C. and Plewis, I. (1988) *Young Children at School in the Inner City.* Lawrence Erlbaum, Hove.

Tomlinson, J. R., Mortimore, P. and Sammons, P. (1988) *Freedom and Education: Ways of increasing openness and accountability.* Sheffield Papers in Education Management 76, Sheffield City Polytechnic Centre for Education Management and Administration, Sheffield.

Wallace, M. and Hall, V. (1994) *Inside the SMT.* Paul Chapman, London.

Watkins, C. (1995) School Behaviour, *Viewpoint No 3.* Institute of Education University of London, London.

West, M. and Hopkins, D. (1996) *Reconceptualising School Effectiveness and School Improvement.* Paper presented at the School Effectiveness and Improvement Symposium of the Annual Conference of the American Educational Research Association, New York: 8 April.

White, J. (1997) Philosophical perspectives on school effectiveness research, Chapter in *Perspectives on School Effectiveness and School Improvement.* Bedford Way Paper, Institute of Education, University of London, London.

Wilcox, B. and Gray, J. (1996) *Inspecting Schools – Holding Schools to Account and Helping Schools to Improve.* Open University Press, Buckingham.

Willms, J. D. (1986) Social class segregation and its relationship to pupils' examination results in Scotland, *American Sociological Review.* Vol. 51, pp. 224–241.

Willms, J. D. (1992) *Monitoring of School Performance: A Guide for Educators.* Falmer, London.

Willms, J. D. and Raudenbush, S. W. (1989) A longitudinal hierarchical linear model for estimating school effects and their stability, *Journal of Educational Measurement.* Vol. 26, no. 3, pp. 209–232.

Witziers, B. (1994) *Coordination in Secondary Schools and its Implications for Student Achievement.* Paper presented at the annual conference of the American Educational Research Association, New Orleans: 4–8 April.

Author Index

Subject Index